The Languages
of Difference

Also by Ronald E. Martin

The Fiction of Joseph Hergesheimer

American Literature and the Universe of Force

American Literature and the Destruction of Knowledge:
Innovative Writing in the Age of Epistemology

The Languages of Difference

American Writers and Anthropologists
Reconfigure the Primitive, 1878–1940

Ronald E. Martin

DELAWARE

Newark: University of Delaware Press

Associated University Presses
2010 Eastpark Boulevard
Cranbury, NJ 08512

The paper used in this publication meets the requirements of the American National Standard for Permanence of Paper for Printed Library Materials Z39.48-1984.

Library of Congress Cataloging-in-Publication Data

Martin, Ronald E., 1933–
    The languages of difference : American writers and anthropologists reconfigure the primitive, 1878–1940 / Ronald E. Martin.
        p. cm.
    Includes bibliographical references and index.
    ISBN 0-87413-904-X (alk. paper)
    1. American literature—20th century—History and criticism.   2. Primitive societies in literature.   3. Literature and anthropology—United States—History—20th century.   4. Literature and anthropology—United States—History—19th century.   5. American literature—19th century—History and criticism.   6. Anthropology—United States—History—19th century.   7. Anthropology—United States—History—20th century.   8. Difference (Psychology) in literature.   9. Primitivism in literature.   10. Race in literature.   I. Title.

    PS228.P7M37   2005
    810.9′3552—dc22   2004019363

This book is dedicated in memoriam *to:*
Lewis Henry Morgan
Henry Adams
Eugene O'Neill
Franz Boas
William Faulkner
Margaret Mead
and
Zora Neale Hurston
For the imagination, originality, and skills
by which they advanced our understanding of what it is to be human

Contents

Preface: History's Parallax

THE GREEKS OF THE CLASSICAL PERIOD HAD AWE-INSPIRING REPRE-sentations of their relationship to the distant forerunners of their civilization: sculptures and frescoes depicting legions of heroes and gods in mortal struggle—entangled in what would become victorious combat—with the satyrs, centaurs, serpents, and beasts from the dim reaches of prehistory. Western culture has this deeply seated motif of rejection of the earlier-stage ancestor. Ancient sculptors depicted it in terms of mortal combat, celebrating the foundation of Civilization as conquest of the unruly, the animalistic, the primeval, by representatives of heroic rationality, of morality and order—rejecting as subhuman and semihuman the creatures of their universe's distant past. Alternatively, other cultures have had quite different myths of the primeval, imagining (as have many Native American peoples) a distant past inhabited by spiritual ancestors whose animal qualities became special endowments of perceptiveness, ingenuity, and courage in the people who were their inheritors.

Not only has EuroAmerican culture been haunted by its fear-and-loathing images of its prehistoric past, but it has tended to classify the differences of contemporary Others according to those same imaginings—to see "primitiveness" in every notable difference of skin color, familial or social structure, or pattern of belief or behavior. The resulting ethnic arrogance has only relatively recently been widely exposed, along with the political and economic exploitations it sanctioned. What I am interested in studying here are the attempts of a few quite original writers and scientists to counter the prevalent, seemingly self-evident notions of the primitive and of such human difference as is included in that term, and to discover more subtle and humane alternatives. Their efforts began in perceptions of the imprecise, complacent and even immoral categories and approaches commonly used to characterize and deal with "primitive" Others. Their struggles toward understanding were ingenious accretions of insight, method, and language. But however insightful, their results cannot stand as definitive. The process of reconceiving those who once were considered "primitive" continues still.

9

Continuously creatively evolving our approaches and our understanding is actually the best we can do by way of conceiving of human
difference: absolute and final definition will always be elusive. Our
languages change, as do our conceptual systems, our viewpoints, our
motives, and even the differences themselves. Thus any project of interpreting human difference becomes a question of time, of categories, perspectives, and the conditions and qualities of humanness
itself. Whatwhen is a seamless, everchanging human dimension, much
like physical spacetime, and the languages of difference, timebound
and perspective-frozen, can offer only limited, inconclusive, mutable
insights.

Furthermore, while actual, perceivable differences are legion, in
any given culture only certain of them are perceived and endowed
with exceptional significance. Why, for example, out of the vast range
of potentially differentiating items, did Western cultures fix on skin
color, technological orientation, religion, as crucial differences? Obviously the perceptions and interpretations of difference are products
of particular cultures, embodying their own preoccupations and biases. And languages themselves embody those preoccupations. A
Western interpreter of difference using a basically analytical, discursive language—even if he or she be vividly aware of the hazards of
ethnocentrism—cannot avoid biases and condescensions deeply infused in the very words, idioms, and grammar of his or her text. And
language *per se* transforms everything into itself: nonlinguistic purposes and significances are obscured; and incomprehensibly rich,
complex, simultaneous, and inconsistent reality-sets—cultures or
peoples for example—become in language simplified abstractions,
made up at least in part of societally shaped convention, experience,
and individual mentality. Thus it is that, for example, *primitiveness*
and *race* as categories of thought based in real apprehensions of difference metamorphose into conceptual entities—abstractive, biased,
and incapable of operational validation.

This sort of realization of epistemological relativity has become a
principal theme of much contemporary criticism of literature and of
anthropology. Henry Louis Gates Jr., on the subject of "writing
race," declares that "we must . . . understand how certain forms of
difference and the *languages* we employ to define those supposed differences not only reinforce each other but tend to create and maintain
each other. Similarly, and as importantly, we must analyze the language of contemporary criticism itself, recognizing especially that
hermeneutic systems are not universal, color-blind, apolitical, or neutral" (1986, 15). James Clifford, on "writing culture," emphasizes
"that science is in, not above, historical and linguistic processes"; he

refers to "the constructed, artificial nature of cultural accounts" and cites "the general trend toward a *specification of discourses* in ethnography: who speaks? who writes? when and where? with or to whom? under what institutional and historical constraints?" (Clifford and Marcus 1986, 2,13). And Marvin Harris particularizes the inadequacy of our language for describing the "behavior stream of events" of another culture by pointing out that although English speakers might be certain about phenomena designated as "church service" or "taxation" within their own culture, "Is a Chuckee séance a church service? Does the Trobriand chief's acceptance of his brother-in-law's yams constitute taxation?" (1964, 25).

The insights and innovations of writing in the 1878–1940 period fed directly into a contemporary revolution in epistemology, as well as into more recent realizations of literature and anthropology as collateral enterprises with common goals and common theoretical issues of perspective, representation, and interpretation. Anthropological writers broached the issues of cultural difference, of on-site particularism, of the observer's standpoint and ethnocentricity, and of the fallible nature of generalization; literary writers opened issues of authorial positioning and voice, of bias of language and discursive form, of societal multiplicity and internal conflict, and of individual social and psychological difference. Today the insights and theoretical ventures of that period have become variously elaborated as theoretical postulates: that language is never the transparent objective medium it had long been assumed to be, that the authority of any interpreter is tainted by her or his personal and cultural perspective, that pure and total intercultural understanding is an impossibility, that no characterization of Others is without significance in the interplay of power and dominance, and so forth. This has been progress, a breaking free of some particularly inhibiting modes of conceptualization, but the new epistemology has its own inhibiting modes—distinctly relativistic, of course—that seem also to lead to contradictions and dead ends. For example, when persons or groups are made the subjects of study, what relative status does this automatically assign to them? In his treatment of this issue Robert Levy points to the irony that "the activity that was supposed to humanize us may in so doing dehumanize them" (1984, 88). And indeed, how are we supposed to relativize and respect those Others who still believe in the absolute transparency of their language and the absoluteness of their general concepts—they, who even lack any systematic anthropology?

Unavoidably in his or her interpretations, the interpreter acquires—however unintentionally, however counter to his or her ideology, however respectful of local expertise—a superior status. A

neoelitism of ethnological positioning and epistemological sophistication replaces the old absolutist elitisms of race and technological superiority. And even as we might try to counter that inequality, we
hear warnings such as that of Regna Darnell to her fellow anthropologists that "respect for ways of being different is deeply ingrained in
us (although the other side of this coin is the potential moral pitfall
of condescension)" (2001, 311), and Marjorie Perloff's that the notion
"that we can now enter a utopia where we approach 'primitive' cultures as 'full and valid alternatives' to our own is perhaps an even
more dangerous myth" than that of simple colonialist superiority
(1995, 352).

That the twentieth-century project of realizing the "primitive"
Other should still be struggling with some residual indeterminacy
and internal contradiction is perhaps a predictable irony, but I would
like to stress two very positive themes underlying the best of the attempts: the fervent moral intent and the creative ingenuity of their
authors. Historically, (as indeed presently) attempts to come to know
and understand the Other have involved a struggle against prevailing
social attitudes and beliefs and persuasive intellectual traditions and
conventions. In the late nineteenth and early twentieth centuries notions of primitive difference were framed in the science of the day,
supported by both official and popular belief, and undergirded and
even sponsored by powerful established interests, all of which made
those notions even more formidable. Striving toward deeper and
more humane understanding of human difference called for the moral
courage to criticize, deconstruct, and antagonize, as well as to launch
new notions, new approaches. Often the new approaches were themselves essentially moral innovations: literary writers pushing the limits of language, of imaginative empathy, of polyvocality in their
works; anthropologists finding ways to achieve greater particularity,
identification with the Other, contextual inclusiveness. Morality-
through-method has come to be an important new factor in this cultural mix, its tendency clearly relativist, multiculturalist. Literary and
anthropological writers have developed several methodological and
rhetorical practices analogously, even mutually, some of the distinctions between their disciplines fading.

In the late nineteenth and early twentieth centuries ethnic researchers had gone into the field and into the libraries with many varied
agendas and subagendas, but most usually with the ethnocentric assumption of objective expert authority and the propensity, in the
standard style of nineteenth-century science, to steer their findings
into the channels of universal truths about human nature and societies. Their gains in understanding were enormous, although their in-

terpretive conclusions and, to some extent, the foci of their investigations were enmeshed in ethnocentric mind-closers like the notion of primitiveness. The anthropologists I study here were thus the inheritors of a great deal of information, conceptual initiative, and endeavor, but—and this is the aspect that I am most interested in examining—they felt they needed to clear away many inherited thought patterns and find new and individual approaches to whatever insights were possible about humankind and their societies. The literary writers were part of an age of experimentation, of "Modernism," of throwing off Truths and conventions and inventing new ways to be new, new ways to envision the human and the social condition.* The period is one of rapid and radical change in the intellectual West, and one with deep and enduring effect.

Henry Adams, Eugene O'Neill, Franz Boas, William Faulkner, Margaret Mead, and Zora Neale Hurston—each in his or her own way was trying to control self-reflexiveness, to avert ethnocentricity, to cancel the vagueness and sweepingly inclusive implications of absolutist language and thought. And in their respective realms they were working toward a respect for the personhood of the Other—possibly as a part of a very different culture, but nongeneric, not constructed as part of a generalized theory of cultures or peoples—and toward a respect for the Other's right to be different and our obligation to try to understand her or him as such. It's a nominalist particularism, a focus on specifics *in situ* that they share, and in evading the mindset and the conceptual system of their own background they invented interpretive and representational modes to embody those specifics. They wouldn't all agree, except in some aspects of their general objectives and intents, but they're all bent on realizing unsparingly candid visions, opening and expanding the range of conceptual possibilities.

They didn't launch us into a sea of absolute relativism even as they loosed us from the tethers of primitiveness and its opposite, but neither did they give us a final and unqualifiedly wiser idea of humanity and human difference. We're still muddling about that, but we know more empirically now, and we know better how to come to know, how not to get quite so badly blocked off in our researches by the things we think we have general categories for, things we think we know.

As I focus on these attempts to reconceive the primitive and the primitivized Other, I am interested in juxtaposing literary and anthropological writing, and in comparing and contrasting them both

---

*See, for example, my *American Literature and the Destruction of Knowledge* (Durham, N.C.: Duke University Press, 1991).

explicitly and implicitly, although evidence of direct influence is quite rare and I do not intend this to be an influence study. There are a number of other worthwhile avenues I plan not to follow. I assume that my readers have some knowledge of sociopolitical conditions of the colonial and neocolonial periods, and there are a great number of studies devoted to those matters, which I don't feel I need to repeat or reinvoke. Popular notions of difference provide a background for the innovations I study here, but they, too, have been extensively studied by other writers, and I will only note them as background or counterpoint. The languages of gender difference is a complex and interesting subject in itself, but one which I address only as it is brought into play by Adams, O'Neill, Faulkner, Mead, and Hurston.

In studying the evolution of the various languages of difference over this period we arrive at nothing definitive. We see a series of stabs at definition and understanding—adding increments of conceptual possibility—a process that has carried us beyond certain phases of ethnocentrism, self-interest and epistemological naiveté, but has left us (even to this day) still in a phase of deconstruction and experimentation. I will claim that collectively it is a heroic process: incapable of ultimate success, perhaps, but absolutely crucial to human welfare—at the tragic extreme, crucial to the survival of particular persons and groups. Perhaps the very variety of approaches and insights is its great strength and hope.

Acknowledgments

I{\small N THE PREPARATION OF THIS STUDY I RECEIVED SOME CRUCIAL HELP} for which I am deeply appreciative. I especially want to acknowledge Carl Dawson for his support both personal and official; Philip E. Coyle III for his encouragement and insight from the inside of anthropology; Susanne Korte for one summer of extraordinarily thorough and intelligent research assistance; Donald Mell for his thoughtful and professional efficiency as Delaware University Press editor; and my wife Barbara for her intelligence, patience, wit, and deep concern, all of which seemed a whole lot like love.

Additionally I would like to acknowledge the following permissions:

From Robert E. Spiller, ed., (1976) *Tahiti by Henry Adams: Memoirs of Arii Taimai* used by permission of Scholars' Facsimiles and Reprints.

"The Fountain", copyright 1919, 1920, 1924, 1926, 1927, 1928 by Eugene O'Neill. Copyright renewed 1946, 1947, 1952 by Eugene O'Neill. Copyright renewed 1954, 1955 by Carlotta Monterey O'Neill, from PLAYS OF EUGENE O'NEILL: VOLUME I by Eugene O'Neill. Used by permission of Random House, Inc.

From LIGHT IN AUGUST by William Faulkner, copyright 1932 and renewed 1960 by William Faulkner. Used by permission of Random House, Inc.

Brief excerpts as noted in the request from COMING OF AGE IN SAMOA by MARGARET MEAD, COPYRIGHT © 1928,49,55, 61,73 BY MARGARET MEAD. Reprinted by permission of HarperCollins Publishers, Inc. WILLIAM MORROW.

Brief excerpts as noted in the request from TELL MY HORSE by ZORA NEALE HURSTON copyright 1938 by Zora Neale Hurston; renewed © 1966 by Joel Hurston and John C. Hurston. Reprinted by permission of HarperCollins Publishers Inc.

The Languages
of Difference

Introduction: Anthropology and Literature Then

IN THE UNITED STATES IN THE YEARS AROUND THE BEGINNING OF the twentieth century, notions of the primitive had a great deal to do with a number of contested social issues and contested interpretations of human nature and human relatedness. The writings and the ideas I examine here were formed in a context of high-stakes contention in which policy, status, and power relationships were being determined and confirmed, and in which scientific theories or literary works could be and were wielded as instruments of validation and justification.

With regard to four major issues this was especially true. Westward expansion and settlement had dispossessed Native American populations and introduced deep ambivalence toward Indians, who, in the words of Philip J. Deloria (following D. H. Lawrence), "served Americans as oppositional figures against whom one might imagine a civilized national Self. Coded as freedom, however, wild Indianness proved equally attractive, setting up a 'have-the-cake-and-eat-it-too' dialectic of simultaneous desire and repulsion" (Deloria 1998, 3). Contention about the morality and the economics of the actual treatment of Indians was more direct, public, and vehement. Second, the Civil War and reconstruction had left the country deeply conflicted about race and the issues of democracy, economic opportunity, and social justice. Justification for white supremacy, for assimilation, or for separation was sought and was readily forthcoming in the discourse of the period, scientific and other. Third, the arrival of immigrants from southern and eastern Europe and from Asia had raised troubling issues of race and of American identity and economic security. The idealism embodied in mottoes like our "Give me your tired, your hungry, and your poor" was mitigated by protectionist theory and policy. And fourth, the idea of extending American commerce and influence out beyond our borders—of civilizing and Christianizing throughout the world—seemed to follow inevitably from assumptions of universal evolution, and it spurred a great deal of argument about the issues of imperialism. As Peter Conn points

19

out, on the question of American occupation of the Philippines, Senator Albert Beveridge insisted that "God has not been preparing the English-speaking and Teutonic peoples for a thousand years for nothing but vain and idle self-contemplation and self-admiration. No! He has made us *the* master organizers of the world to establish system where chaos reigns. . . . He has made us adepts in government that we may administer government among savages and senile peoples." This end-of-century imperialist enthusiasm was tempered by the misgivings of *Harper's* editor E. L. Godkin, who lamented the way that "we fell to shouting and yelling for distant islands to govern" (Conn 1983, 9,8).

Thus many of the contended issues of the day that involved interpretations of human difference and relationships to the Other—Indian displacement, race, immigration, and imperialism—involved conjuring some rationale out of the notion of the primitive. Even the post-Darwinian American keynote of progress was commonly measured off in our difference from primitives. For example, David Nye recounts how an electrification exhibit at a turn-of-century world's fair could typically link the notion of progress to a specific vision of the primitive:

> One of the most common ways to illustrate progress was to evoke its opposite, primitiveness, and most exhibitions included "ethnological" villages—compounds representing the life of Mexicans, Cubans, Blacks in the Old South, Filipinos, or Africans in the jungle—where the visitor could see staged versions of earlier forms of social evolution. At the St. Louis fair these villages were arranged in a "historical" sequence. Electrification thus became embedded in a social Darwinist ideology of racial superiority. Only the most advanced societies had electrified machines and lighting. Darkness was a metaphor for the primitive; light was the exemplification of Christianity, science, and progress. (1990, 35–36)

While imperialist polemics and demeaning characterizations of "primitive" Others did occasion a good deal of opposition, the basic ground of the discourse on policy and on issues—and a good deal of their language—was frequently determined by simplistic racial preconceptions and quasi-scientific theoretics. In what Robert F. Berkhofer, Jr. refers to as "the dominant interpretation of United States history, . . . Frederick Jackson Turner's so-called Frontier Thesis, . . . the Indian was pictured as an obstacle to White settlement and the coming of civilization." Indeed, he also points out that "[b]oth popular and academic historians of the last decades of the nineteenth century accepted the premises of Indian inferiority and the necessity for the disappearance of Native Americans before the westward move-

ment of White civilization" (1978,108–9,108). The extremely influential eugenics movement provides another example. Regarding
human behavior, character, and morality as determined by racial and
individual genetic inheritance, advocates of eugenics urged measures
to insure racial purity and social progress by discouraging interbreed-
ing, to manage birth rates of supposedly superior and inferior types,
and to radically limit immigration. As historian Kenneth Ludmerer
points out, "In order to preserve the superior racial quality of the
American people, it became an important feature of 'negative eugenics' to urge that immigration to the country be limited to those of
Nordic stock" (1972, 23). Simplistic notions of the primitive were
both endemic and vastly influential at the turn of the century.

The very form of nineteenth-century scientific thinking largely put
the writers and anthropologists of the early twentieth century in a
situation where the principal terms available to them were absolute
definitions and distinctions, reified generalizations, and language-
bound designations of laws of nature. Looking backward from a century or so later, we can be amazed at the ways that fundamental sureties had so often been little more than intuitive, biased, or *ad hoc*
hypotheses. The category of the primitive provided one such surety.
Basically a reification of an indefinite property abstracted from various not-necessarily-related characteristics of some widely divergent
cultures, it summed up for many Victorian and early twentieth-century thinkers the principal essence of Other. That this construction
was formed reflexively, around its sheer otherness, is an insight
strongly urged by Adam Kuper in *The Invention of Primitive Society*:

> The anthropologists took . . . primitive society as their special subject, but
> in practice primitive society proved to be their own society (as they un-
> derstood it) seen in a distorting mirror. For them modern society was de-
> fined above all by the territorial state, the monogamous family and private
> property. Primitive society therefore must have been nomadic, ordered by
> blood ties, sexually promiscuous and communist. There had also been a
> progression in mentality. Primitive man was illogical and given to magic.
> In time he had developed more sophisticated religious ideas. Modern man,
> however, had invented science. . . . [Anthropologists] looked back in order
> to understand the nature of the present, on the assumption that modern
> society had evolved from its antithesis. (1988, 5)

The satyrs and centaurs were dying hard, even down through the intellectual culture of the late nineteenth and early twentieth centuries.
Mary Louise Pratt suggests that the process of "othering" is the operative element in the process of primitivizing, its signs as evident in the

text of an eighteenth century explorer (John Barrow's 1801 account of Africans) as in latter-day ethnography:

> Any reader recognizes here a very familiar, widespread, and stable form of "othering." The people to be othered are homogenized into a collective "they," which is distilled even further into an iconic "he" (the standardized adult male specimen). This abstracted "he"/"they" is the subject of verbs in a timeless present tense, which characterizes anything "he" is or does not as a particular historical event but as an instance of a pre-given custom or trait. . . . Through this discourse, encounters with an Other can be textualized or processed as enumerations of such traits. This is what happens in modern anthropology, where a fieldwork encounter results in a descriptive ethnography. It also happens in ethnography's antecedent, the portrait of manners and customs. (Pratt 1986, 139)

Variously affected by these tendencies toward reflexiveness and "othering," early twentieth-century conceptions of primitive difference were rationalized within three distinct, apparently opposed paradigms growing out of the master notions of race, civilization, and culture. In time these notions would come to be seen in sociocultural terms, as founded on intuitive, imperfect science, fallible in their epistemology and suspect in their social implications. But for the thinkers using them they were the most advanced and accurate categories of human classification and characteristics going.

Human difference as conceived of in terms of race was biologically based, on a fixed set of hereditary essences, hierarchical in respect to particular peoples' levels of potential and achievement, and timeless. Primitiveness was an essential, permanent condition. The notion of racial purity as a condition to be rightfully preserved generally came with this paradigm, casting racial intermixture as "miscegenation" and against nature and human welfare. Subsequent developments in genetics and physical anthropology would reveal insufficient evidence of race as a consistent and reliable category of difference, and the term virtually went out of use in science. As Nancy Stepan points out, in its place "we find discussions of populations, gene frequencies, selection and adaptation." Still, she notes that people do indeed believe races exist as discrete entities and are fundamental to human categorization, despite the recent reorientation of biological and anthropological thought (1982, 171,182). As Audrey Smedley sums it up, "Despite referential discrepancies, the social categories of 'race' are very real" (1993, 6). And, of course, those same social categories had a great deal to do with the formation of the race-based scientific paradigm in the first place.

The civilization paradigm was based on time and the idea of progress. Evolutionist theory was central to its articulation and justification, so that it too was biologically oriented, but by the biology of development rather than the biology of classification. For evolutionists, primitiveness was a temporary first stage in human development. The idea that societies would evolve, even had to evolve, fit nicely with the Western world's sense of its own magnificent progress, just as evolution's inbuilt universal society-ranking scheme flattered its assumption of preeminence. Certainly this paradigm, too, was hierarchical, but it did not involve marking any peoples as absolutely, hereditarily inferior, but only as to some degree and for some reason—climatic or historical, say—slower in their development as a society. As an evolutionary notion it of course came with a motif, often an implied undertone, of competitive struggle for survival, but also with a tacit moral obligation to help the less developed to attain a higher level of civilization. In time the unilinear aspect of this model of social evolution would come into question, as would its assumptions of a uniform pattern of development of diverse and widely separated societies, and of a universal state of civilization toward which they all developed. Societies certainly evolved, but not as uniformly and formulaically as that early paradigm would have it, and not with its burden of difference-as-*ipso-facto*-inferiority.

The culture-based paradigm came somewhat later than the other two, and was formed partly in reaction against some of their principles and implications. Its advocates attempted to develop a relativistic, non-ethnocentric approach, avoiding racial essentialism and judgmental comparisons and hierarchies of any kind. The specific culture, conceived of as an integrated unit with its own unique history, was the determinant of character, institutions, mores, and what Westerners perceived as difference. Subsequently the totalizing, functionally integrative tendencies of this paradigm would come in for criticism (see, for example, Said 1978, and Clifford 1988, 2, 272–73). What were called cultures came to be seen as internally disparate, contentious, continuously changing, and somewhat artificially designated entities. But historically the culture-based paradigm introduced a new explanatory framework of difference and relegated to virtual disuse the notion of the primitive as an ethnographically descriptive category.

There is a rough historical progression observable here, as the explanatory dominance shifted from terms of "race" to "civilization" to "culture," although utilizations of each of them were roughly contemporaneous throughout the period I am examining. And in their particular applications none of these conceptual paradigms was entirely free of the others, as we shall see. Still, each functioned as a particular kind of window on human difference, each with its own system of language and perspective, of corollaries and social resultants, each with its own particular created truth, its own particular blindnesses.

In the early twentieth century, oddly, anomalously, almost as an object lesson in the inconsistency of cultures, a new strain of interpretation and attitude initiated a radical alteration in the way the primitive was regarded. Cutting across the traditional sense of the primitive as crude, bizarre, superstitious, ignorant—as something to be regarded with revulsion or condescension as well as wonder—was a new sense of the primitive as universally primal, essential to the human makeup—as something to be rediscovered beneath the veneer of civilization and to be indulged or at least accommodated and learned from. Cultural historians offer a number of explanations for the burgeoning of this new strain of thought: the sudden vogue of depth psychology, of Freudianism and its emphasis on primal, unconscious drives, most prominently, of course; but also the revolution in sexual mores, neoromantic idealization of the noble savage, emerging modernist antirationalism, and so forth (see, for example, Bone 1965, 59 and Bell 1972, 57).

The discovery of the new value of the primitive was especially evident in the visual arts, where "primitive" forms and values provided striking alternatives to confining conventions, and where, in the words of Robert Goldwater, the assumption reigned "that the further one goes back—historically, psychologically, or aesthetically—the simpler things become; and that because they are simpler they are more profound, more important, and more valuable" (1986, 251).*
The whole phenomenon of the psychologizing of the primitive changed the prospect before both anthropology and literature enough that in chapter four I will take a break from Americanness to study the impetus given it by Frazer, Freud and Jung.

Thus notions of the primitive and human difference, for a number of reasons and in a number of sociocultural areas, took on new significances, shifting, to a certain extent, some of their implications of power and status and morality. But still contention raged, on both the old terms and the new, much of it naive fulmination. In Thomas Dixon's notorious 1905 novel *The Clansman*, as George Fredrickson recently pointed out,

> Dixon intensified his efforts to demonstrate the bestial propensities of the blacks. The character who speaks most directly for the author describes

---

*It is worth noting (as Goldwater does, 1986, xvii)—in the interest of maintaining our recognition of the artificial nature of such categorization—that the African and Polynesian artifacts admired as "primitive art" were strictly neither "primitive" nor "art" in the sense in which early twentieth-century culture used those terms.

the Negro as "half child, half animal, the sport of impulse, whim, and conceit, . . . a being who, left to his will, roams at night and sleeps in the day, whose speech knows no word of love, whose passions, once aroused, are as the fury of the tiger." (1971, 280–81)

As opposed to a racist with an absolute and color-based sense of difference, new primitivist William J. Fielding could insist, in a 1922 book called *The Caveman Within Us*, that

> *under the cultural veneer*, all human beings are essentially alike. . . . [N]otwithstanding its higher qualities and potentialities, the nervous system is inherently and inescapably primitive . . . [and] [i]f some . . . expression is not given to the innate forces that are surging up from the jungle of the past, and that have their roots firmly intrenched within us—that are literally the fundamental part of our being—then they will assert themselves no less, but in abnormal and pathological ways. They will not be denied. (1922, xvi, 32, 63)

At the turn of the century American writers were not yet attuned to the attractions of psychoanalytic theory (although they soon would be), but neither were they much affected by either the ethnology of their time or an empirical understanding of the lives and cultures of the presumedly primitive. In their representations of peoples regarded as primitive many of them simply used popularized or sentimentalized stereotypes. For example, Bret Harte and Mark Twain, as Berkhofer explains, seemed to take a view of Indians like that of so many of their compatriots that, "continued to be derived as much from the polemical and creative needs of Whites as from what they heard and read of actual Native Americans or even at times experienced" (1978, 71). Likewise, in White writers' representation of Africans, African Americans, and Asians, stereotyping of every type was endemic, as has frequently been pointed out (see, for example, Cooley 1982, Fredrickson 1971, Gossett 1997, Said, 1993, Torgovnick 1990).

For turn-of-the-century writers of literary works, there was relatively little interest in the "primitive" peoples of faraway lands: "realism" was a predominant fashion—literature's forerunner/analogue to anthropology's sanctioning of the participant-observer—and few American writers had experience outside of their own or European societies. Jack London wrote a number of South-Seas and distant-past-age stories (many of them potboilers) that merely confirmed racial and ethnic stereotypes on their way to their ironic or melodramatic climaxes, although he also wrote a few that challenged conventional notions of primitive-versus-civilized character; Frank

Norris, less experienced and dying younger, operated only within the primitivistic stereotypes.

America's literary culture excluded or marginalized writing by the nonwhite peoples themselves until some time later. "[T]he Indian novel proper can hardly be said to have begun before the 1920s," according to Berkhofer (1978, 106). African American writers, despite significant exposure of nineteenth-century slave narratives by Frederick Douglass, Harriet Jacobs, Sojourner Truth, and others, received little public notice until the manifold accomplishments of the writers of the Harlem Renaissance in the twenties and thirties. Then the perspective was shifted away from that of the white majority, and alternatives to its values and terms of social analysis burgeoned.

Developments in literary technique associated with the emerging fashion for realism predetermined, however, some alteration in the very notion of the primitive. Realism's first-hand detailed documentary observation mitigated against stereotyping, and its demand for unsparing candor, along with its critical stance toward society and society's support system of conventional verities, undermined the ethnocentric complacency of many earlier approaches. Beyond realism's frame (in the directions modernist writers would go) the problematizing of narrative authority and the relativizing of point of view and of language would further substantially affect the reconfiguring of primitive difference, as we shall see. Henry Adams would couch his study of the history of Tahiti in the perspective of one of his Tahitian informants and produce a telling indictment of the callous stupidity at the heart of western imperialism. Eugene O'Neill would shift the position of his audience into the skin of a black protagonist—not only black but black and imbued with the values of a greedy white "civilized" culture—and show his "emperor's" psychic and civil fallibilities in contrast to the humbler but deeper humanity of the very people he has been exploiting. William Faulkner would anatomize a whole Southern community and its interrelationships and incongruities by focusing fictionally in the minds and in the disparate languages of a set of characters caught up in a vortex of racism and self-justification. But more about these as the study progresses. From our perspective, American literature of the early twentieth century seems to be characterized by increasingly more innovative, more "modernist" approaches, and increasingly more negative representations of American society.

The anthropology of the period seems no less revisionary, but in its own particular way. Discovering and interpreting rather than inventing was the anthropologists' calling. The difference of the presumedly primitive Other was their fascination, their stock-in-trade and the justification of their whole endeavor, and how it was framed and understood was a matter of prime importance. But interested in putting the study of human similarity and difference on a basis that was systematic (scientific, that is, in whichever way that seemed possible), they also had to pick their way through the public controversies, struggle against longstanding opinions, manipulate the institutions and publications, and display the usefulness of their work and their discipline, all in a field that was complex, conflictual, and undergoing rapid change. Outside there were the political and bureaucratic and economic apologists anxious to find scientific (or pseudoscientific) support for their ideals and programs, and inside the field there were constant efforts to define and direct the courses of theory and field investigation.* And there was an emerging self-analysis of methods and their implications. Brand new in the early twentieth century was the effort to professionalize the field, to sanction certain goals and procedures and to develop a course of study and a system for certifying professional status.

In those respects (and in some others as well: see chapter six, below) the history of American anthropology practically becomes the story of the achievements of Franz Boas. This attribution is a standard judgment in the history of anthropology; Marvin Harris (ultimately no fan of Boasian ethnology) cites Boas as "one of the most influential figures in the history of the social sciences," pointing out that "His mission had been to rid anthropology of its amateurs and armchair specialists by making ethnographic research in the field the central experience and minimum attribute of professional status" (1968, 250). As early as 1910 we can see domination of *The American Anthropologist* by the Boasians: Paul Radin, Alexander Goldenweiser, Edward Sapir, Robert Lowie, Alfred Kroeber. And of course, in time there were also Ruth Benedict, Melville Herskovits, Ruth Bunzel, Leslie Spier, Margaret Mead, and many others who went on to build and practice anthropology along Boasian lines. Significantly, they each developed approaches, techniques, and conclusions of their own; what Boas gave them was not a specific program or set of *a priori* categories or conclusions, but a sense of the indispensability of empirical evidence gathered in the field, and a critical wariness about conventional habits of cultural generalization and about the inescapable ethnocentricity of their own assumptions. The discourse of difference had been dominated by evolutionists and racial essentialists with their predetermining paradigms; the emerging Boasian alternative offered not a new school of thought but a new approach to interpretation.

---

*For cogent studies of the former, see Gould 1981 and Stepan 1982; for the latter, see Harris 1967 and Stocking 1968.

"For Boas the position of the observer was the fundamental fact of science," Regna Darnell asserts. "The observer must deliberately manipulate standpoint, the angle of vision, to transcend his or her own biases" (2001, 111,112). Such readjustment of perspective away from that of the detached, presumptively omniscient observer was of course an integral part of the movement away from secondhand library research and toward firsthand field experience. Marilyn Strathern traces this relationship in the work of Bronislaw Malinowski,* which she compares in its effects with the work done by Frazer: "The contrast between this modernism and Frazer's historicism was embodied in a new version of primitiveness—a version that incorporated a new relationship. The difference between 'us' and 'them' was conceived not as a different stage in evolutionary progression but as a difference of perspective." And so focusing in a single society "led to a view of individual societies as entities to be interpreted in their own terms, so that . . . societies so identified were seen as organic wholes" (Manganaro 1990, 99,87).

Thus, "culture" would become the key term in anthropological analysis and description: again according to Darnell, "[John Wesley] Powell and Boas agreed that 'culture' was the appropriate unifying concept for the emerging professional discipline of anthropology and, further, that culture was a mental construct, a symbolic form" (1998, xiii), although George Stocking maintains that "It was not Boas but his students who were largely responsible for the elaboration and development of the anthropological concept" (1968, 231). It was a revolution of sorts in the study of humankind, and from its several sources it developed into an interrelated package: firsthand onsite research, near-relativistic viewpoint, and the notion of different cultures as valid, integrated, determining social units. Freed from the necessity of interpreting other peoples according to some absolutistic and basically *a priori* general theory of race or biology or progress, anthropologists had created for themselves a framework of relativism very much in keeping with the modernism so prevalent in literature and many other fields in the early twentieth century. As Darnell puts it, "Cultural relativism was *the* anthropological message of the interwar years" (2001, 327).

But even that revolutionary dogma was an item of some contention during the years of its heyday, and more recently the implications—especially the moral implications of its more extreme applications—

Malinowski is often cited as the originator of the participant-observer ethnographic technique, although others cite Boas or show that such fieldwork had been carried on by a number of earlier Americans out west.

have been subject to dissent from within and without the profession. Michele M. Moody-Adams, for example objects that "any adequate conception of culture must meet, most notably the recognition that cultures are not self-contained, internally consistent wholes," and that to "optimistically assert the 'equivalence' of all practices and ways of life typically demands toleration of all ways of life as equally valid" (1997, 8–9,17). But, as part of the considerable gains of the revolution, again quoting Darnell, "Use of the term 'primitive' without qualification is no longer acceptable, in or out of anthropology. . . . The critical problematic, then, is to disentangle the now distasteful, indeed immoral, concept of 'the primitive' from the historical roots that produced anthropology as a discipline" (2001, 311).

Early twentieth-century anthropology, in the newness of its negatives—its antiethnocentricity, its antiabsolutism, and its rejection of the sort of universal authority assumed by most previous practitioners—had a great deal in common with the emerging literary practices of the day. How we know what we know was becoming a live and complicated issue then in many realms of inquiry from physics to philosophy, and the positioning and the knowledge base of the observer/interpreter was a crucial epistemological matter in the writing of both ethnographic and literary texts. In the new regime much more than in the past, the source of authenticity was local, relativistic, personal.

But given that common epistemological base, anthropological and fictional approaches diverged. In the double-faced relationship of expositor/narrator to subject and to audience—to the people being described and to the people being addressed—the anthropologists of the early twentieth century, avowing (at least implicitly) their own locally limited standpoint, represented their own academicized selves as the expositor/narrator and positioned themselves well over on the audience side, as unquestionably one of us looking in at the others, even when sincerely concerned to realize those others in their native terms. The period's literary writers, on the other hand, felt free to create fictional personae or fictional selves to do the narrating, positioning them wherever revelation and impact could be maximized: with the subjects, with the audience, or with any combination. Empathy and identification with the Other came more readily, more vividly, by the literary route, although with no warrant that verisimilitude hadn't been compromised by the essential reflexiveness of the fictional process. For the anthropologist—staying outside the subject-Other while still trying both to understand what the subject might feel and to block the obtrusion of his or her own cultural conditioning—it was perhaps even more difficult to not-create the observed subject than for the fiction writer to create plausible others. Authorial positioning is a crucial determinant in the texts I have chosen and of the sense of human difference they project. There is a great deal of fictionalizing in them—but in no case is any of them only fiction.

Both anthropology and literature of the early twentieth century had strong leanings toward psychological interpretation. The tendency in itself was neither new nor unusual in the practice of either of those disciplines, but the new and unusual addition of the several depth psychologies to the age's intellectual mix tempted some anthropologists and writers toward such interpretive approaches and language, although seldom without explicit reservations and denials. In the main, though, the language basic to both disciplines was a language of empirical specificity. Anthropologists increasingly regarded a deep familiarity with the language of the object people as necessary to understanding their perception of the world and their place in it, and literary writers had a longstanding fascination with the lingoes of others as representations of their minds and motives. And the details of everyday life, of relationships, of the intersection of social, institutional and individual experiences especially required a very particularized telling in either genre. Thus, just as fiction writing was essentially quasi-ethnographic, cultural anthropology was essentially reliant on the imaginative empathy of its participant-observer.

Of course anthropological writing was the reporting on what we necessarily and simplistically must regard as real people—real people who could be revisited to confirm or refute or modify the original report. And even though, as Stocking points out, "cultural anthropology focusses on complex phenomena whose elements seem to be connected only in the mind of the observer" (1992, 340), and, as James Clifford presents as a recent general recognition, "literary procedures pervade any work of cultural representation" (Clifford and Marcus 1986, 4), it is a *science*, its generalizations subject to scrutiny and its methodologies subject to refinement, revision, or repudiation. Its temporality is inbuilt—progress as well as obsolescence—its growth, in the words of I. C. Jarvie, "involving as it does critical appreciation of past theories and methods combined with their refutation and replacement" (Manganaro 1990, 123).

Typical of all scientific theories and perceptions, the solid knowledge for which anthropologists strove was prone to obsolescence in a way that literary visions were not, and this was to a great extent because of the different function of generalization in the two types of discourse. Anthropological writing was expected to produce general interpretation of its specific information, but the very conceptions that could provide both analytical access and justification for the whole anthropological project also determined the selectivity of the presentation (and possibly of the prior data-gathering and assembling) and tied the resultant text to an obsolescence-prone set of categories. Its specific observations might still be useful, but one might need to discount the tendencies of their general envelope. Literary works had no implied requirement to generalize; whatever it was that writers meant to fit their expression to—considerations of genre, literary tradition, experimentalism, publishability, audience effect, or opposition to conventional judgments and conclusions—left them freer to invent means of representing their possibly quite unorthodox visions. Generalizing was in no way a requirement of their craft. Their visions of human experience could never be more than suppositional (exempting any theory of divine inspiration), but their works were far less vulnerable to the temporal decay that could so affect generalized interpretation when science moved on or intellectual discourse inevitably changed.

For writers in both disciplines, the topic of myth had special importance to the notion of the primitive in various ways at various times. Many anthropological theorists in the late nineteenth and early twentieth centuries were fascinated with myth, seeing it as the special provenance of primitive belief and expression, a key sign of primitive difference. They might differ on whether this story- and image-purveying was a superstitious barbarism linked to dreams and bizarre rituals or a kind of prescientific thinking, but it was clearly different (in one typical comparison) from civilized religious and ethical thought and (in another) from civilized cause-and-effect rationalism. Such interpretations flourished comfortably within the race and civilization paradigms, but in time and with the shift in anthropological focus toward cultures and functions-within-cultures, myth lost much of its defining status, being treated more as a kind of culturally-specific concoction having any of a variety of uses or significances, determined by a particular people's traditions, needs, contact with other cultures, and so forth. Boas's folklore studies were especially important in producing this shift.

Anthropological interpretations growing out of depth psychology tended, however, to posit or imply a sense of myth as a portal to the deepest reaches of a universal human nature. Such interpretations resonated with the modernist primitivist initiatives and their ambition to reach to something primal and elemental in the human makeup. For most twentieth-century American writers of literature, such concerns were far more interesting than were notions of barbarism-in-contrast-to-civilization or the subtleties of intracultural functionality. Additionally, psychoanalytically slanted myth interpretation was congruent (in some respects in a new way) with the sense of universality that was, since time immemorial, Western literature's undergirding theme and broadest justification. But what of interpretations of the past's and other peoples' myths: were they realizations or projections? And since interpretations so often seemed in time to shift and alter or even die, what exactly was their status? During this period, then, the issues of whether myth was primitive or civilized or both, universal or culture-specific, its significance intrinsic or attributed, fixed and final or ever-changing, were live, open, and diverse questions. Their answers (or their presumptions) depended on the conceptions and intents of the answerer.

In the study that follows, I mean to detail the ways that early twentieth century forms of reconceptualization and "literary procedures," especially those involving standpoint/point-of-view and generalization/symbolization, bear on the subject of the primitive in anthropological and literary writing, and how certain insights and rhetorical and linguistic techniques enabled several writers in those disciplines to reconfigure the idea of the primitive. I present the discourse on the primitive as evolving in the direction of more humane and more useful understanding, and the engine of that evolution as the creativity and original insight of individual writers and anthropologists. It is this originality that I am most interested in tracing—in celebrating, actually—and in that interest I devote a chapter to each of several writers, selecting texts in each case to demonstrate originality and the new senses of human difference it was able to produce. I don't claim that the writers I am presenting here are the only ones or the only important ones who contributed to the reconceiving; in fact I have chosen texts to some extent for their variousness, ranging from the enormously influential, widely admired (and later bitterly reviled) *Coming of Age in Samoa* of Margaret Mead to the very inconspicuously published *Tahiti: Memoirs of Arii Taimai* of Henry Adams, which in spite of its negligible contemporaneous influence was a landmark in method and point of view. Each of my choices is meant to reveal particular innovations in the deconstruction of absolutes and in the dedication to specifics *in situ* that have contributed so profoundly to the intellectual and social cultures of the twentieth century. I am hoping for a broader effect, too, whereby my limited and fairly narrowly focused study stimulates further such humanistic analysis of these and other writers and thinkers, of these and other matrices of connection.

I begin my study with an attempt to establish a context: a study of the civilization paradigm of the evolutionists, the dominant new conception at the close of the nineteenth century. It provided new and broadly, intricately articulated concepts of the primitive. Subsequently a great deal of reconfiguring would then have to contest its prevailing preconceptions, language, methods and conclusions.

1

Evolutionizing Difference I: Some Concepts and Complications

THE PRIMITIVE WAS A PASSION WITH ANTHROPOLOGISTS IN THE LATE nineteenth and early twentieth centuries, not only because of its exoticism (that powerful attraction for general audiences), but because so much could be signified by the sheer difference. And the introduction and wide dissemination of the idea of evolution provided a new conceptual framework—very enthusiastically received and applied—for understanding human nature and transforming the whole study of human populations. Here was a framework that could envision a universal, unilinear scheme of development that synthesized all human knowledge and offered the possibility of understanding-at-a-distance, of prediction, of cultural comparisons seen in a whole new light with new significances. The new insights and new limitations on understanding that came with this revolution in thought are the subjects of this chapter and the next.

To the evolutionist, human difference—cultural, social, behavioral, moral, and even in some versions physiological—was basically temporal: not a quality or a categorical essence, but a phase or stage. His approach put him at odds with a number of more traditional notions: with various theories of heredity-based difference, like polygenism and racism; with religion-based theories involving special creation, teleological purpose, and the widely subscribed notion that savages were of races fallen from a higher state of civilization through some cosmic disobedience; and of course with the romantic secular notion of the noble savage. Instead of such absolutely differentiating aspects, evolutionism brought along with it the presumption of what many evolutionists called "the psychic unity of mankind," the idea of the uniform potential (the uniform capacity to evolve) of all humankind. It brought the understanding that all cultures are constantly in a state of change, and that developments in one area of life, like survival technology, have correlative changes in other areas, like social organization. As Henrika Kuklick describes it, "Each stage of evolution was represented as an integrated cultural complex, an amalgam of interdependent habits, beliefs, and social structures"; although she goes on to observe that "evolutionists collapsed all of the dimensions of human variation onto a single axis" (1991, 84).

The "single axis" was, of course, a significant problem, and one very much characteristic of nineteenth-century thought with its penchant for conceptual absoluteness. To represent a universally explanatory framework, an actual Law of Nature, and to assemble a staggeringly diverse range of details in its categories involved a nearly absolute trust in language's capacity to represent sociocultural and psychological phenomena, even where differences were extreme and where essences were (presumably) really temporal stages. But the evolutionists' language was steeped in the biases and preconceptions and judgments of their own EuroAmerican cultures, so that in many ways what they intended as wholly objective syntheses of the populations of the world took on many characteristics of near-jingoism. The tendency of their language and categories to fall into patterns of ranking is an example: peoples and cultures came out as "higher" or "lower" on the evolutionary scale, with, of course, the Caucasian/Western coming out on top, the standard by which all others were judged. Ethnocentricity is inherent in the very situation of evolutionary theorizing: the explanation of the system of evolution automatically positions itself as evolution's highest product.

The data of the evolutionists also posed problems, their methods of filling in the details of their universal human pattern vulnerable, but to some extent unavoidably so. Information about other societies was spotty in those days before the systematic effort to gather information about the peoples of the world. Most nineteenth-century anthropologists relied most of the time on information in texts. A number of non-Europeanized societies had been written about from relatively reliable points of view, but for some remote societies the only texts were by travelers, explorers, missionaries, or conquistadors, and were heavily biased by the predispositions of their authors. And the need to complete the evolutionary pattern pushed anthropologists even beyond the use of questionable source material, into filling in with hunches and *ad hoc* hypotheses where information was entirely lacking. They were fearless in their comparisons and categorizations, however, of cultures past or present, near or far, on the basis of apparent similarities. The "comparative method" it was called, and it was an essential postulate of their method by which they felt they could draw far-ranging conclusions about the evolutionary stages of any given culture. The method could be a route to insightful comparison and discovery, but by discounting the particularity in a culture's history or makeup and the factor of intercultural transmission, it also closed them off from a number of perceptions about their object cultures.

In their representations of the peoples they designated as primitive, the evolutionists were undeniably paternalistic. Their term "primitive" was basically derogatory, primarily meaning "crude," or "rudimentary." In various degrees, from their systemically superior cultural standpoint they saw primitive peoples as developmentally inferior, childlike. They tended to represent the primitives' psychological processes as prerational, their myths as inferior science, their social organizations as crude totemistic forerunners to the property-based monogamous system characteristic of higher development, and their religions as animistic superstitions only rudimentarily like the rationalized and benevolent European faiths. The paternalism and cultural complacency implicit in evolutionist views of course comfortably suited the West's imperialist agenda, although the empirical impetus of the emerging science of human cultures often did not. And there were always individuals whose experience with native peoples belied the standard developmental stereotypes.

But even granting that evolutionist interpretations of primitive difference were culturally made-to-order, were ego- and ethnocentric and complicit in colonialism, the question still remains: What kind of understanding of human difference has been offered by this stream of thought, so crucial in the development of our contemporary world?

The master theorist of nineteenth century evolution—and the Victorian age philosopher with by far the greatest impact on American culture—was Herbert Spencer. What Darwin's *On the Origin of Species* did in 1859 by way of synthesizing biological phenomena, Spencer's *First Principles* did in 1862 for all phenomena in the universe, although he had been working on his formulation for some time entirely independently of Darwin. Spencer's formula for universal process basically involved an evolution from simple to complex, "from an indefinite incoherent homogeneity to a definite coherent heterogeneity" (Spencer 1897b, 472), an evolution characteristic of embryos or species, people or populations, customs or institutions, solar systems or stars. Individual psychology worked this way, whether as development from childhood to adulthood or from the mentality of the primitive to that of the civilized. Societies developed that way too, from homogeneous horde to heterogeneous civilization, with increasing complexity, differentiation and coherence of organization.*

Spencer was in no modern sense an anthropologist; he in fact "did" no science, but he was an omnivorous reader who adopted, adapted, and incorporated theory and fact and hearsay from every congenial quarter, quoting from classical and biblical literature as well as from scholars of history and archaeology, language and religion. His range of information is truly awesome in *The Principles of Sociology* (1876) (as it is in his separate studies of psychology, biology, and *First Principles'* survey of nearly all fields of knowledge). His homogeneity-to-heterogeneity formula unifies and determines the significance of all phenomena: by its means, all reality is rationalized; all phenomena are represented in terms of their utility in the universal tendency toward higher, more complex forms; and all changes are seen as subtle, coherent gradations in a plenitudinous chain of process. Spencer did not see his own society as the end-point in evolution (although it had supplied the norms by which other societies were graded), nor did he see evolution as a perpetual one-way street (he theorized that processes of regression and even universal devolution were inherently inevitable in a universe thus describable). But he had hit upon a system of astounding convincingness and explanatory power for America's science-minded, imperialistically-inclined culture. As a system of explaining phenomena, especially human and social phenomena, it was highly specialized: just as it illuminated certain human situations, it distorted or obscured others.

The primitive for Spencer was not a people or a race but a universal evolutionary stage. One knew its characteristics by knowing how the human mind developed (as Spencer presumptively did, having written *Principles of Psychology* twenty years before *Principles of Sociology*), and using the basic developmental formula to construct a kind of psychocultural childhood of humankind. The process was fundamentally deductive, although supporting and illustrative details, copiously gleaned from all kinds of texts about other peoples and other eras, could be packed into the discussion at the appropriate levels of the evolutionary construct.

Spencer felt no qualms whatever about imagining (quite definitively) what the mental and emotional life of the primitive man was like. The primitive tended to be impulsive; he was improvident and inconstant, deficient in understanding general facts and distant re-

---

*Interestingly, the notion of universal process seems to have come around again with the 1990s complexity theorists, of whom Spencer is a generally unacknowledged precursor.

sults, and unable to concentrate on anything complex or abstract. Thus he was vague about causality; he was credulous and unsceptical, undiscriminating about dream and reality; his language was correspondingly vague and undiscriminating. He was lacking in benevolence (a trait Spencer particularly associated with the higher stages of civilization); and he had a very weak proprietary sense. The primitive society could likewise be defined with total confidence, regardless of local or temporal considerations. It was loosely organized, relatively undifferentiated, weak in specific bonds and connections, rife with ancestor worship and superstition, and informal in its arrangements about property.

"The intellectual traits of the uncivilized . . . are traits recurring in the children of the civilized" (1897c, 91), he explains (in a common analogy that Sigmund Freud would also later adopt), and he repeatedly refers to civilized childhood to interpret primitive belief and behavior. But another *a priori* source of ideas about what primitives must be like is the simple negative of the characteristics of Spencer's own society: judge the difficulty, he challenges, of displacing primitive supernatural beliefs "where the few facts known remain ungeneralized, unclassified, unmeasured; where the very notions of order, cause, law, are absent; where criticism and scepticism are but incipient; and where there is not even the curiosity needful to prompt inquiry" (1897c, 224). And the characteristics Spencer derives from his comparisons with childhood and his negative projection of civilized mental habits and social forms constitute necessitous stages in a fundamentally deterministic evolutionary system: of the typical sorts of primitive beliefs, he asserts, " these ideas which the primitive man forms, are inevitably formed. The laws of mental association necessitate these primitive notions of transmutation, of metamorphosis, of duality; and, until experiences have been systematized, no restraints are put on them" (1897c, 122).

The notions about human culture and society in Darwin's biologically based *The Descent of Man* (1871) had less impact on nineteenth-century anthropological theory than Spencer's, but they were essential components in his effort to discriminate between and stratify primitive and civilized peoples, and to situate them on a time line that progressed toward Western culture. His version of evolutionary progress was driven by natural selection—the survival of better-adapted varieties—rather than by an inherent tendency of things to progress in a certain way. For example, societies tended to become more moral in time, he theorized, because "There can be no doubt that a tribe including many members who, from possessing in a high degree the spirit of patriotism, fidelity, obedience, courage, and sympathy, were always ready to give aid to each other and to sacrifice themselves for the common good, would be victorious over most other tribes; and this would be natural selection" (1981, 166). A basic ethnocentricity still permeates Darwin's views, however: about the evolution of religious ideas he theorizes, "The idea of a universal and beneficent Creator of the universe does not seem to arise in the mind of man, until he has been elevated by long-continued culture" (1981, 395). And he recalled with a full measure of Victorian revulsion his own unfortunate encounter with primitives:

> The astonishment which I felt on first seeing a party of Fuegians on a wild and broken shore will never be forgotten by me, for the reflection at once rushed into my mind—such were our ancestors. These men were absolutely naked and bedaubed with paint, their long hair was tangled, their mouths frothed with excitement, and their expression was wild, startled, and distrustful. They possessed hardly any arts, and like wild animals lived on what they could catch; they had no government, and were merciless to every one not of their own small tribe. (1981, 404)

He avows that he would rather be descended from a monkey who could show some unselfishness of action than from these Fuegian savages who seemed to him, in the shock of this passing encounter, to have no civilized virtues.

The work of British and American anthropologists of the late nineteenth century, beginning in the study of human phenomena rather than of cosmic process or biological selection, was not as intuitive-deductive as Spencer's and not as committed to the mechanism of natural selection as Darwin's, but it too was generally patterned by the notion of evolutionary progress and in that way inherently ethnocentric. But the work of these people—including, among others, Britons Edward Tylor, Sir John Lubbock, John McLennan, and Andrew Lang, and Americans Lewis Henry Morgan, Daniel Brinton, John Wesley Powell, and W. J. McGee—employed a great deal of creative curiosity about other peoples, and, as it greatly expanded available information about other cultures, moved in the direction of modifying attitudes as well.

I do not plan a survey of their particular contributions here. Other available historical and biographical studies do that quite well. My concern is to call attention to several of the key concepts in their characterization of the primitive, discuss their problematical relationship to the idea of race, and then to consider in some detail a work of some originality but still very much a part of that first-wave evolutionist anthropology, Lewis Henry Morgan's *Ancient Society*.

One of the great disadvantages of the work of the early evolutionist anthropologists was their (necessary) reliance on textual sources that came loaded with very particular biases and preconceptions. Looking back at that time, E. E. Evans-Pritchard makes this point especially clearly: in the writings of travelers and missionaries

> [m]agic, barbaric religious rites, superstitious beliefs, took precedence over the daily empirical, humdrum routines which comprise nine-tenths of the life of primitive man and are his chief interest and concern: his hunting and fishing and collecting of roots and fruits, his cultivating and herding, his building, his fashioning of tools and weapons, and in general his occupation in his daily affairs domestic and public. These were not allotted the space they fill, in both time and importance, in the lives of those whose way of life was being described. Consequently, by giving undue attention to what they regarded as curious superstitions, the occult and mysterious, observers tended to paint a picture in which the mystical . . . took up a far greater portion of the canvas than it has in the lives of primitive peoples . . . and the natives were made to look childish and in obvious need of fatherly administration and missionary zeal, especially if there was a welcome bit of obscenity in their rites. (1964, 8)

Anthropologists were of course part of that same culture of interpretation, and their own preoccupation with matters of mentality, belief and ritual tended to shape the most prominent characteristics of their version of primitive difference. It was Briton Edward Burnett Tylor who proposed *animism*—"the theory which endows the phenomena of nature with personal life" (From "The Religion of Savages" [1866] Kuper 1988, 80)—as a defining characteristic of the primitive mind. According to this notion, widely (although not universally) adopted in the anthropological community, savages saw spirit in everything they experienced, waking or dreaming. A specific elaboration of animism, linking that mental characteristic to social forms and structure, was John McLennan's widely adopted idea of *totemism*, which hypothesized that primitive peoples often regarded a type of animal, bird or natural phenomenon as their particular tribal talisman, having special spiritual significance and efficacy for them. According to George Stocking "McLennan wanted to show that 'totemism' was a general stage in the evolution of man" (Stocking 1995, 48).

Totemism and correlative theories of exogamy were subjects of a great deal of controversy in nineteenth-century Anglo-American anthropology: according to one source quoted by Stocking, "there had been over twenty different theories of totemism" (Stocking 1995, 177). Anthropologists were quick to perceive evidences of animism and totemism in primitive societies and to distance themselves from them. Especially to distance: they recognized what they called "survivals" of primitive beliefs in their contemporary culture. And while they saw that "survivals" might be interpretively useful as analogies in their quest to understand human evolutionary history, such beliefs and practices still signified the presumably animalistic heritage their culture was trying rationalistically (in the very act of anthropologizing, for example) to overcome. Shades of the satyrs still haunted a culture insecure about its own state of civilization.

Anthropologists could accomplish the distancing by their characterization of primitive religion and their relative positioning of it on the evolutionary scale. Here is Sir John Lubbock in 1870 differentiating, apologizing, predisposing:

> I shall endeavor to avoid, as far as possible, anything which might justly give pain to any of my readers. Many ideas, however, which have been, or are, prevalent on religious matters, are so utterly opposed to our own that it is impossible to discuss the subject without mentioning some things which are very repugnant to our feelings. Yet, while savages show us a melancholy spectacle of gross superstitions and ferocious forms of worship, the religious mind cannot but feel a peculiar satisfaction in tracing up the gradual evolution of more correct ideas and nobler creeds. (1895, 205)

And Andrew Lang, for whom the myths and beliefs of savages were failed attempts at both science and religion, says of the stories he regards as the repositories of primitive wisdom,

> No more need be said to explain the wild and (as it seems to us moderns) the irrational character of savage myth. It is a jungle of foolish fancies, a *walpurgis nacht* of gods and beasts and men and stars and ghosts, all moving madly on a level of common personality and animation, and all changing shapes at random, as partners are changed in some fantastic witches' revel. Such is savage mythology, and how could it be otherwise when we consider the elements of thought and belief out of which it is mainly composed? (1968, 52–53)

Lang sees an absolute discontinuity between the wisdom of his own culture, founded on "an elevated conception of a moral and undying Maker of Things, and Master of Life, a Father in Heaven" and the terrible stuff of savage belief. "In the civilized races the genius of the people tends to suppress, exclude and refine away the wild element, which, however, is never wholly eliminated. . . . It can only be subdued by Christianity, or rather that break between the educated classes and the traditional past of religion which has resulted from Christianity" (Lang 1968, 160, 53). Is there a note of fear behind all the hyperbolic negativity of these characterizations, and of that insistence on a historical break in the evolution of belief? But in a paean to science's triumph over myth in the 1888 *American Anthropologist*, American John Wesley Powell, influential director of the Bureau of American Ethnography, picking up on the tripartite categories *savagery*, *barbarism*, and *civilization* promoted by Lewis Henry Morgan, shifted the grounds of difference from Christianity to chest-thumping culture pride:

> The greatest intellectual discovery of savagery was the discovery of the difference between the animate and the inanimate, between the organic and the inorganic, between the living world and the dead world; but the discovery having been made, the animals were deified and believed to be the authors and movers of the world of phenomena. The greatest intellectual achievement of barbarism was the discovery of the limited powers of animals; but the discovery having been made, the powers and wonders of nature were deified and given the forms of men. The greatest intellectual achievement of civilization was the discovery of the physical explanation of the powers and wonders of the universe, and the intellectual superiority of man, by which he becomes the master of those powers and the worker of wonders.
> In savagery, the beasts are as gods; in barbarism, the gods are men; in civilization, men are *as gods*, knowing good from evil. (Powell 1970, 75)

There were, of course, exceptions to the kind of differencing prevalent in most evolutionist interpretation. As one example, Daniel Brinton, one of the most prominent American anthropologists of the late nineteenth and early twentieth centuries (and a Quaker), insisted that religious myths of all kinds had not only an absolute referent but a divine source. They had evolutionary gradations, to be sure, from animistic to Christian, but the "laws of the human mind," being essentially similar the world over, the universality of religious inspiration meant not only that "in every race, in all ages, have men's prayers ascended to 'Our Father who art in heaven,'" but that "the lowest religions seem to have in them the elements which exist in the ripest and the noblest; and these elements work for good wherever they exist" (1897, 167, 215). Like Lubbock, Brinton was ashamed of many primitive ritual practices, but humane paternalist throughout, he would contrive an excuse rather than an apology for the violations of Victorian sensibilities:

> There were, indeed, and often, licentious rites, deliberate indecencies, practised under the cloak of religion by unscrupulous rulers and debased

priests. These were alienations and prostitutions of religion. In the genuine and primitive faiths, the symbols of the reproduction and transmission of life were frequent and public, and were not associated with thoughts or acts of debauchery. They were visible emblems of that Spirit of Life which, beyond all else, was the unifying instinct of religious expression. (1897, 167)

An exception of a very different sort was provided by on-site ethnologist Alice C. Fletcher, who reported in the *Journal of American Folk-Lore* in 1891 on the Cheyenne people's incorporation of Jesus and the imagery of messianic Christianity into their pagan vision. Fletcher represented their religious change not as the hoped-for upward movement of a primitive people toward civilization but a terribly ironic consequence of the destruction of a culture, with the attendant characteristically human reaction to oppression and alienation:

> In view of all the facts, it is not surprising that these Indians, cut off from exercising their former skill and independence in obtaining their food and clothing; growing daily more conscious of the crushing force of our on-sweeping civilization; becoming, in their ignorance, more and more isolated from a new present, which is educating their children in a new language and with new ideas,—that these men of the past, finding themselves hedged in on all sides, and shorn of all that is familiar to their thought, should revert with the force of their race to their ancient hope of a deliverer, and to confound their hero with the white man's Messiah, who shall be able to succor the failing Indians, feed their half-famished bodies with the abundant food of old, to reunite them with their dead, and give back to them sole possession of their beloved land. In a rudely dramatic but pathetic manner this "Messiah craze" presents a picture of folk suffering, and their appeal for the preservation of their race, to the God of their oppressors. (Fletcher 1891, 60)

Race was a category that should not have been a problem for evolutionist anthropology, but it was. For Darwin and Spencer, the issue was clear. Darwin reasoned that "the variability of all the characteristic differences between the races . . . indicates that these differences cannot be of much importance; for, had they been important, they would long ago have been either fixed and preserved, or eliminated." He went on to characterize racially differentiated humankind as a "protean or polymorphic" form in that "their variations being of an indifferent nature, . . . they escaped the action of natural selection" (1871, 249). Spencer insisted that to try to maintain that there were profound innate racial differences in the capacity to evolve while acknowledging "that the human type has been evolved from lower

types" was a "marvelous inconsistency" (1897c, 294–95). Nevertheless, race was an unavoidable consideration in the latter nineteenth
century. It was, of course, in ordinary experience a primary classifier
that designated the way people saw themselves as members of definite
groups and different from others. In sociopolitical contexts, it was the
matrix of profound differentials of status and power. In the study of
human populations and characteristics, it provided anthropologists
with a typology that seemed both natural and essential.

Although the evolutionary scheme marginalized it, the analysis of
human populations seemingly couldn't do without it. In a very basic
sense the static, essentialist nature of the concept of race was, in nineteenth-century terms, incompatible with the process-oriented concept of evolution. The thinkers who tried to unite the two notions as
major conceptions in a single frame were led into reductionism, self-
contradiction, or *ad hoc* improvisation. Even Darwin, as Nancy
Stepan has pointed out, compelled by "the type of argument he was
making," striving for "continuity," "closed the mental and moral gap
between man and animals by using the savages as a point of comparison." "At the heart of Darwin's argument for evolution, therefore
was a reliance on the traditional chain of races . . . [by which] scientists would find it only too easy to interpret Darwin as meaning the
races of man now formed an evolutionary scale" (1982, 54–55). There
simply weren't terms subtle and inclusive and compatible enough
with which to frame an understanding of the whole human population and its history.

The incompatibility of the prevailing concepts was manifold. If race
were in some sense a pure and essential human characteristic, the evolutionary postulate of the mental unity of humankind was compromised. Additionally, the relative openness of the developmental
parameters of evolving forms was negated. Insofar as the hierarchical
habit of thought, so common in nineteenth-century thought, determined the relative positioning of the races, the absoluteness implied
in such positioning also contravened evolutionary principles. Evolutionary theory had difficulty with the origins and the very existence
of races: supposedly they had evolved, but in recorded history they
only seemed to have intermixed and marginally blended, so what was
the mechanism of their formation? Some kind of radical climatic effect? And were races, as such, themselves in competition in natural
selection? But wasn't such a notion a kind of macro-reductionism
that overrode all other aspects of natural selection?

In the anthropologists' discourse we see presumed expertise falter
and self-contradict. Daniel Brinton, so vigorous in his affirmation of

evolution and "the psychic unity of mankind" is, in passages of different intent, equally affirmative about race as an absolute category:

> The traits of the race . . . overslaugh the variable characters of the family, the sex or the individual, and maintain themselves uniform and unalterable in the pure blood of the stock through all experience.
>
> This fact is the corner-stone of the science of Ethnography, whose aim is to study the differences, physical and mental, between men *in masses*, and ascertain which of these differences are least variable and hence of most value in classifying the human species into its several natural varieties or types. (1890, 18)

The notions of "pure blood" and "uniform" and "unalterable" traits are clear derivatives of polygenist, essentialist thinking, and the intent to "classify the human species into its several natural varieties or types" entails countering the temporal orientation of evolutionary thought.

With that project of classifying in mind, anthropologists tended to look for what could be comparatively regarded as typical physical characteristics of the races (like the relative skull capacity, angle of forehead slope, width of nasal aperture, length of arm, time of closing of fontanel or appearance of wisdom teeth of each), and typical mental and cultural attainments (like the relative sophistication of the language, agriculture, metallurgical technology, or religion of each). Brinton provides a representative interpretation of such comparative data: after a list of characteristics such as "wide nasal aperture," "prominence of the jaws," and "early appearance of wisdom teeth," he declares,

> When all or many of these traits are present, the individual approaches physically the type of the anthropoid apes, and a race presenting many of them is properly called a "lower" race. On the other hand, where they are not present, the race is "higher," as it maintains in their integrity the special traits of the genus Man, and is true to the type of the species.
>
> The adult who retains the more numerous fetal, infantile or simian traits, is unquestionably inferior to him whose development has progressed beyond them, nearer to the ideal form of the species. . . .
>
> Measured by these criteria, the European or white race stands at the head of the list, the African or negro at its foot. (1890, 48)

Brinton in his writings is by turns (and inconsistently) generous, understanding of difference, tolerant, condescending, paternalistic, and superior. But in respect to the category of race, what is operational is racism and self-justification. The one who defines "the ideal form of the species" has a mirror-model in mind.

Historian Peter Conn suggests some of the effect of the close tie between science and racism around the turn of the century by juxtaposing two significant sources. With one, he cites W. E. B. Du Bois's 1898 appeal to settle society's problems in accordance with its "highest ideals" by essaying "to study those problems in the light of the best scientific research." Conn points up not only "the grimly ironic trap [that] lay in wait for the confident Du Bois" in the racist slant of most of the social science of the period, but also how such presumptive expertise was disseminated in, for example, the essay on "Negro" in the ninth and eleventh editions of the *Encyclopedia Britannica* (1889 and 1911). The ninth characterized the African aborigines as that people which "by the nearly unanimous consent of anthropologists occupies . . . the lowest position in the evolutionary scale . . . ," while the eleventh claimed that "the negro would appear to stand on a lower evolutionary plane than the white man, and to be more closely related to the highest anthropoids . . . Mentally the negro is inferior to the white . . . The arrest or even deterioration in mental development is no doubt very largely due to the fact that after puberty sexual matters take the first place in the negro's life and thoughts" (Conn 1983, 138–41,329).

It was principally in the popular white imagination and the minds and works of negrophobe apologists like Thomas Dixon (*The Leopard's Spots*) and Charles Carroll (*The Negro a Beast*) that that motif of unbridled sexuality fulminated threateningly in the supposed conjunction of dark skin, primitiveness, and a position on the evolutionary scale relatively closer to the animals. In terms of the characterization of the darker races, the evolutionists, in concocting their developmental hierarchies of races, were playing the same reflexive, self-aggrandizing game as the essentialists, and supporting, actually, their characterizations and their attendant social programs. For example, just as Francis Galton (*Hereditary Genius*) could look on the possibility of selective mating as an evolutionary opportunity to improve the human stock, Madison Grant (*The Passing of the Great Race*) could look on the breeding habits of the respective fixed racial types as a threat to the survival of civilization.

The issue of racial mixing was of course an especial crux of the evolutionists' discussion of race. Their intellectual heritage predisposed them toward the ideas of "pure blood" and racial purity, and that line of thinking often involved the polygenist notion of the weakness or inviability of mixed-race individuals. There were even theories (of sociologists William Thomas and Franklin Giddings) that racial prejudice itself was instinctual (See Fredrickson, 1971, 315–16). Anthropologists addressing the issue thus again brought their fledgling discipline into a preconfigured and highly charged field. Of the two basic theoretical positions the evolutionists were able to take—that intermixture was detrimental to the species or that it was beneficial—both involved struggles with the heritage, and each was determined, ultimately, by the moral predilections of its proponents.

Brinton's articulation of the issue in his 1890 book *Races and Peoples* is in some ways quite typical and in some ways quite personal, although the personal reaction is very revealing about the objectivity of much turn-of-the-century anthropology. Treading gingerly at first, he acknowledges the sensitivity of the problem linguistically: of the American term *miscegenation* he says, " The fact that we have manufactured this 'recent and ill-formed word,' as Webster's *Unabridged* calls it, is evidence that the questions involved in this problem touch us nearly." He goes on to recognize on the basis of anthropological evidence that "the results of race-crossings differ with races and with evironment [*sic*]." But as he proceeds, what he conceives of as racial characteristics take on the force of essences unrelated to social or cultural conditions: "It seems, for instance, tolerably certain that the cross between the white and black races produces offspring (mulattoes) who are deficient in physical vigor. It is well ascertained in the United States that they are peculiarly prone to scrofula and consumption, unable to bear hard work, and shorter lived than either the full black or the white." He later recognizes the effect of social factors, at least generally: "It is also true that in perhaps ninety per cent of the cases, these mixed unions are illegal, and the children suffer under the stigma of illegitimacy. This means more or less deficiency in home training, education, legal protection, and social recognition."

But Brinton cannot maintain this scientifically objective persona, as the very thought of miscegenation on a personal level, especially between a white woman and a black man, breaks through to the personal moral revulsion underlying his whole discourse:

> There can be no doubt but that any white mixed race is lower in the scale of intelligence than the pure white race. A white man entails indelible degradation on his descendants who takes in marriage a woman of a darker race . . . Still more to be deplored is the woman of the white race who unites herself with a man of a lower ethnic type. It cannot be too often repeated, too emphatically urged, that it is to the women alone of the highest race that we must look to preserve the purity of the type, and with it the claims of the race to be the highest. They have no holier duty, no more sacred mission, than that of transmitting in its integrity the heri-

tage of ethnic endowment gained by the race through thousands of generations of struggle. That philanthropy is false, that religion is rotten, which would sanction a white woman enduring the embrace of a colored man. (1890, 283–84, 286, 287)

A good deal of evolutionary anthropology had a different theoretical/moral slant, however—different, that is, but not substantially more sanguine about the capacities and likely fate of the dark-skinned Other. The position that intermixture was a long-run benefit to humanity was the position of arch-evolutionist John Wesley Powell and a number of his colleagues of the Bureau of American Ethnography (BAE). Powell saw the homogenizing of the races, the blending of difference, and even the loss of distinct racial identity as inevitable and hopeful correlatives of that evolution that was moving humanity in the direction of progress and stability. As historian Curtis Hinsley describes Powell's position, "While the 'synthetic chemistry of social life' was bleaching black Americans, the American Indian was rapidly fading as a distinct race as well. Powell predicted that within three generations there would be no pure Indian or Negro blood in North America: 'Civilization overwhelms Savagery, not so much by spilling blood as by mixing blood, but whether spilled or mixed, a greater homogeneity is secured'" (Hinsley 1981, 133). BAE anthropologist William McGee recognized the fallibility of the idea of the superiority of pure blood ("the predominant peoples of the world are of mixed blood"), and he affirmed that "the human genus . . . is steadily drifting toward unity of blood and equality of culture." And mixture was strength for McGee. Again according to Hinsley, he decided that "the mingling of peoples had gone so far that the American had become 'the world's most complex ethnic strain,' and American culture embraced all others." Therefore "America stood at the head of advancing humanity" for McGee, precisely because of racial and ethnic mixing (1981, 247).

Finally, although it seemed to turn-of-the-century anthropologists that race was a natural, inevitable category of human classification, there was, as Thomas Gossett has recently pointed out, no real agreement what constituted a race, nor how many different races there were—that is, whether there were three, four, nineteen, sixty-three or whatever number. For out-and-out racists, Gossett points out, scientifically classifying presumably racial characteristics did not matter, since "they did not really need proof for what they *knew* was there" (1997, 82–83). But regarding evolutionary anthropologists of any and every stripe, we might discover with dismay what seems to be another unconsciously categorical aspect of their thought: that the hierarchies of however many races, however characterized, were always scaled according to color, the darkest being the lowest. In consideration of race, on the vast scale of human evolution primitive was a color.

2

Evolutionizing Difference II: Lewis Henry Morgan and *Ancient Society*

ONE OF THE NINETEENTH CENTURY'S MOST INFLUENTIAL TEXTS IN evolutionist anthropology, American Henry Lewis Morgan's *Ancient Society* (1878), is an amazing confluence of absolutism and empathy. Like a great deal of Victorian science, it booms with macrocosmic generalization (what latter-day anthropologist Meyer Fortes would refer to as Morgan's "preposterous scheme of social stages" [1969, 7]); but at the same time it has a basis in painstaking empirical detail, a carefully defined and delimited method of drawing scientific conclusions from it, and remarkable tones and overtones of admiration and empathy in treating the noncivilized Other.

"It can now be asserted upon convincing evidence that savagery preceded barbarism in all the tribes of mankind, as barbarism is known to have preceded civilization. The history of the human race is one in source, one in experience, and one in progress" (Morgan 1878, xxix–xxx). Thus Morgan presents the sweeping generalization that is his thesis for unifying all human societies, past and present. Along with this universal perception comes the sense of great drama of all human history considered as a single narrative:

> There is something grandly impressive in a principle which has wrought out civilization by assiduous application from small beginnings; from the arrow head, which expresses the thought in the brain of a savage, to the smelting of iron ore, which represents the higher intelligence of a barbarian, and, finally, to the railway train in motion, which may be called the triumph of civilization. (1878, 553)

Of course this was the standard culture-pride of the nineteenth-century EuroAmerican, the sort of attitude later associated with so much of the world's intolerance and tragedy.

But Morgan had come to pontificating only fairly late in his career, and *Ancient Society*, his culminating work, was based on a good deal

49

of thinking of a very different sort. Morgan was a lawyer all his working life—never really a professional academic, social scientist, or philosopher—and he came to the study of human societies in an amateurish and unusual way. As the events are cogently traced in Carl Resek's biography (1960, 23–40), Morgan in the 1840s was working as a lawyer in Rochester, New York, when he persuaded his fellow members of the public-spirited fraternity "The Gordian Knot" to change their focus to one more indigenously American and become "The Grand Order of the Iroquois." In the words of Philip Deloria, whereas the fraternity originally "sought literary inspiration in the familiar mixture of Greco-Roman classicism and the natural antiquity of the New World," they "eventually turned from nostalgia toward rationalized, objective scientific investigation," and their effort "to define a literary national identity took on a modern, ethnographic character well suited to the American social elite of the late nineteenth century" (1998, 72,73).

Morgan himself established personal connections with Iroquois Indians ("informants," anthropologists would later term such connections), and also so close an involvement with contemporary Indian affairs that he acted as the representative of the local tribes to Albany and Washington in that crucial time of the Indians' struggle to prevent displacement from their lands in the face of white men's concerted use of the law, propaganda, bribery, and intimidation to get the territory for themselves. Upon his requesting the honor, Morgan was even adopted into the Seneca tribe.

Morgan collected artifacts and studied the Indian languages, he knew all the published writings of American missionaries and frontiersmen, but most important in terms of his contribution to subsequent anthropology and the development of its scientific method were his contacts with the Indians themselves. He had informants (like the articulate Ha-sa-ne-an-da, Ely Parker to the whites) from whom he got extensive and deep information, and he had scores of short interviews, which he inevitably turned toward the subjects that mattered the most to him. He toured the Midwest and West extensively (at some cost to his family and professional life), interviewing at every opportunity. He even embarked on a program of sending questionnaires to potential informants he could not contact personally. The empirical, emic aspects of Morgan's work are still highly valued by anthropologists of our day, like Thomas R. Trautman, who says that Morgan's reliance on fieldwork seems quite modern when compared with his contemporary "anthropologists of the library": "again and again he sought to get the data of his work by direct interrogation and observation rather than by ransacking libraries." His series of works thus record "the successive attempts to rationalize by generalizing the original intense, meaningful, and baffling encounter with the cultural other" (1987, 9–10).

It was the special line of inquiry that Morgan pursued in his investigations that made him able to rationalize the "cultural other" in ways that proved highly congenial to empirical investigation, empathetic with his subjects, and, in both respects, unusual in nineteenth century anthropology. What Morgan focused on was kinship terminology—how the members of a given tribe would designate a cousin, the daughter of a cousin, the husband of the daughter of a cousin, and so forth—and what the kinship relationships had to do with the social and political organization of the people, from family to tribe to confederation of tribes. This sort of investigation was original with Morgan—he *invented* kinship as an anthropological category, Trautman claims.

As Marvin Harris points out, Morgan "systematically avoided" the subject of religions at a time when that matter "was actually given priority by most the other evolutionists" (1968, 199). In his own words, Morgan avoids the subject of "the growth of religious ideas" because "religion deals so largely with the imagination and emotional nature, and consequently with such uncertain elements of knowledge, that all primitive religions are grotesque and to some extent unintelligible" (1878, 5–6). To a lay observer, kinship and social organization have little of the exotic appeal of the strange and very much "other" religious beliefs and practices of "primitive" cultures. But they have the potential to project the anthropologist more specifically into the social structure and the human experience of the people being studied. How do their family relationships work? With which of the people around them do they feel the nearest ties? What is the source of authority in their culture? How do they solve their interpersonal and social problems? These are questions that could take one inside their lives and give a nuanced sense of how they live day to day. As Meyer Fortes points out, "a kinship terminology represents a body of specialized knowledge which is indispensable for the individual in regulating and organizing his social relations" (1969, 25). By comparison, focusing on the apparently religious aspects of a culture was far more likely to impress the anthropologist with a people's atavistic otherness in notions or practices that differed greatly from those of his or her own home culture. The regnant myths of primitive difference may well have followed from the European preoccupation with religion and myth. The study of kinship initiated by Morgan, however, pointed anthropology in the subsequently very useful directions of the emic investigation of cultures and relativized conceptualizations of cultural organization.

The major works that Morgan produced before conceiving of *Ancient Society* had yielded some interesting insights and perspectives. *The League of the Iroquois* (1851), *The American Beaver and His Works* (1868), and *Systems of Consanguinity and Affinity in the Human Family* (1871) presented Morgan's discoveries that the Iroquois society was basically matrilineal in the passing on of property and political influence, that the basic unit of Indian societies was familial (as he termed it, "gentile"), that the Indians' gentes were organized into remarkably democratic confederations, that it was by rational rather than instinctual processes that adaptation was achieved by the beaver (a finding which very much interested Charles Darwin), and that kinship systems were broadly comparable among different peoples. A great deal of the material of these works was directly incorporated into *Ancient Society*, and their basic insights provided much of its intellectual framework.

But it was the idea of evolution that gave Morgan's insights their master framework. Like Spencer and Comte and Darwin, but apparently not at all very directly indebted to them, Morgan came to see that the way to understand and unify the phenomena of human society was through the notion of universal progress. The model of Iroquois familial/social organization seemed to prevail also among other Indian peoples, and Morgan's discovery that it seemed to be characteristic of a number of oriental cultures as well suggested the idea of the unity of human potential and experience: "It may be remarked finally that the experience of mankind has run in nearly uniform channels," he maintains in *Ancient Society*; "that human necessities in similar conditions have been substantially the same; and that the operations of the mental principle have been uniform in virtue of the specific identity of the brain of all the races of mankind" (1878, 8). Viewed around the world and down through the passage of time, this human unity entailed the existence of a uniform and universal evolution indicated in the subtitle of this work, *Researches in the Lines of Human Progress from Savagery through Barbarism to Civilization*. In *Ancient Society*, then, Morgan's original Iroquois model, the comparative method, and the notions of universal progress and the unity of mankind come together to form a unified vision of all human experience.

In following all "lines of human progress" through all "ancient" societies, Morgan develops a complex, highly rationalized grid for organizing and presenting his exposition. This of course was customary in nineteenth-century social theory: witness Spencer, Comte, Hegel, and others. Morgan's scheme involved the three major periods of "savagery," "barbarism" and "civilization," each divided into "lower," "middle," and "upper" stages; he set out to examine the succession of stages with respect to four general aspects—"inventions and discoveries" (intelligence and the arts of survival), "social and civil institutions," "the family," and "property"; correlative with the nine general stages was a succession of five phases of family development; and overarching this grid of notions was the general movement from precivilized forms of sociopolitical organization based on family structure and toward organization based on property and territorial boundaries. The intricate meshing of this network of notions is not important to us today, nor is even the relative accuracy of its applications (some are amazingly apt and others wildly, obsoletely speculative). Morgan's originality is worth noticing, however, as well as the wonderful example *Ancient Society* affords of Victorian age rationalism and universalism struggling with sheer multiplicity and inescapable reflexiveness in conceptualizing the cultural Other.

Morgan refutes or ignores many of the categories of prior and contemporary anthropology—the notion of animism as the foundation of primitive belief, the essentialist definition of human difference in polygenist racial terms, and the Christian myth that savage societies have degenerated from a state of grace, for example—all categories, it is worth noting, that served to increase the sense of separation of the Westernized observer from the non-Westernized Other. But a new social theory is in essence not an escape from bias but the substitution of different bias, and for Morgan, as we shall later see, the idea of the universal sameness of all mankind carried some distinct overtones of universal Americanization.

Morgan's scheme of classifying societies is both synchronic and diachronic: Archaeology and contemporary anthropology are intermixed in this affirmation of human uniformity, and "in studying the [contemporary] condition of tribes and nations in these several ethnical periods we are dealing, substantially, with the ancient history and condition of our own remote ancestors" (18). The "ethnical periods" themselves have a consistency to their elements: "The weapons, arts, usages, inventions, dances, house architecture, form of government, and plan of life of all alike bear the impress of a common mind, and reveal, through their wide range, the successive stages of development of the same original conceptions" (151). Thus he can postulate, in a remarkably relativistic way, that in general "the spirit of the government and the condition of the people harmonize with the institutions under which they live" (214). And human evolution is continuous and coherent for Morgan: "The principal institutions of civilized nations are simply continuations of those which germinated in savagery, expanded in barbarism, and which are still subsisting and advancing in civilization" (321). We can see in all of Morgan's postulates the effort to establish a sense of commonality with the Others' cultures, or at least a sense that however different, they have every right to be the way they are (or were). And this in spite of the enormous ethnocentric pull of evolutionary theory itself.

Of the lowest of the three stages of savagery Morgan claims there are no examples in the nineteenth-century world; it had "commenced with the infancy of the human race, and may said to have ended with the acquisition of a fish subsistence and of a knowledge of the use of fire." The people of this stage subsisted on fruits and nuts, Morgan supposes, and they are to be credited with "the commencement of articulate speech" (10). Morgan's system by its very nature needs all the stages to be filled in, and unfortunately the first stage to be described is one about which there is no empirical information, only a range of likelihoods, generated systemically out of what is more surely known. And the process is risky. Fish subsistence as a cultural marker might (or might not) be relevant for peoples of eastern North American, but Morgan must also hypothesize an "original restricted habitat" (10) to make it plausible. And when he (admittedly) hypothesizes the earliest stage of sociosexual relations as a system of utter promiscuity, it is apparent that this notion is little more than a retrograde projection of an evolution to monogamy, implied in the rationale of his unified, all-inclusive system. The earliest stage of social life is lost in the dimness of the past and must be constructed out of back-projections and negatives.

Middle and Upper Savagery are the stages to which Morgan attributes the spreading of population across the earth, the invention of the bow and arrow and, eventually, of the art of pottery. These latter phases include "the establishment of two forms of the family, and possibly a third, and the organization into gentes which gave the first form of society worthy of the name" (42). Contemporary Polynesia and Australia are "the best areas for the study of savage society," (463) he claims, although having first warned his gentler readers that examining the Australian system "carries us into a low grade of human life" (50). "Australian humanity, as seen in their cannibal customs, stands on as low a plane as it has been known to touch on the earth" (374). The Africans Morgan seems especially unable to treat—even to classify—partly because of lack of information and partly because of incursions by nonindigenous cultures:

> In Africa we encounter a chaos of savagery and barbarism. Original arts and inventions have largely disappeared, through fabrics and utensils in-

troduced from external sources; but savagery in its lowest forms, cannibalism included, and barbarism in its lowest forms prevail over the greater
part of the continent. Among the interior tribes, there is a nearer approach
to an indigenous culture and to a normal condition; but Africa, in the
main, is a barren ethnological field. (371)

Morgan tends to use the term "primitive" very sparingly, usually
in reference to the very earliest stages of human evolution, and he insists that peoples in the savagery stage are fully humanly endowed,
although crudely underdeveloped. Take the case of that cannibalism
marker, for example, Morgan's sign of the furthest extremity from
civilization. From the beginning, cannibalism had been practiced, he
claims, because of the scarcity of food sources. Thus,

> the acquisition of farinaceous food in America and of domestic animals in
> Asia and Europe, were the means of delivering the advanced tribes, thus
> provided, from the scourge of cannibalism, which . . . there are reasons
> for believing was practiced universally throughout the period of savagery.
> (24)

Thus as the food supply increased, the human population could make
the utilitarian (and moral?) decision to move to a higher stage of development. To Morgan, mind was rationality and the making of useful
decisions, whether on some human level, savage or civilized, or on the
level of the beaver.

Morgan's treatment of the peoples he designates as savage is curious—a blend of evolutionist ethnic superiority and a genuinely tolerant relativism. On the one hand "savagery" and "barbarism" were
hardly neutrally connotative terms in themselves, and Morgan's exposition at times would project characteristically Victorian hierarchical
judgments: "The Australians rank below the Polynesians, and far
below the American aborigines. They stand below the African negro
and near the bottom of the scale. Their social institutions, therefore,
must approach the primitive type as nearly as those of any existing
people" (51).

But just as historical stages of cultural development could so typically become spatialized as "higher" and "lower" in Morgan's mind,
on a number of occasions he would go to considerable lengths to
point out the relative legitimacy of the different, earlier social forms,
and the Western tendency to judge them narrowly and ethnocentri-
cally. The low Western assessment of the Hawaiians he attributes to
the accounts of the first American missionaries, who, when they discovered among them a family system far different than that of their
own monogamous culture, "It seemed to them that they had discov-

ered the lowest level of degradation, not to say depravity." As Morgan is at pains to establish, the Hawaiians had, as was evolutionarily appropriate to their particular stage of culture, a "Punaluan" family system, in which "the males were living in polygyny, and the females in polyandry." Thus "It is probable that they were living as virtuously in their faithful observance, as these excellent missionaries were in the performance of their own" (414). To Morgan this is a lesson in the "profoundness of the expanse which separates civilized from savage man."

In one framework it seems characterizable as the impact on "the high moral sense and refined sensibilities" of the civilized man of "the feeble moral sense and the coarse sensibilities of a savage man" (414). But in another framework, "there could never have been a time in human experience when the principle of morality did not exist" (415), and every society has organization, moral principles, and family structure appropriate to its particular developmental stage. There is this kind of struggle in Morgan's thought between reflexive ethnocentrism on one hand and relativism on the other. Reflexiveness was structured into the very terms of cultural discourse, however, and even a specific effort to avoid ethnocentrism was apt to be futile.

But let us see how Morgan builds upward from the state of savagery in his social paradigm. Briefly surveying the evolutionary patterns of family, society, and property, his nineteenth-century American bias is quite obvious. The family he sees as beginning with that (very questionable) state of original promiscuity, in which descent was matrilineal (of course: paternity would be impossible to determine in such circumstances). Subsequent stages would, step-by-step, restrict the mixing and mating (groups of brothers or sisters sharing their mates in the "Punaluan" system, for example) until with the state of monogamy the threshold of civilization was attained. The shift to monogamy entailed a shift to a paternalistic system too, and (somewhat paradoxically, we might feel) a gradual appreciation of the sentiment of love and a respect for women.

A discussion of the Mayan custom of arranged marriages leads Morgan to this general conclusion: "In a matter so personal as the marriage relation, the wishes or preferences of the parties were not consulted. No better evidence is needed of the barbarism of the people" (457). Notice not only the bias but also the pejorative use of the term "barbarism" here. "The passion of love was unknown among the barbarians," Morgan later asserts: "They are below the sentiment, which is the offspring of civilization and superadded refinement" (476–77). The treatment of women in the Homeric poems he regards as typical of social forms in classical times—his period of "upper bar-barism"—and he finds it reprehensible:

> The premature destruction of the ethnic life of these remarkable races is due in no small measure to their failure to develop and utilize the mental, moral, and conservative forces of the female intellect, which were not less essential than their own corresponding forces to their progress and pres-ervation. (479–80)

Thus the domestic insights of the liberally enlightened Victorian-age American male shape the contours and meanings of this version of human evolution.

Morgan's theories of social organization grow out of the same set of cultural expectations. Democracy is the key he discovers in observ-ing the lower-barbarism Iroquois: "The simplest and lowest form of the council was that of the gens. It was a democratic assembly because every adult male and female member had a voice upon all questions brought before it" (85). The gentes even elected the chiefs, he points out, and thus, "a powerful popular element pervaded the whole or-ganism and influenced its action. . . . In this and the next succeeding ethnical period democratic principles were the vital element of gentile society." And examination of the similar structure of ancient Greek society "shows further how deeply inwrought in the human mind the principle of democracy had become under gentilism" (144). In the course of evolution gens democracies gradually banded into phratry democracies and then into confederation democracies (like the Iro-quois peoples had, and, yes, the United States of America).

Morgan regarded monarchy as a kind of aberration of a certain few societies in their early paternalistic stages. Basically, people banded together rationally, for defense and survival; democratic structures became dominant because they were wiser choices—they just worked better. The fall of the patrician-dominated, imperialistic Roman Em-pire illustrates just this lesson for Morgan the rationalist and demo-crat: "The human race is gradually learning the simple lesson, that the people as a whole are wiser for the public good and the public pros-perity, than any privileged class of men, however refined and culti-vated, have ever been, or, by any possibility, can ever become" (335).

The evolution of the idea of property followed along the lines of the development of tools and implements and the things that could be possessed: savages had little, and little sense of ownership; barbarians (with their increased reliance on agriculture, more highly developed crafts, and more secure and elaborate housing) had increasingly more, along with more elaborate arrangements for transferring or inheriting it; and civilized peoples were increasingly preoccupied with (and in too many cases virtually ruled by) the business of its accumulation. As Morgan says, "Its dominance as a passion over all other passions marks the commencement of civilization" (6). And "the monogamian family owes its origin to property" (389). As the upper barbarian societies like the Greek and Roman grew in size and demographic complexity, governance by gentes proved too exclusionary and too unwieldy, he theorizes, and shifted (or was shifted) to a system based on private ownership, inheritance through the male line, and citizenship within a certain territory. This more than anything else was the defining step to civilization. And it brought the theoretical possibilities of all past human evolution up to the stage of Morgan's contemporary America.

But what are the engines of this complex human evolution? What causes the progress? Morgan the humanist, the rationalist, lived in an age of rampant scientific determinism—spurred by Herbert Spencer's idea of the universal evolution of force in increasingly complex and heterogeneous configurations, and by Darwin's notion of Natural Selection as the universal mechanism of the evolution of living species. Thus Morgan is ambivalent about whether these changes come because of human choice and effort or because they simply must come. As a deeply dyed rationalist, he envisions human beings surviving and improving their lot by making good practical and moral decisions, "work[ing] their way up from savagery to civilization through the slow accumulations of experimental knowledge" (3). In numerous passages he shows the adoption of new and better techniques and social arrangements as indications of mankind making the best choices.

He is somewhat vague and inconsistent about whether those were conscious or unconscious choices—whether the rationality is intentional or really an unconscious principle of the operation of the human mind. At one point, he credits Theseus, Solon, and Cleisthenes individually with devising Greece's shift to a territorially based political system (273). At another, he states that "the institutions of mankind have sprung up in a progressive connected series, each of which represents the result of unconscious reformatory movements to extricate society from existing evils" (59). At times, his reliance on rationalistic assumptions is grotesquely exaggerated, as when he credits savages with abandoning cannibalism when they are able to fill their need for protein food in less revolting ways, or when he sees them forgoing sexual promiscuity and incestuous mating for more socially stabilizing behaviors.

In a larger theoretical framework, anthropologist Elizabeth Colson has discounted *Ancient Society*'s sociopolitical rationalism by pointing out that "Morgan's political theory rested upon the assumption that men developed their social orders through conscious thought and rational choice," the governmental model he had in mind all along being Locke's contract theory, "which had already been explored by earlier political thinkers and was under attack by contemporaries" (1973, 9,13). Indeed, at his most extreme Morgan can carry his faith in reason (and the implied social contract) to extremes, as when he describes the fundamental political shift teleologically: "The people were seeking to transfer themselves out of gentile society, in which they had lived from time immemorial, into political society based upon territory and upon property, which had become essential to a career in civilization" (217). Somehow, we might feel Morgan had too few explanatory options and too little control over language to focus this question of the rational element in the process of evolution.

Morgan's designations of the causes of progress that were nonrational or outside human control are also vague and inconsistent. Human factors like the "unconscious reformatory movements" are subtly and not very consistently woven into a fabric in which the human mind, "limited in the range of its powers, works and must work, in the same uniform channels, and within narrow limits of variation" (255). Thus there is uncertainty as to whether the changes happen because of human adjustments, conscious or unconscious, or because there are only very limited paths for change to take. And the force of tradition is strong in determining the changes in a number of Morgan's formulations. There are "a few germs of thought," out of which "have been evolved all the principal institutions of mankind" (61). The principles of human society "grow naturally, with time, out of pre-existing elements," he claims, and the specific direction of progress is necessarily determined (123). In one summation of the impersonal, necessitarian version of human progress, he states, "In the grand aggregate may still be recognized the few primary germs of thought, working upon primary human necessities, which, through the natural process of development, have produced such vast results" (255). So germination, limitation, necessity, and time become the factors designating the nonrational, nonvolitional elements with which the rational are variously mixed in his envisioning of evolution's causes.

Morgan's discussion of barbarism is in substance and importance the centerpiece of *Ancient Society*, and because it is so reliant on his firsthand expertise about the American Indian, it is the book's most original and enduring feature. Morgan classifies the Iroquois and the Eastern Amerindians among the lower barbarian cultures. The middle barbarians in his scheme are the village Indians of New Mexico, Mexico, and Central and South America. The upper barbarians are principally those of the historical cultures of ancient Greece and Rome and the later Germanic tribes (464–65). In terms of the technological advancements within its long span, "the great period of barbarism was signalized by four events of pre-eminent importance: namely, the domestication of animals, the discovery of the cereals, the use of stone in architecture, and the invention of the process of smelting iron ore" (42).

But barbarism was, in the social organization of its peoples, democratic and familially gentile-based from the very beginning. This insight was at the heart of Morgan's discoveries about the American Indians, and it led him to show them in a light very different from what was customary either in American society at large or in the anthropological fraternity. Here were these primitives, now being classed with the most respected of the progenitors of Western society in terms of principal, if not locally transient, cultural forms:

> When the gens of the Iroquois, as it appeared in the Lower Status of barbarism, is placed beside the gens of the Grecian tribes as it appeared in the Upper Status, it is impossible not to perceive that they are the same organization, the one in its archaic and the other in its ultimate form. The differences between them are precisely those which would have been forced upon the gens by the exigencies of human progress. (231)

Thus, "the archaic form of the principal domestic institutions of the Greeks must even now be sought in the corresponding institutions of the American aborigines" (17). The comparison of course can now be recognized as a carryover from the Greco-Roman preoccupations of the Gordian Knot/Grand Order of the Iroquois fraternity, as well as being one of the riskier sort of applications of the comparative method, but in its time it revealed Indian societies in a subtler, more respectful and (seemingly) more scientifically authentic light, and gave evolutionary anthropology new corroboration that human difference was cultural and developmental, rather than essential.

Morgan's chapters on the Iroquois and the American Indian peoples are rich in detail and undisguised in their tones of admiration. He gives an extensive exposition of the historical development of the tribes of the eastern United States (101–7,136–37). He describes the organization and functioning of the Iroquois Confederacy and its subdivisions in careful detail, paying special attention to its mores and ceremonies. He specifically details a Senecan funeral ceremony (96), a Confederacy meeting (135–43), and the ceremony for the investiture of sachems (141–44), dwelling on the formality and high seriousness of those occasions. In these passages Morgan is attempting not only to preserve and communicate a record of this people's culture, but also to indicate their humanity and wisdom. Of the ceremony for a deceased sachem he notes, for example, "It was certainly a more delicate testimonial of respect and affection than would have been expected from a barbarous people" (142). Although they lacked written history (it would evolve at a later stage), Morgan explains with admiration the Iroquois' use of wampum belts to symbolize particular episodes in the history of the tribe, used by the tribe's oral historians in recounting those details (143).

The Iroquois' system of electing two war-chiefs instead of only one showed wisdom in power-balancing; even the Romans had lacked that precaution, Morgan points out, much to the detriment of their democracy (318). By Morgan's account, the Iroquois' commitment to democracy was both pervasive and subtle, and is an everlasting credit to them:

All the members of an Iroquois gens were personally free, and they were bound to defend each other's freedom; they were equal in privileges and in personal rights, the sachem and chiefs claiming no superiority; and they were a brotherhood bound together by their ties of kin. Liberty, equality, and fraternity, though never formulated, were cardinal principles of the gens. (85)

This structure alone, Morgan asserts, "serves to explain that sense of independence and personal dignity universally an attribute of Indian character" (86). On the broader governmental level, Morgan finds their wisdom similarly compelling, ranking them very nearly (and note the condescension here) with the Aryan:

The Iroquois were a vigorous and intelligent people, with a brain approaching in volume the Aryan average. Eloquent in oratory, vindictive in war, and indomitable in perseverance, they have gained a place in history. If their military achievements are dreary with the atrocities of savage warfare, they have illustrated some of the highest virtues of mankind in their relations with each other. The confederacy which they organized must be regarded as a remarkable production of wisdom and sagacity. One of its avowed objects was peace; to remove the cause of strife by uniting their tribes under one government, and then extending it by incorporating other tribes of the same name and lineage. . . . Such an insight into the highest objects of government is creditable to their intelligence. Their numbers were small, but they counted in their ranks a large number of able men. This proves the high grade of the stock. (149)

Interesting to observe in Morgan's exposition are the numerous and sometimes subtle strategies for drawing the reader into sympathy with the Indian culture. The outspoken admiration is one, and the designation of the Indian cultural forms in the language of American democracy is another, but a subtler strategy is the attempted familiarization of the exotic: "Grace was said before the feast commenced. It was a prolonged exclamation by a single person on a high shrill note, falling down in cadences into stillness, followed by a response in chorus by the people" (143). Thus Morgan uses every means at his disposal to achieve an identification of his readers with the Indian culture. "However little we may be interested in the American Indians personally," he urges, "their experience touches us more nearly, as an exemplification of the experience of our own ancestors" (148).

One vindication of the method of *Ancient Society* came in the area of one of its greatest challenges, that being the classification of the indigenous peoples of Mexico and Central and South America in terms of the criteria of barbarism. Not only did he lack direct empirical information and reliable contemporary ethnographic studies, but extant accounts, historical records of the Spanish conquistadors and settlers, where they made any statements at all about the social organization of the Indians, assumed patriarchal, monarchical structures that were absolutely inimical to the scheme Morgan had developed in extending his findings about the Iroquois. His solution was to reject essentially all of the available interpretations of those cultures (insisting on their reflexiveness), proceed to find in them whatever minor indications he could of matrilineal gens-centered democratic social forms, and insist on the applicability of his general pattern of the evolutionary stage of barbarism despite all opinion to the contrary: "Without ascertaining the unit of their social system, if organized in gentes as they probably were, and without gaining a knowledge of the system that did exist, the Spanish writers boldly invented for the Aztecs an absolute monarchy with high feudal characteristics, and have succeeded in placing it in history" (213). "Monarchy is incompatible with gentilism," he claims, "It belongs to the later period of civilization" (124), he says in another discussion, and uses that general theory to counter what he identified as the Spanish writers' ethnocentricity in assuming that if the Indians had a government, they must have had a king or emperor. "The story has been so well told and so completely finished that it is next to impossible to overthrow the cunningly wrought fable" (Letter to Francis Parkman, Resek 1960, 132), Morgan had earlier written, but overthrow it he did. At least partly on the basis of his revision of theory, subsequent anthropologists revised the earlier assumptions and began new ethnographic interpretations of those societies.

Finally, Morgan's absolute faith in his theoretical construct is both

Ancient Society's strength and its weakness. It enabled him to make unprecedented leaps of interpretation, but it also produced a text bristling with classifications, rationalizations, and forced illustrations. The knowledge base Morgan demonstrated is enormous and varied: about Indian languages and mores, travelers' and explorers' accounts, and the literature of ancient Greece and Rome, for instance. He was candid about much of the information he found unattainable, but the demands of his universal system forced many potentially embarrassing gaps and guesses. As anthropologist Robert Lowie observed, looking back from the 1930s, "Along certain lines he was incomparably ahead of his period; in others he neglected data that should have been at his fingertips" (1937, 57).

In terms of our present humanistic context there are two points especially worth noting. First, that all Morgan's systemics and all his first- and second-hand particulars are focused on the ways people do get together—their ties and loyalties and the fabric of their societies. Second, that insofar as he is able, he treats each culture as a rational, self-regulated group with an organization and a morality (!) appropriate to its situation. He tends to familiarize, de-exoticize difference. And he explicitly attempts to articulate a system that gives each culture its own evolutionary course, and by implication, its own rights. This aspect has important political correlatives, as biographer Charles Resek correctly points out:

> Progress, Morgan observed, was inherent in all cultures, civilized or not, and each must advance along its own course. In his letter to President Hayes he wrote, 'We wonder why the Indian cannot civilize, but how could they, any more than our own remote ancestors, jump ethnical periods.' Civilization was a process; it could not, in Senator Beveridge's terms, be administered. Morgan's theories were useless as imperialist doctrine. (1960, 156)

Morgan could see the impact of an "administered" evolution on the Indian tribes around him, and it prompted him both to intervene as legal counsel and to attempt to record and thereby preserve, at least as text, the culture of this people. For as he observes with regret in *Ancient Society*, "American civilization and intercourse necessarily administered a shock to Indian institutions under which the ethnic life of the people is gradually breaking down" (173).

Although Morgan's own modern American society supplied the implicit referent for all his ethnological describing and evaluating, he could still see anthropology's mirror as such, and stepping out of its reflection address social ills he saw around him. He could warn his fellow countrymen that, although the dedication to property had brought them to the stage of civilization, their increasing obsession with property must be bridled and finally transcended for mankind to go on to the next evolutionary stage. Here is anthropology in the service of home society reform (and not the last example we shall see of such in this study):

> Since the advent of civilization, the outgrowth of property had been so immense, its forms so diversified, its uses so expanding and its management so intelligent in the interests of its owners, that it has become, on the part of the people, an unmanageable power. The human mind stands bewildered in the presence of its own creation. The time will come, nevertheless, when human intelligence will rise to the mastery over property, and define the relations of the state to the property it protects, as well as the obligations and the limits of the rights of its owners. . . . A mere property career is not the final destiny of mankind, if progress is to be the law of the future as it has been of the past. (552)

Thus the lesson of evolutionary anthropology for Morgan is that intelligence must master materialism.

The writings of the evolutionist anthropologists about primitive societies were bound to be relative to their own cultural moment, expressive of their own preoccupations, preconceptions, and social forms as well as of the details of the subject cultures. Their project was noble: to advance their understanding of other cultures and to build an overarching theory of all human culture. In their preoccupation with the primitive and their discourse about peoples they so designated, the only language available to them was structured around terms with specific cultural definitions and traditions, like *democracy*, *property*, *religion* and *myth*; terms with strongly biased loading, like *savagery* and *barbarism*; and terms with implications of superior worth or status, like *higher* and *lower*. Likewise, their mental habits and the traditions of their discourse entailed the kind of intellectualism that mandated the organization of perceptions around general, rationalistic concepts, just as it predisposed them toward the assumptions of utilitarian motivation, of hierarchies of cultural levels, and of material and social progress.

And there is no doubt that a principal purpose of their endeavor was the improvement of the human condition. "To impress men's minds with a doctrine of development, will lead them . . . to continue the progressive work of the past ages," said Briton Edward Tylor back in the 1880s; and, he went on,

> It is a harsher, and at times even painful, office of ethnography to expose the remains of crude old cultures which have passed into harmful superstition, and to mark these out for destruction. Yet this work, if less genial, is not less urgently needful for the good of mankind. Thus, active at once in aiding progress and in removing hindrance, the science of culture is essentially a reformer's science. (Tambiah 1990, 44)

But counterpoised against such evolutionary sanguinity were a few voices from other cultures, such as that of Charles Eastman, a former Indian warrior who, in his 1916 autobiography, after earnestly avowing the value of becoming part of what he saw as the civilized Christian world, expresses these misgivings:

> Why do we find so much evil and wickedness practised by the nations composed of professedly "Christian" individuals? The pages of history are full of licensed murder and the plundering of weaker and less developed peoples, and obviously the world to-day has not outgrown this system. Behind the material and intellectual splendor of our civilization, primitive savagery and cruelty and lust hold sway, undiminished, and as it seems, unheeded. . . . When I reduce civilization to its lowest terms, it becomes a system of life based upon trade. The dollar is the measure of value, and *might* still spells *right*; otherwise, why war? (1931, 194)

3

The Historian's Art as Ethnography:
Henry Adams and *Tahiti: Memoirs of Arii Taimai*

HENRY ADAMS WAS A HISTORIAN, NOT AN ANTHROPOLOGIST, BUT A historian with a flair for literary innovation and an unconventional sense of the significance of cultural processes. When he journeyed to the South Seas in 1890 he had absolutely no intention of writing anything other than letters to his friends, but circumstances and his own predilections determined otherwise, and he wound up producing an anomalous little book that had a very slight readership at the time, but that anticipated by eighty or so years the evolving canons of ethnographic method. Its principal innovation—and this was an enormous one, setting it apart from other contemporary accounts, anthropological, historical, or journalistic—was in Adams's presenting his principal informant as narrator, expressing (insofar as he was able) her perceptions and values through her point of view.

Here was an unusual text that largely gave the narration over to the native informants; that scrupulously followed indigenous concerns, often couched in indigenous nomenclature, legend, and song; that eschewed the imperialistically loaded classifying terminologies such as "primitive," and "barbarism"; that in fact very candidly and directly impugned the whole competitive European colonial project; and that after its completion as text was even resubmitted to the informants for revision and approval. With the combination of materials available to him and his own sense of discursive purpose and presentation, Adams produced a work of considerable ethnographic value along lines virtually unanticipated in the late nineteenth century—and one that projected a highly unorthodox view of the presumed "primitives" who inhabited the South Sea isles.

The story of the inception of his Tahiti text, of its composition and its publication, is both unusual and personally, typically Adamsian. He had gone to the South Seas with his artist friend John La Farge for diversion and renewal. His labors on his monumental history of the United States had just been completed, and his recovery from the suicide of his wife some five years earlier was still woefully incomplete, but by the midpoint of his long excursion he certainly seemed to be picking up the Polynesian tempo and to be fascinated by what he saw as the true native ways. Hawaii had been a disappointment, its indigenous culture tragically adulterated by Western economic interests. But Samoa still seemed unspoiled, and, as he thought, took him close to a human condition he venerated as "archaic."

The opportunity to go on to Tahiti was a bit less attractive, in proportion to the generally less "archaic" state of Tahitian society, but he and La Farge very fortuitously happened to meet an American who was married to a daughter of Tahiti's leading family, the Tevas, and who gave the travelers a personal introduction to them (Chalfant 1994, 602–3). Adams seems from the first to have been fascinated by the matriarch of this family group, the elderly Arii Taimai, now widow of English Jew Alexander Solomon, and mother of ten children (including Marau Taaroa, divorced consort of Pomare, recognized by the colonial powers as the king of Tahiti). The Tevas welcomed Adams and La Farge into their circle—they were all fluent in English, all except the old matriarch. Of her, Adams wrote to his friend John Hay,

> but the old lady, their mother, whose names or titles are so many that she herself does not know them all, was far the most interesting member of the household. She is pure Tahiti of the old source. . . . Evidently she was pleased by our attentions, and developed into a sort of coquetry that reminded me of our Samoan taupo. Every evening at sunset, the mats were laid on the grass by the sea-shore, where the heavy surf rolled in through an opening in the reef; and when I lay down at her side, she told me to ask questions. So I asked all the questions I could imagine, especially about the women of pagan times, and she talked by the hour, bothering her daughter and grandson terribly because they did not understand her old-fashioned Tahitian words, and scolding them because they did not know their own language. Tired of asking questions, I begged her on our last evening, to tell us legends; and she started in on a sort of fairy story that held us on till twelve o'clock. (1982, 3: 432–33)

When urged by Hay to write a Polynesian romance, Adams had declined, saying, "I am not the man to write Polynesian. My methods are all intellectual, analytic and modern" (1982, 3: 434). But here was material of great interest. Focused in the right way, it not only might accomplish the time-honored purposes of historian (and anthropologist!) of preserving the traces of a culture that was fast becoming just another part of the EuroAmerican colonized world, but it also might be gratifying and socially or politically useful to the Tevas.

The purposes might be realized later, but a combination of opportunity and whim seems to have got the project started, and in a direction somewhat tangential to its end product. The opportunity was a tediously extended delay during which Adams was unable at any price to get transportation away from Tahiti. "Another week of exasperated idleness," he complained. But the Teva history fascinated him, so he made a suggestion to the daughter Marau, the former queen of Tahiti:

> By way of excitement or something to talk about, I some time ago told Marau that she ought to write memoirs, and if she would narrate her life to me, I would take notes and write it out, chapter by chapter. To our surprise, she took up the idea seriously, and we are to begin work today, assisted by the old chiefess mother, who will have to start us from Captain Cook's time. (1982, 3: 471)

Two weeks later, Adams reported that his suggestion to Marau had become a high-energy family project:

> Being now thoroughly adopted into the Teva family, I find myself provided with occupation, for I have at last got them into a condition of wild interest in history. My interest appears to have captured the old lady, who astonished her children by telling me things she would never tell them; and as they had to act as interpreters, they caught the disease one by one, till at length they have all got out their pens and paper, and are hard at work, making out the family genealogy for a thousand years back, and tracing their collateral connections in every direction. (1982, 3: 478)

Their different accounts didn't always agree, and this caused some difficulties that Adams regarded as "very amusing," but quite suddenly "every day a crop of new stories, legends or songs, turn up, until a year's work would hardly be enough to put them in shape" (1982, 3: 478). These quasi-Westernized members of a culture without a written history were suddenly excited by the prospect of having one, and of participating in its production.

It took Adams more than a year to put the reminiscences in shape (with continued consultation with Marau and her brother Tati even after Adams was back in residence in Washington). He remained faithful to the original plan of presenting Marau's memoirs by titling the work *Memoirs of Marau Taaroa, Last Queen of Tahiti*. He published it privately, in a very small edition, in Paris in 1893. But the real focus of that work, and of much interesting material not includable as Marau's memoirs, was what had been remembered or reconstructed by her mother. So with Marau's encouragement, Adams expanded the text, refocused its presentation, and published it (again privately in Paris) as *Memoirs of Arii Taimai* in 1901.*

Despite representing the works as a Tahitian woman's memoirs and himself as standing aside merely as "editor," Adams's own role went considerably beyond that. At one relatively early point in the composition, he admits to a friend,

> I have rewritten two chapters, making a very learned disquisition on Tahitian genealogy, mixed up with legends and love-songs. The thing would be rather pretty if I only knew how to do it, or perhaps it might be better if I were writing it on my own account; but as it is for Marau in the first person, I have to leave out everything risky. (1982, 3: 479)

At a later point, writing from Washington, he pleads with Marau for livelier material:

> but if we only can make a lively story of it, so that our ancestors will be amusing, the more, the better. But to be amusing, the men, and especially the women, must be real Tahitians with no European trimmings. Nowadays in Europe and American, we are getting to like our flavors pretty strong. We want the whole local color. Tahitian society today is frightfully proper, but in old days it was almost as improper as Europe, and very much more frank about it. The memoirs must be *risques* to be amusing; so make Tati, I supplicate, translate all the legends for me literally, so that I can select what suits our time. I see no reason why you should tell the story merely to suit the *jeune personne* of a French pension. (1982, 4: 82)

Adams wanted to make it a good story, but he was first of all extremely scrupulous about genealogical details, asking again and again about the relationships and lines of descent. (Ernest Samuels points out that "the 1901 edition has become a standard authority on Tahitian history and genealogy" [1964, 606, n. 45]). And Adams saw the importance of the memoirs' revelations about the European powers, their competition for colonial possessions, and their blundering, self-righteous intrusion into Tahitian life. To bolster that part of the story line Adams would need a broader range of information, to put the Tahitian experience against the perceptions and intentions of the colonialists, and so he did some research of a more customary kind; according to Samuels,

---

*For information about the texts, see Robert E. Spiller's Introduction to his edition, *Tahiti by Henry Adams* (Adams 1947. New York: Scholars' Facsimiles and Reprints). Spiller's text, a facsimile of the 1901 *Memoirs*, is the one I shall be using here. See also Samuels 1964, 606 n. 45.

> While in Paris and London on his way home from the South Seas, he had scoured the bookshops for materials on Tahiti and had acquired an impressive collection on the subject, nearly thirty titles in French, twenty in English, and one in German, and had patiently worked out the puzzles presented by the wilderness of phonetic spellings. (1964, 100)

Perhaps he had too many objectives in writing this little book, perhaps sensing but not fully developing the many valuable but diverse possibilities in the project. And judging by the activities recorded in his correspondence while he was finishing the text back in Washington, the project was only incidental to a great variety of other tasks and activities that were engaging him at the time. For whatever causes, *Tahiti* has not drawn much admiration or even interest from either the reading public or Adams scholars. Recently Eugenia Kaledin has cited the book as "an accurate description of an intricate real world destroyed by . . . Western civilization with its diseases, its intrusive capitalism and its self-righteous Christianity," and as evidence that by both ethnic and gender categories "Adams chose . . . to identify with the powerless and exotic" (1993, 74, 75); and Robert Hume, in 1951, had acknowledged the book's "quality of pity and anger" (128).

But typically Adams criticism has been negative to lukewarm about *Tahiti*, viewing it basically as a way-station on the road to *Mont-Saint-Michel and Chartres* and *The Education,* and finding in it none of the literary mastery of the later works, and only vague shadowings of the major Adamsian themes. In 1947, Robert Spiller introduced the standard text, with the judgments that "it is the product of a lull in his writing and it marks the transition between the two phases of his career, as historian and as man of letters." It projected "parallels between Arii Taimai's story and his own" in terms of the marginalization of a previously prominent family, Spiller claimed, but "it does not quite succeed in filling out the meaning of its massed data, largely because there was no central symbol like the Virgin or the Dynamo about which to group fact and idea" (Adams 1947, v). Ernest Samuels impugned the book's point of view: "By throwing the narrative into the form of an autobiographical memoir, he paid his hosts a pretty compliment, but the device prevented his giving the complex recital the artistic unity he longed to achieve." Samuels went on to point out that Adams's use of historical source books falsified "the pretended point of view," but still could not redeem the text in terms of "the larger and more universal bearings of the history, those which made it a parable of the decline of the West" (1964, 100–101). Elizabeth Stevenson's biography also observed Adams "losing his Tahitian voice" in bringing in the textual historical materials (1961, 212), and recently

William Stowe, studying the text in the category of travel accounts, referred to the "evasive narrative voice" that produced "an ambiguous anonymity," determining that the book be "an exercise in self-distancing" (1991, 188).

Although we can easily understand the Adams scholars wanting the book to reveal more about the author and his own attitudes, or to foreshadow the literary contours of the later, major works, it is important to respect Adams as a project-specific designer of literary genres and approaches (indeed that kind of originality is what we most respect about *Mont-Saint-Michel* and *The Education*), and to try to understand *Tahiti* in its own context. I doubt that read thus, the work will seem a great deal more readable or satisfactory as a literary production, but if we regard Adams as trying to maximize the value of the available materials, we can discover him trying to present the particular otherness of the Tahitian culture as set against the notions and intents of the European colonialists. In this interpretive framework the book's value is historical—and ethnographic in ways unanticipated in its own time.

In its own bizarre way, *Tahiti* was the culmination of a number of Adams's enthusiasms, fancies, and deep concerns. The *Voyages* of Captain Cook, and Herman Melville's *Typee*, had inspired him in his youth, and his adult ambition to learn to paint was motivated at least partly by the intent of illustrating *Typee* for his dear friend Elizabeth Cameron (Chalfant 1994, 570, 884 n. 6). *Typee*'s romanticism could, of course, easily focus wanderlust, especially for one yearning to escape overcivilization. And its thematic burdens—of the fascination of unspoiled peoples and landscapes, of the ugly, self-serving depredations of the colonial powers, of the mysterious but dignified demeanor of the cultural Other, and of woman and of sexuality in a wholly different cultural context—these notions are conceivably strong background factors, not only for Adams's journey to the South Seas, but for the thematic contours of his book as well. Kaledin's study interestingly reveals Adams's emerging ethnographic curiosity and concern by surveying the contents of *The North American Review* (*NAR*) under his editorship in the 1870s: "He tried to record details about the Native American cultures he saw on the brink of being wiped out; and he included essays on a variety of other societies in order to expand the consciousness of the parochial American" (1993, 62).

Such interests and his work on the *NAR* quite naturally connected Adams with Lewis Henry Morgan. Morgan had been an *NAR* contributor before Adams's tenure, and Adams continued the relationship, soliciting reviews, articles, and information from the man he came to regard as preeminent in anthropology. According to Morgan biographer Carl Resek, "Morgan had no more confirmed disciple in Boston than Henry Adams" (1960, 149). In Adams's collected letters we can follow the relationship, as Adams congratulates Morgan on a devastating review of historian George Bancroft, requests a copy of Morgan's out-of-print work on the Iroquois, poses some questions about the political and judicial organization of the American Indians, proposes the hypothesis that the American Indians and the Indo-European races sprang from common stock, rejoices at learning of the publication of *Ancient Society*, and several times solicits Morgan's opinions about the very earliest stages of cultures and their relation to the American Indian. Adams declares that "our American ethnology is destined to change the fashionable European theories of history to no small extent," and that Morgan's study of the American Indians "must be the foundation of all future work in American historical science." In the process of developing some intercultural anthropological ideas of his own, Adams asks Morgan, "Can you tell me where I can find any information on the customs regulating marriage among our Indians?" (1982, 2: 271, 311).

In asking about Indian marriage customs, Adams was preparing a lecture for the Lowell Institute in 1876, the only lecture he was ever to give in public, and the one that he later published as the first piece in his *Historical Essays*, "Primitive Rights of Women." In it he propounded an evolutionist view, very akin to Morgan's, of the earliest cultures: "communistic," with "no idea, or only a rudimentary idea, of private property"; matrilineal, "a system of relationship through women . . . the germ of future family organization"; and species-wide, since "in all countries and through all ages its traces have been found." Women had rights in the earliest societies, Adams asserted, and invoked the example of American Indian social organization (as described by Morgan) to support that fact. And far from judging primitive societies as manifestly inferior to his own dominant culture, Adams claimed of them that, "within the bounds of their own society they succeeded in constructing a social fabric that compared with any that succeeded to it for successful adaptation of means to ends." Although, like Morgan and Brinton, he evaluated civilizations by their treatment of women, he nevertheless pointed out how "the rise of Christianity" had actually "marked the diminution of women's social and legal rights" (1891, 3–4, 5, 36).

Without a doubt Adams brought to the "editing" of *Memoirs of Arii Taimai* a potpourri of not-quite-compatible predispositions. In terms of research method, he combined a devotion to texts and textual research with a passion for immediate experience, especially experience of the sort that bends or breaks customary categories. Fortified before his journey to the South Seas with novels, travel accounts, friends' letters and word-of-mouth accounts, and even a little ethnography, and fortified in the act of composition with an array of explorers' and colonialists' texts, he nevertheless involved himself with the Polynesian people and their culture as immediately and as deeply as he could. His traveling companion John La Farge records this characteristic of him in the Samoan setting:

> he is patient beyond belief; he asks over and over the same questions in different shapes and ways of different and many people. . . . But everywhere one comes right against some secret . . . something that cannot be well disentangled from annoyance to the questioned one. For instance, in the question of genealogy, Seumano told us that had he been interrogated some years ago in such a direction he should have struck the questioner down on the spot. Still we have hope, and if any one can manage it, Atamo ["Adams" to the Samoans] will. Web after web I have seen him weave around interpreter and explainer. . . . As many times as the spider is brushed away, so many times he returns. (Chalfant 1994, 601)

It was in that spirit that Adams had questioned old Arii Taimai and listened to her legends and reminiscences through the night. And likewise he carefully observed the details of the Polynesians' lives and technology: he wrote to friends about their squid fishing, the use of stone and wood for tools and weapons, their clothmaking, and even their fly swatters (see, for example the letter to William Hallett Phillips, 1982, 3: 368–69). Of Samoan politics he said, "though I loathe the very word, and of all kinds of politics detest most those of islands, I am just soaked with the stuff here" (1982, 3: 293). His careful taking of measurements of the bodies of the Samoan *taupos* and daughters of chiefs no doubt had a more complex agenda, but still expressed the same yearning for unmediated knowledge.

This level of immersion even produced a sense of cultural change in Adams, as he fantasized in a letter to Elizabeth Cameron, "I find myself now and then regaining consciousness that I was once an American supposing himself real. The Samoan is so different from all my preconceived ideas, that my own identity becomes hazy, and yours alone remains tolerably clear" (1982, 3: 292). How gratifyingly appropriate it was that later the Teva family not only confided in him, but adopted him, and gave him a Teva family name. He proudly and playfully wondered over his radical personal reorientation: "Sometimes I half feel as though I really were Taura-atua i Amo, and never should know more of the world than that the ocean is big and blue" (To Elizabeth Cameron, 1982, 3: 479). Whatever his Western-world textual orientation, Adams seems to have experimented with immersing experientially in the cultures of those Others and trying to feel and think in their ways.

His emic ambitions of course had limits, growing out of habits of perception and judgment both personal and cultural. One of those limits related to class: it is not the society of the Samoans or Tahitians that is his object but their Society. From Samoa he wrote back, "[w]e have associated only with the first society—the families of the powerful chiefs—and I know nothing of the common people except as I see them pass by"; and from Tahiti, "[t]he chiefs interest me much more than the common-people do, for they are true aristocrats and have the virtues of their class, while the common people would sink to the level of the Hawaiians if the chiefs were to become extinct" (1982, 3: 301, 377).

Another limiting factor was his predisposition toward the "archaic" and the natural. He sought such qualities knowing they would be there. Even granting their undeniably ennobling effect, they still characterized the natives as interestingly different, picturesque, primitive, or childlike—and by implication intellectually and politically inferior. He continually tried to see the Samoans and the Tahitians as contemporary versions of the ancient Europeans (shades of Morgan's classification of the correlative stages of Barbarism): "in many respects, the race has preserved a sort of pre-Homeric quality which tells the story of its origin. Its physical beauty goes with its refinements and especially its order of intelligence," Adams writes to Clarence King, in a letter that also had broached his theory of the Polynesians' Indic origin. "Historically, the Samoan *taupo* is archaic," he goes on, "Homer's women—Penelope, Helen, Nausicaá,— are modern types compared with Faauli and Leolofi" (1982, 3: 465, 467).

While seeing these people as possessing the nobility and elemental simplicity of the ancients, Adams also saw them as manifesting the intellectuality and the temperament of children: "They are the happiest, easiest, smilingest people I ever saw, and the most delightfully archaic. They fight bravely, but are not morally brave. They have the virtues of healthy children,—and the weaknesses of Agamemnon and Ulysses" (1982, 3: 346). And in a less admiring frame of mind, he writes to King, "Children! No American child is so childish. All, except the greatest chiefs, are cast in one mould, physically and mentally; and all are made only to wreathe garlands and dance and kill each other,—the true objects of true life" (1982, 3: 465). This statement certainly carries a freight of polygenism and a conviction of the natives' difference as both essential and specifically limiting, both notions in contrast to his otherwise admiring attitude toward their highly developed indigenous culture and social class system. We can see implicit in the characterization of the natives as childishly archaic the suggestion of a rationalizable colonialism, although in Adams's mind that characterization tended to bolster his condemnation of the repulsiveness of the actual European dominance.

Of that colonialist adventure he is certainly unambiguous: "[t]he three foreign powers have made a mess, and the natives are in it," he writes of the English, French and German Polynesian policies and treaties (1982, 3: 293). Morally, the natives were being deprived of their beliefs and behavioral customs by Christian teachings, while at the same time being infected with every sort of vice and disease by the European presence. Socially and politically, their society was being destabilized by foreigners ignorant of or negligent of their institutions. And economically—the driving motive of all this disruption— they were having their very lives redefined by intruders interested only in their own profit-and-power agendas. Viewing Samoa, Adams writes back to his friend, former Assistant Secretary of State and later Ambassador to Great Britain John Hay,

> I am inclined to profanity when I think that religion, political economy and civilisation so-called, will certainly work their atrocities here within another generation so that these islands will be as melancholy a spectacle as Hawaii is, and the dignity of [contract] labor will be asserted as God's own lesson to Polynesia. (1982, 3: 302)

And later, from Tahiti, viewing what the French have done (and they not even getting any actual profit for it!) he writes to Hay,

> Year by year Tahiti loses activity and character. The natives become more and more diseased and weak. The society becomes less and less polished. Presently, in twenty or thirty years, the Americans will swoop down, and Tahiti will become another Hawaii, populated by sugar-canes and Japanese laborers. (1982, 3: 412)

Whatever the contradictions within Adams's own predispositions and perceptions, he certainly was far better attuned to Polynesia than were Morgan or Brinton. Not only had he been there, and seen and talked with actual Polynesians (as they hadn't), but his understanding of the natives' culture was not subsumed as an application or validation of evolutionism or another theory of cultures. He could see what he could and decide what he would without *that* intellectual mediation. How different was Morgan's approach. That Morgan's theoretical framework was in fact a substantial impediment to his understanding of Polynesia is a point well made by Robert Lowie in the very specific continuation of the passage I quoted in the previous chapter:

> Along certain chosen lines he was incomparably ahead of his period; in others he neglected data that should have been at his fingertips. His treatment of the Polynesians is inconceivable. Though Captain Cook's observations must have been accessible, Morgan puts this horticultural, sophisticated people in the same class with the Australian hunters. Lacking bow and arrow, both races are degraded to the middle status of Savagery—below the level of the rudest North Americans. This is taking a classificatory device far too seriously! (1937, 57)

Without metacultural theorizing or systematic classifying, Adams's Tahiti text could elicit this admiration from Tati Teva from inside the Tahitian culture:

> The Memoirs have been studied over and to me it is a wonder, the amount of patience you must have taken to search for reports of the island, takes us all by surprise. You may say what you like, but I have already said that you knew more than anyone else the history of this island. It has been translated to our mother, and as I have done so as well as, the others, she detects the difference at once, so that since the arrival of the document, we are continually talking of it. Some rectifications, only in the spelling of the native words, has been added to it. Why Tahiti was quite a place in the old days. (Samuels 1964, 109–10)

The narrative that ostensibly comes from the principal informant herself in *Tahiti: The Memoirs of Arii Taimai* mainly focuses on the ruling classes of the various Tahitian peoples as viewed from the perspective of Teva family. It is chronological in a general way, moving from the legendary origins of the Tevas ("Our Tevas claim by tradition a descent from the Shark God" [Adams 1947, 12]); through the earliest struggles to establish and consolidate a complex system of ruling families in the various locales. It then details the arrival of the first European explorers and their impact; the impact of the missionaries on the ruling families, institutions, and welfare of the various peoples; the emerging struggle of England against France for control of Tahiti; and finally, Ariitaimai's own interposition to bring peace to the islands in the decisive 1840s conflict pitting the French and their Tahitian allies against a substantial faction of Tahitian insurgents abandoned by the English. The precolonial stages of the story are drawn from native legend, story, and song. The stories of the arrival of the European explorers and colonials use European diaries and reports, modified by Tahitian memories and opinions. In the final stages, the account intermixes with and relies increasingly on Ariitaimai's own memories. *Tahiti* holds in general to this chronological structure, although with a good deal of digression and background explanation, some probably part of the reminiscence situation and some an attempt to make the narrative more comprehensible to a Western audience.

Unfortunately, the level of comprehensibility of this text is nevertheless not very high, and its quality of readability is highly questionable. Given the vast differences between Tahitian and Western cultures, the book seemingly couldn't be both readily comprehensible for a Westerner and authentically Tahitian. Tahitian names are one great problem: Not only do individual natives have several alternative names, but they have different names in different locales, and often sons have the same names as fathers. Intermarriage frequently mixes ruling families, names as well as heredities, and clan names and locale names are frequently difficult to match. "Ariis" aren't kings or even chiefs in the usual Western sense, "Maraes" aren't exactly shrines; there are precise and not quite logical distinctions between gestures of homage and of humiliation. Since telling the truth, for historian Adams, entailed avoiding readers' misconception, these matters and many more like them had to be rather painstakingly brought into the Western frame of reference, in Adams's own terms if not in Ariitaimai's. In this instance, the greatest drag on the book as a literary performance is exactly what makes it ethnographically valuable.

The stories that make up the precolonial stage of the Ariitaimai/ Adams reconstruction of Tahitian history deal primarily with the founding of the Teva line and their battles with neighboring clans in maintaining their territory, prerogatives, and interclan dignity. Genealogy is the backbone and often the point of the stories: "[W]e have no history apart from genealogy" (162). Before the time of Westernized written records, genealogy was preserved in the stone Maraes (monuments with altars, in specially sanctified locations, that had familial significance for individual clans), and in the songs and legends, most of which, as the female narrator appropriately enough observes, center on women. Along with the genealogical charts and the list of Maraes and their locations, the narrator offers stories of wives abducted and avenged ("If one is to believe history, men never fought about themselves"[23]), and of chiefesses who supplicate and who scheme, who accept and who refuse important marriage alliances.

One such story from the mid-seventeenth century tells of a wife lent and not returned and of a revenge not taken, which tale embodies (and reinforces) several important Tahitian customs, while implicitly symbolizing the expansion and consolidation of power by the clan, which at that time became dominant throughout Tahiti. Tavi was the chief of a large and powerful district, confident and generous ("All chiefs were obliged to be generous, or they lost the respect and regard of their people; but Tavi was the most generous of all the chiefs of Tahiti" [23]). The chief of another district, a man who was then head of the Teva clan, yearned after Tavi's wife Taurua ("the most beautiful woman of her time" [23]) and requested Tavi lend her to him, formally pledging to return her in seven days. Tavi reluctantly acceded ("in the Polynesian code of manners, such a request could not be refused without a quarrel" [24]), but when the seven days were over, the borrower chief Tuiterai was too madly in love with Taurua to give her up. ("The Tevas still sing the song of Tuiterai aurorua replying to Tavi's messenger who came to demand Taurua . . . :

E ore e pa iau. no fea e pa iau.
I will not give her up! Why should I give her up?

Teuraiterai ono rai ono. e ura piria mai tau orio.
I, Teuraiterai of the six skies! the Ura [bright gold] that clings to my eyes!

E ura ahuahu mai Raratoa mai e te ipo iti e.
The Ura, sunshine from Raratoa, my dear treasure. . . .

"This was an outrage of the most grievous kind, such as he might perhaps have inflicted on a very low man—a man fit only for a human sacrifice—but not on a chief; least of all on a chief of equal rank with himself" [23–24].) So Tavi's people went to war with Tuiterai's, but when they had defeated them and Tuiterai lay bound and helpless, the Tahitian story "has a charm of its own" because Tavi doesn't do "what any Greek or Norse chief would have done" and kill, sack, and burn. Tuiterai makes to his captors the argument "forcible to a Polynesian, that a great chief like himself could not be put to death by an inferior. . . . None but Tavi must kill Tuiterai" (26). And this put Tavi in an especially Tahitian dilemma:

he must forfeit his character if he put Tuiterai to death with his own hand in his own house. The wars of Tahiti were as cruel and ferocious as the wars of any other early race, but such an act would have shocked Tahitian morality and decency. Tavi felt himself obliged to spare his rival's life, but between complete vengeance and complete mercy the law knew no interval.

Another Teva ballad memorializes Tavi's generous decision, not only to spare his rival but to give him his beloved wife too:

A mau ra i te vahine ia Taurau.
Tou hoa ite ee. e matatarai maua e. . . .

Take, then, your wife! Taurau! my friend! we are separated, she and I!
Taurau, the morning star to me. . . . (27)

In terms of ethnographic content the story thus reflects Tahitian customs of class and interclan relationships, of romance and gender relationships, of warfare and generosity. It (and other stories like it) show Tahiti as being from the earliest times a complex and highly formal, yet unstable, system of chiefdoms with a complex history of the use of force and finesse. As the Ariitaimai/Adams narrator observes of Tavi's sacrifice of his wife, "Nevertheless, the overthrow of [Tuiterai's district of] Papara was too serious a revolution not to affect the politics of the island. Tavi became by this triumph the most powerful chief in all Tahiti" (27). In terms of ethnographic method, the Taurau story constitutes a thoroughly reworked transcript of an informant's narrative, complete with analogies to European myth and history. But interestingly enough, it preserves the Tahitian moral attitudes and narrative selectivity, the tradition of presenting history as it had been preserved in song, and in the Tahitian language at that.

So keen is *Tahiti*'s narrator, in fact, to convey the idea of the nature of Tahitian poetry and the impossibility of translating it in any but a very rough and approximate way into the language and poetic traditions of another culture that she/he gives an extensive digression on its untranslatable characteristics. On language, after the bilingual presentation of a later tradition-laden love song, "The Lament of Taura-atua":

> Paraphrase is all one can try for, where languages are so hopelessly different. The native figures have no meaning in English. The Uriri passes the power of translation. Perhaps *rumaruma* may convey an idea of branches weighed down by their leaves, but the leaves of the bread-fruit and the palm are something different from those of the oak and beech. The Ura—the reddish feathers of the parrot or parroquet—may perhaps pass for orange-red or golden; but local terms like Paepaeroa, Moua, Outu, and the like, need a long education to slip gracefully on the tongue or through the mind. (38)

And on Tahitian poetics, following "Aromaiterai's Lament," the song of an exiled chief—a very simple yet evocative (for Tahitians) song of yearning for the homeland he could see across the bay, the narrator explains, viewing the chasm separating cultural traditions:

> Europeans, who are puzzled to understand what the early races mean by poetry, look for the rhythm as likely to explain a secret which they cannot guess from the sense of the words; but Polynesian rhythm is, if anything, rather more unintelligible to European ears than the images which are presented by the words. Tahitian poetry has rhythm, but it is chiefly caused by closing each strophe or stanza by an artificial, long-drawn, e-e-e-e! The song is sung with such rapidity of articulation that no European can approach it or even represent it in musical notation, and as for the sounds themselves, one can best judge of them by glancing at the native words.
>
> Other Polynesian dialects have a way of using indifferently *k* or *t*. Tahiti is then Kahiki; Tamehameha, the king of Hawaii, became Kame-hameha. We use *t* always, and the *l* becomes *r* in Tahitian. The Mariage de Loti is properly the Mariage de Roti. The dialect is never guttural or harsh; the verses seem to run off the tip of the tongue with a rapidity impossible to any one but a native. Singing was as natural as talking, and one danced as naturally as one walked. (36)

Thus the narrator tries to take the Western audience inside the precolonial Tahitian culture, its mind-set and language and poetry as well as its history and cultural traditions. It is worth noting that feelings, too, get to be a matter of ethnographic import in such a poetry-laden account: the emotional life of Tahitians, its conventions and standards. Complexly informing across time and cultural difference seems to be a very basic aim of the text.

From its perspective, Tahiti's colonial period began with a series of European blunders. Each of the English explorers—Wallis in 1767, Cook in 1769, and Bligh in 1788—unfortunately landed on a side of the island away from the peoples (and the chiefs) of the highest social standing and political significance. Wallis, not knowing the language or anything about the sociopolitical system, assumed that the first natives he encountered who seemed to be of significance were the rulers of the entire island. After subduing the natives in a pair of battles well known to Europeans, he had little contact with them until one of his crew came back from an exploratory foray and, in Wallis's words, "'came on board with a tall woman, who seemed to be about five-and-forty years of age, of a pleasing countenance and majestic deportment'" (48). The majestic deportment and the obvious deference paid her by other natives convinced Wallis that this was the queen of Tahiti.

In fact, as the narrator informs us, she "was herself a guest, whose presence there was due to her relationship with the chief" (50). Wallis was immensely impressed with her, which the narrator (the Adamsian side of the narrator, no doubt) is moved to treat quite satirically:

> This visit first opened the island to the Englishmen, as Wallis instantly noticed; but he was so much more interested in his introduction into good native society that he quite lost sight of politics. From this moment until he sailed from the island, July 27, his narrative ran almost wholly on the subject of "my princess, or rather queen," until it ended in a burst of sentiment which, as far as I can learn, stands by itself in the literature of official reports as the only case of an English naval captain recording tears as part of his scientific emotions, [as he described his feelings as the "queen"] "bade us farewell, with such tenderness of affection and grief as filled both my heart and my eyes." (48–49, 52)

Shortly after Wallis's Tahitian experience, the French explorer Bougainville came for a short stay, and, the text explains, "both these explorers returned to Europe with such glowing accounts of Tahiti as created lively interest" (53). This interest was largely due, according to our narrator (undoubtedly Adams again here), to the Rousseauism then sweeping Europe, in which framework the Tahitians represented untroubled people living in a state of nature—especially in a sexual state of nature, free and uninhibited. The naiveté and destructiveness of this misconception are excoriated in the text, as Adams uses the Tahitian situation to vent his opinions about European colonialism:

> [T]he interest felt in France for the state of nature in Tahiti was largely caused by the eternal dispute about marriage and the supposed laxity of Tahitian morals in regard to the relations between men and women. I say "supposed" because no one knows how much of the laxity was due to the French and English themselves, whose appearance certainly caused a sudden and shocking overthrow of such moral rules as had existed before in the island society; and the "supposed" means that when the island society as a whole is taken into account, marriage was real as far as it went, and the standard rather higher than that of Paris; in some ways extremely lax, and in others strict and stern to a degree that would have astonished even the most conventional English nobleman, had he understood it. The real code of Tahitian society would have upset the theories of a state of nature as thoroughly as the guillotine did; but, when seen through the eyes of French and English sailors, who had not the smallest sense of responsibility, and would not have been sorry to overthrow all standards, Tahiti seemed to prove that no standard was necessary, which made the island interesting to philosophers and charming to the French people, never easy under even the morality recognized at Paris. So there again our

aunt Purea, Wallis's queen, played a part in the drama, for, in an island which seemed to have no idea of morals, she was a model of humanity, sentiment, and conduct—the flower of a state of nature. (55–56)

Yes indeed, Wallis's "queen" was, the text finally reveals, Ariitaimai's Aunt Purea, but the European misreading of her status and her philosophical significance was only the beginning of the mischief brought by the colonialists. The English, under the command of Captain Cook, so misconceived the sociopolitical structure of the Tahitian culture that they took one of the lesser chiefs, Tu of the Pomare family, who happened to be particularly in evidence and (for personal reasons) helpful to them when they arrived, and regarded him— essentially *made* him—the king of Tahiti. Then when Cook went away and the other Tahitian chiefs took steps to reassert the traditional order of things, Tu protested to the English. They returned and by force of arms helped Tu to regain what they thought of as his rightful position as supreme ruler. Through warfare and subversion and intermarriage, Tu and his successor son, also "Tu," essentially tried then to destroy in their own interest the whole intricate structure of clan hierarchy and jurisdiction.

In recounting these events—dismal for the Teva family, and for Tahiti—the narrator is highly judgmental about the shortsighted Eurocentrism of the English. Cook "never quite succeeded in understanding their position [the chiefs'] or his own," she/he claims: "Tahitian genealogy at best was hard to understand, but Captain Cook's struggles with it, aided by English rules, were almost pathetic" (61, 67). The root of the trouble was the European notion of the necessary and divinely ordered structure of society: "Every one who has tried to tell the story of Tahiti has had to struggle with this idea of kingship. . . . [U]ntil one has dismissed from one's mind the notion of government such as Europeans conceived it, one must always misunderstand the South Seas" (6–7). And the misunderstanding was mutual, the cultural difference incomprehensible to either side except in its own reflexive terms. With Cook's elevation of Tu,

> The Ahurai and Attahuru people were furious, and Cook was quite unable to understand that they had reason to be so. Ahurai and Paea had never before been treated as the inferiors of a Purionuu chief, and they could understand Cook's conduct as little as Cook could understand theirs. To them Cook's infatuation for Tu must have seemed a deliberate insult. (94)

Narrator Ariitaimai contributes her knowledge of the chiefly structure and attitudes of the Tahitians, while "editor" Adams juxtaposes that with an insider's view of the European perspective: "in his [Cook's] eyes Tu was King by divine right, and any attack on his authority was treason in the first place and an attack on British influence in the next" (96). Thus with our single-faced, double-identitied narrator we get a very early study in intercultural misunderstanding, a revelation of how reflexiveness inhibits understanding of cultural difference.

As the narrator's account goes, the arrival of Lieutenant Bligh and his ship "The Bounty" caused further and faster degeneration of Tahitian society. With this new incursion of the English—patently "to bring breadfruit from Tahiti, to be domesticated as a fruit of peculiar usefulness in the various tropical colonies of Great Britain" (98)— politically it was a case of more of the same, only worse. Bligh blindly accepted Cook's view of Tahitian politics, affirming the absolute kingship of Tu of the Pomares, and "showed not the slightest interest or curiosity in any one but the Tus, father and son, and their immediate connexion" (100). Bligh focused on putting the English support behind Tu in every way short of actually fighting his battles for him. Supplying him with guns and equipment was, however, part of the relationship, and it was instrumental in reshaping Tahiti.

The mutiny on "The Bounty" was so widely publicized and discussed in the Western world, so "dramatic" and "picturesque," that the fate of the Tahitians had drawn no more attention than the program to propagate breadfruit. "[T]he part of the story which was most serious to us is the part which has been least noticed by the world. . . . [N]o one has taken the trouble to tell how great an influence Bligh and his mutineers exercised over the destinies of Tahiti, and especially of its old chiefs" (98). Sixteen of the mutineers, with their guns, joined up with Tu in his campaign to establish and solidify his rule over as much of Tahiti as possible. As the narrator says, the war that followed "deserves to be called the War of the Mutineers of the Bounty" (102). And to the narrator's mind it was an assault on the whole fabric of Tahitian society for the selfish purposes of a tyrant:

> Pomare could gain his object in no other way than by destroying one after another the whole of the old chiefly class. As long as one of them survived he was sure to be the champion of the great body of islanders who detested the tyranny of a single ruler, and knew what such a tyranny meant for them. If their legends show nothing else, they show that the natives knew much more about tyranny, and had much more reason to dread it, than the English or the French had known for many centuries; and against such a despotism as Europe could not realize, their tribal system, with its chiefs, was their only protection. They clung to it, and Po-

mare had no choice but to succumb, or to destroy it. . . . [He] knew that what he was trying to do could be done only by wholesale destruction, and that, in order to do it, he must depend on outsiders. (138–39)

Missionaries came to Tahiti with their particular agenda and an interest in island politics only insofar as it might assist in the spread of Christianity. They, like the colonialists attempting to normalize and solidify civil administration according to their own perceptions (and interests), were, by their own admission, somewhat baffled by native politics: " 'Though the wheels of political government are not so many in this as in our native island, yet they are more in number than any would conceive from the rude and barbarous state the nation is in' " (127). The observation of Ariitaimai/Adams about this sort of statement is "With better reasoning the natives looked at the missionaries as a kind of children, or idiots, incapable of understanding the simplest facts of island politics or society, and serving only as the unconscious tools of the Tu family" (128). At times, the narrator uses this kind of textual duel to confront the views and records of the missionaries with a contrary interpretation from the other side of the chasm between cultures. At other times, she/he is either heavily ironic or directly accusatory about the callousness (conscious or unconscious) of the men bearing the Christian message to the Tahitians. Basically men of peace and forbearance, the missionaries could be coopted in the causes of natives professing Christianity and even be persuaded to obtain firearms to help them secure their dominance over neighboring clans. Of a bloody war to stabilize Tu's dominion they could record the reaction " 'The Lord does all things well' " (142). For an impending war, native against native, they could easily enough find divine justification:

"We rejoice that the Lord of Hosts is the God of the heathen as well as the Captain of the armies of Israel; and while the potsherds of the earth are dashing themselves to pieces one against the other, they are but fulfilling his determinate counsels and foreknowledge." (143)

From the point of view of one of the potsherds, the moral is vastly different:

Alternately praying for peace and helping Pomare and Tu to make war, the missionaries innocently hastened the destruction of the natives, and encouraged the establishment of a tyranny impossible for me to describe. Pomare was vicious and cruel, treacherous and violent beyond the old code of chiefly morals, but Pomare was an angel compared with his son Tu. (143)

To the Paparan Teva family, the missionaries' agency seemed especially immoral: "They were satisfied to give Tu muskets and gunpowder to conquer Papara and destroy its chiefs without their knowing their own victim" (147).

The rivalry between Great Britain and France for control of Tahiti put the Tahitians in the middle—both prize and pawn—and this time even the ruling Pomares were uncertain which way to lean. According to the narrator, "in 1836, two French missionaries landed at Tahiti to convert, not pagans but Protestant Christians, to the faith of Rome" (179). They were soon ejected by the British, but shortly afterward had their (and imperialist France's) claims reinforced when "King Louis Philippe sent a frigate to Papeete with the usual message of great powers to little ones,—an ultimatum, to which the Queen [Pomare] naturally acceded, as small powers always have done, and always must do, before great ones" (179). Then with the British returning, the natives found themselves caught between two Christianities and two colonial powers. Unsurprisingly, some leaned toward regarding themselves as under the protection of the British, and some as under the French. Again they were to be the losers, although this time, partly because of the intervention of Ariitaimai herself (for now the narrative had come down to her own time and the events she herself had witnessed), the losses were not as disastrous as might have been the case.

According to the narrator, England had refused to become more deeply involved with a distant quarrel between missionaries. The French were more immediately and frequently present in Polynesia, so, she/he affirms, "the chiefs broke loose from the missionaries, and in September 1841, decided that, between such masters as England and France, they could not hope to maintain independence or even a good understanding; and since England would not undertake to protect them, they would try to obtain protection from France" (179). But just when the chiefs had the papers ready for Aimata (Queen Pomare IV) to sign, a British frigate arrived and, with her British allegiance reinforced, she decided not to sign. Instead she went into nearby exile, her many loyal followers left behind becoming a rebel insurgency.

At this point the narrative begins a new section, subtitled (within Chapter XVII) "The Story of Ariitaimai, 1846" (181). Previously Ariitaimai had personally appeared in the narrative when she diagrammed and explained her placement in the genealogy of the Teva family and the chiefly class, recorded a traditional song of the heritage of her mother's side of the family, pictured herself as a girl as her father's favorite (able to get confidences from him that no one else could get), and recounted how her marriage had come about despite a British prohibition against Tahitians marrying foreigners: "Finally I decided to marry Mr Salmon, an Englishman who had general esteem and consideration in the island; and Aimata suspended the law in order to enable her friend to be married" (177). But at this crucial point in the history of Tahiti, Ariitaimai becomes an active agent in determining the fate of her country. An old woman friend alerted her to the fact that the French were about to launch an attack on the insurgent rebels, and pleaded with her (in words that Samuels has shown to be largely Adams's [1964, 104]), "I cry for my land of Tahiti. Our people will soon be at war with the French, and they will soon be opened like a lot of chickens? . . . Don't you know that you are the first of the island, and it remains in your hands to save all this and your land?" (181).

With the French field commanders positioning their troops for battle and Queen Aimata out of contact with the situation in exile on another island, still unwilling to accept the prospect of French domination, Ariitaimai rushed out to try to avert the disaster. She did first things first: got an audience with the French governor and with his permission rushed both to the frontline village and to the field headquarters of the French forces, and persuaded in dramatic fashion first the chiefs and then the French commander to hold off on the battle to give her the chance to journey to the queen's place of exile to bring back herself or at least her capitulation. But when confronted, Queen Aimata refused, saying she would only trust the English, and it took considerable persuasion by Ariitaimai and her English husband, considerable time and anguish, and even an intervening battle. Finally Queen Aimata relented, and the Tahitians were spared the terrible bloodshed that would otherwise have accompanied their inevitable capitulation. Then the narrative closes with Ariitaimai being honored for her role in bringing the peace: "The peace of the island was then decided upon. On arriving at the governor's house, we found all the commanders of the troops and vessels there, and before them I was thanked by [Governor] Bruat for what I had done for my country" (196).

In terms of Western literary values, the story of Ariitaimai's success gives the book closure, and that on the sort of positive note that usually establishes the justification of memoirs. But an underlying sense of failure and cultural tragedy attends this conclusion, since the success was really a capitulation to the colonial forces. A certain very considerable amount of bloodshed was avoided, but the Tahitians had thereby acquiesced in the continuing destruction of their cultural autonomy, their social structure, and, actually, their population. The text had heretofore been insistently anticolonialist, making the theme of cultural tragedy absolutely dominant. The dual narrator had been basically culturally relativistic, affirming that traditional Tahiti had had a substantial population *"better fitted than any other possible community for the conditions in which they lived"* (136; my emphasis). And as one particularly forceful passage points out, while the Westerners were forcing inappropriate societal adaptations on the natives, their virulent diseases "found a rich field for destruction." "For this, perhaps the foreigners were not wholly responsible, although their civilization certainly was; but for the political misery the foreigner was wholly to blame, and for the social and moral degradation he was the active cause" (137). And those were the foreigners who would control Tahiti in the future, the narrative neglects to point out.*

Melville's *Typee* is especially worth considering in its intertextual relationship to *Tahiti*: there are similarities in its authorial use of personal impressions, and in Melville's strong image of the violation of a native culture's self-sufficiency by a corrupt, imperialistic, and hypocritically Christian West. In some ways Melville's novel might be imagined to be, in an implicit way, the very kind of "central symbol like the Virgin or the Dynamo" that Spiller felt *Tahiti* lacked. But there are still significant differences. Adams, working with his native informants and not writing a novel, does little of Melville's sort of naive exaggeration of the natives' state of unspoiled happiness when unaffected by the civilized world, and he can see the structure of the native society as more complex and sophisticated than Melville imagined it to be. In those respects Adams's work has a greater feel of authenticity in its representation of Polynesia. But Adams's commitment to the point of view of the Teva family, determining that Ariitaimai's emergency diplomacy be regarded as the triumph and resolution of both the event and the historical text, went directly counter to Melville's view of that same event (tacked on to *Typee* as an appendix in the very year of Queen Aimata's capitulation) that it was a "piratical seizure" by the French. Oddly and coincidentally, Melville had been there in person:

> The author of this volume arrived at Tahiti the very day that the iniquitous designs of the French were consummated by inducing the subordinate

---

*Ernest Samuels makes the point that although the fact "was apparently unknown to Adams," Ariitaimai's husband Salmon "perceived that a French protectorate would greatly enhance his wife's extensive estates" (1964, 105). In that case, of course, we can see reasons other than the purely historical or literary for the unquestionably positive tone of the final capitulation she helped to bring about. Is this an early example of the hazard of totally trusting a single family of informants?

chiefs, during the absence of their queen, to ratify an artfully drawn treaty, by which she was virtually deposed. Both menaces and caresses were employed on this occasion, and the 32-pounders which peeped out of the portholes of the frigate were the principal arguments adduced to quiet the scruples of the more conscientious islanders. (Melville 1968, 254)

Adams gives no sign of having read this appendix to the very novel he had worked at illustrating while on Samoa—Did he indeed not see it? Not think it was accurate? Not feel willing to submit its construction of the events for the approval of the Tevas? Whatever Adams's reason, the Melville account does offer us what we might have expected was the case: that the climactic event of Ariitaimai's memoirs was open to alternative interpretation.

In terms of its ethnographic and epistemological values—that is, in terms of the insight it gives us into a people who are Other, and into the means by which Others are to be understood—*Tahiti* offers some models of approach and problematizing that are fascinating and well ahead of their time. The project of letting "primitive" people virtually write their own history, of helping them to present their non-Western experience in Western language and historical/literary format, was unusual enough in its day to raise some interesting questions about the style of intercultural interpreting and theorizing most anthropologists were then doing, if any of them were paying attention. Granted, the narrative point of view of the book is a kind of inconsistent nuisance—and every one of its critics has noticed that. It raises the question: Who or what are we to imagine is behind this voice, this old woman speaking of her people's sad tribal tribulations so often in the lingo and referential context of an ironic Western intellectual? The book indeed seems to be compromised in its credibility by this mishmash of voices, especially since the title page of the 1901 Paris edition apparently presented only the name of a single author—"*Memoirs of Arii Taimai*," it said,—and a reader would have had to be either clairvoyant or Tahitian (or both) to know that the *Tauraatua I Amo* on the bottom line of the subtitle was the honorary Tahitian name of a certain American historian who was exceptionally cagey about putting his own name on his writings.

But we have all the way through the book observed the collision of the Tahitian and the European: their habits, morals, institutions, social structures, myths, traditions, and even their languages and poetics. This collision has been interculturally informative, and it has been produced by the dual narrator's alternations in voice and perspective, sometimes passage-by-passage, sometimes point-by-point. The mishmash contradicts and corrects as it juxtaposes. There is thematic and political significance in the fact that while we are learning of the Tahitian systems of precedence and rank, of the way that councils of chiefs are called, the way in which a woman can inherit the chiefship or supplicate neighboring chiefs to right an injustice, the relations of Maraes to birthrights, the position of children in the family, the ordering of domiciles and of sleeping arrangements and so forth, those details are being illuminated with analogies from Western cultures and myth and given broader, intercultural significance by juxtaposition with the contemporary political struggles between European powers. To compare Tahitian warriors with Homeric heroes or Tahitian women Ariis with Catherine of Russia or Maria Theresa of Austria is certainly to sacrifice ethnographic accuracy as well as consistency of point of view, but it does achieve some gain in late nineteenth-century intercultural understanding, some reorientation of Western insights and attitudes. As both Ariitaimai and Adams knew, the European understanding of Tahitian history was spotty, one-sided, and in many instances grossly distorted, and the correction and expansion of the existing textual accounts was obviously one of their projects in this book.

But the European texts were indispensable too, and Adams as the master of so many of them: Tahitians having "no history apart from genealogy," in the memories associated with the Maraes, and (not even wholly retrievable anymore) in the songs, had a history that was narrow, highly selective and fast fading. Thus *Tahiti*'s reliance on European accounts for population estimates, chronology, and records of events was essential. Neither Tahiti nor Europe could separately produce a history of the island, but together—complementing and conflicting—some approach to that could be made. And of course the pervading theme of the tragedy of imperialism inheres in the juxtapositions and the oftentimes ironic interplay of the perspectives of the two cultures. For thematic and ethnographic purposes, there can be richness in incompatibility.

In comparison with the evolutionary paradigm so prominent in Morgan's and Brinton's conception of primitive difference, the Ariitaimai/Adams vision seems far less schematic—more complex, subtle, and nuanced—and that is part of its critical political message. And this is certainly no typically condescending study of a primitive society by a civilized observer. *Tahiti*'s representation of the behavior of the Western societies that destroyed Polynesian culture certainly subverts an evolutionary ranking of cultures: The Westerners' spreading of "civilization" is, for purposes of this text, only a form of self-interest and a manifestation of intercultural blindness. To some extent, *Tahiti* implicitly regards Western societies as more highly evolved: They have superior navigation and transportation; and military; communication (writing and publishing) and history-preserving abilities; and a far wider intellectual sociocultural context than the Tahitians. But in terms of personal morality, social ethics, intercultural understanding, reflexiveness, and the general happiness and satisfactoriness of life, there is difference but no progress. Evolution, if that indeed is a category applicable to cultures, is not general and uniform, but aspect-specific.

The text represents and reflects difference in complex and not wholly compatible terms. For the dual narrator, differences in morality and social organization are simply culture-specific characteristics: each culture having its share of fallibility, potential for destructiveness, potential for peace and stability, and so forth. Differences in language and cultural heritage are formidable, but generative of mutual curiosity and respect. Racial difference is a matter of essence. It is very important that the Tahitians have Aryan racial heritage, because that (the operative assumption runs), accounts for their higher level of intellectual and cultural achievement. Also, racial stocks seem to have certain characteristic traits, for which their particular social organizations and cultural mores are appropriate.

A strong message of relativism abides: it is perfectly natural that societies have different mores, morals, social and familial organization, language, belief system, arts, and so forth, each appropriate to the specific people (the *Tahiti* text even resists expression of revulsion or disapproval for the human sacrifice and infanticide practiced in historical Tahiti). There are for Ariitaimai/Adams, however, certain supra-cultural values and characteristics: social stability; natural class hierarchy; civility; and gender equality in intelligence, courage, determination, and capability for governing. There seems to be a natural aristocracy in every people, following from both heredity and personal capability.

In sum, *Tahiti: Memoirs of Arii Taimai* is an unappealing, difficult-to-follow, ambivalently voiced text that, speaking in two languages of difference, portends some challenging standards for conceiving of primitive difference. In its own peculiar way it manages to mitigate reflexive and ethnocentric factors, to represent a culture emically, to demonstrate the gulf between cultures, and to establish a framework for cultural relativism. Virtually unnoticed, it posed a challenge to anthropology and to anthropological and historical writing that would remain unmet for several decades to come.

4

Mythologizing Nondifference: The Influence of Frazer, Freud, and Jung, and the Internalization of the Idea of the Primitive

And he [the cultural anthropologist] is disposed to think that if the resemblances between the neurotic and the primitive which have so often been pointed out are more than fortuitous, it is not because of a cultural atavism which the neurotic exemplifies but simply because all human beings, whether primitive or sophisticated in the cultural sense, are, at rock bottom, psychologically primitive, and there is no reason why a significant unconscious symbolism which gives substitutive satisfaction to the individual may not become socialized on any level of human activity.
—Edward Sapir, Cultural Anthropology and Psychiatry, (1932)

A WHOLE NEW FRAMEWORK FOR THE UNDERSTANDING OF HUMAN difference was brought into the anthropological arena by Sir James Frazer and the depth psychologists. Ethnologically they were still largely under the sway of the older anthropology, with its evolutionist paradigm of progress from primitive to civilized, its reliance on the traditional secondary and tertiary writings for its data, its comparative method, and its notions of universal animism, totemism, and such. But in focusing their analyses on human interiority—not just on beliefs and behaviors but on motives and urges—they attempted to bring deeper and more universal insights to the understanding of human nature and variability. They focused on symbol and myth, on dream and fantasy, on ritual and compulsion, and on the endeavors and conditions—like religion, art, and neuroticism—that most embodied those elements. In investigating the reconfiguration of the primitive in American culture, we can hardly overlook the effects of its articulations in the new psychology.

We start with some cautions, however. Frazer, Freud, and Jung were interested in causality that was prerational or irrational, and they tried to account for such "deep" psychic phenomena by gridding them on quasi-scientific frames fashioned in (and by) rationalistic, technical nomenclature and cause-and-effect grammar. In terms of ethnography and the understanding of human difference, two problems immediately arise. First, explaining human behavior and mentality in terms of its basis in unconscious urges predisposes the question of exactly what order of explanation is suitable and adequate. Such determinants as environment, economy, and political structure are ignored or radically subordinated. Secondly, the translation of (presumably) irrational behavior into universal categories of understanding is entirely a matter of *interpretation*, and subject to all the biases and vagaries of cultural and personal reflexiveness. So in using symbol, myth, and ritual as their keys to "deeper" human likeness and difference, Frazer, Freud, and Jung are bypassing cultural and temporal matrices and ignoring the reflexiveness of their interpretive processes and categories.

And the reflexiveness is multiple. For none of these three thinkers is the description of the primitive Other the primary objective. Each is in his own way fascinated with primitivism for what it can reveal about his own culture, as both product and determinant of contemporary psyches. Their own culture is both the starting point and the teleological objective of their inquiries. Their involvement with other cultures is a kind of psycho-intellectual imperialism, as they try to identify and locate, and then control the psychic commonality.

But just that psychic commonality is one of their most profoundly influential insights. Their designation of the relationship of primitive to civilized psyche imparted to the concept "primitive" new meaning, in much the same way that Picasso's modernist appropriation of the visual forms of African masks and sculpture tended to revise the way those artifacts came to be viewed. No longer a synonym for "rudimentary," or "backward," "primitive" came to mean, from the perspective of this particular cultural moment, something more like "elemental," or even "essential." In the lexicon of the psychoanalysts (although I'll exempt Frazer from this judgment) "primitive" no longer meant merely something to be condescended to, but something we very much needed to be in touch with in order to fully understand ourselves. As Marianna Torgovnick shrewdly points out, "to study primitivism's manifold presence is to recontextualize modernity" (1990, 193).

The explorations of the presumably primal influenced the modernist high culture, and especially its writers, profoundly, while the work of more seemingly mundane researchers into the survival skills, the daily habits, and the familial and institutional interrelationships of the people of different cultures had little appeal and drew little attention outside of *National Geographic* types of popularization. The new psychology and its popularizations in many ways stimulated and supported the radical rethinking of tradition, religion, rationalism, and normalcy. Experimentation in art and literature, like that in sexual behavior now could be (now *needed* to be) sited in a realm that included depth psychology. Thus the artistic products of this high cultural moment seem to have had more to do with mythical symbolism, inherent religious impulses, and deep psychic figuration than with the more prosaic-seeming realm of societal facts and arrangements. (Even postmodernity finds more of interest in T. S. Eliot than in John Dos Passos.) Additionally, of course, depth psychology greatly affected the theory and practice of anthropology. Questionable though it may have been in its simple evolutionist ethnology, it introduced a focus on individual psychology into a social science previously tending to be rather totally involved with the description of cultural averages and groups of generic individuals. Depth psychology awakened anthropologists (like the above-quoted Edward Sapir) to new possibilities of analysis.

Frazer's *The Golden Bough* is a massive, diverse, and unruly compendium of ritual, magical, and religious beliefs and practices from all cultures and all times, culled from all sorts of textual sources: an imbrication of interpretations. It is rationalized (insofar as that ambition could be realized) by systems of classification and explanation designed to affirm the standard evolutionary paradigm and solidify the superior status of Western scientific rationalism. It envisions the primitive as the superstitious, which in all its avatars, bizarre and familiar, pagan and Christian, is evolutionarily inferior to science.

Freud's anthropological work, subsequent to his clinical preoccupations, deriving from and supplementing them, was also heavily dependent on certain notions of nineteenth-century anthropology that especially fitted his psychological paradigms. Especially useful to him in *Totem and Taboo* were the concepts in Frazer's *Totemism and Exogamy* and the examples in *The Golden Bough*. In Freud's characterization, the primitive Other was closer to his instincts than were civilized people, somewhat more subject to unconscious ambivalence, and profoundly inhibited—analogous to the civilized neurotic in his lack of rational self-understanding and control. And, characteristically, Freud saw even the earliest "savages" as inhabiting a myth-scenario of inherited Oedipal guilt that all humans shared and always would share, despite the civilizing struggle to maintain rational control.

By contrast, Jung expresses reservations about rationalism. In his system, accessing the primitive in oneself or in the world at large is a way of maintaining a healthy balance with one's civilized intellectuality. Like Freud, he designates the difference between primitive and civilized as difference in relative levels of influence of the unconscious, of instinct, and of primal imagery, but adds the mechanism of a universal collective unconscious rather than that of a particular inherited sexual guilt as the unifying psychic factor. But "primitive" for Jung is a shifting concept: at times signifying something essential, elemental in the human makeup; at other times signifying something dark and threatening, destabilizing to civilization.

The three theorists are far from being in agreement about the primitive and its markers: about myth, for example, and its significance for difference. For Frazer, myth is basically intuitional pre-science: a distinctly primitive mode of thought associated with magic and inefficacious cause-and-effect. For Freud, it is not so much a way of thinking as an encoded set of symptoms of essential human drives and inhibitions, and a figurative means of accommodating to the inescapable determinants of nature and society. For Jung it is in many of his frames of thought a revealing, rejuvenating symbolic access to our deepest inherited characteristics, from which modern man often strays too far.

All three systems were engaged with an outmoded notion of universal unilinear human evolution, but in the filiation Frazer to Freud to Jung we can see "primitive" morphing from crude-and-backward to essential-and-modernist, inhabiting not only external Other but internal self as well. And its correlative, "civilization" (the underlying subject of each of these theorists), is it contemporarily in need of: (1) protecting its ideal rationality by extirpating the survivals of prerational beliefs and rituals? (2) discovering and controling its essential psychic urges and subconscious residues? or (3) freeing itself from the trammels of a superficial rationalism? The sequence clearly entailed the internalization of the primitive, and anthropologists and writers would need to pursue their truths in such a field of influence and contention.

Sir James Frazer's massive, eclectic, bizarre work *The Golden Bough*—produced in various versions and editions from the late 1880s to the early 1920s—has become a cultural anomaly: a text that defined much about the sensibility of the new age while being thoroughly grounded in the theory and information base of the previous one; a text too that despite a cool reception within its discipline had amazingly disproportionate circulation and cultural impact. And today *The Golden Bough* is an anthropological white elephant studied not for its insights into primitive mentality, religious ritual, or social evolution, but for its traces in the work of Freud, Jung, T. S. Eliot, and D. H. Lawrence. Frazer's position in anthropology, and its justification, has been superbly summed up by his biographer Robert Ackerman:

> Frazer is an embarrassment. The man who has had more readers and who was arguably a better writer than any other anthropologist writing in English does not appear in any of the professional lineages that anthropologists acknowledge today. The reason for this is plain enough: he wrote vast, assured tomes about primitive religion and mythology without ever leaving the library. He based his comprehensive theories on the often crude and ethnocentric reports of explorers, missionaries, and traders. He lacked the idea of culture as the matrix, both conscious and unconscious, that gives meaning to social behavior and belief, and thus had no qualms about comparing items of culture from the most disparate times and places. He was a hard-line rationalist who used ethnographic facts to try and knock the last nail in the coffin of religion in the name of objective science. If from time to time he achieved a kind of prophetic power, it is because he was the spokesman for an imperialist confidence that has now been swept away. It is no wonder that no one wants him for a professional ancestor. (1987, 1)

"[M]y intention merely was to explain the strange rule of the priesthood or sacred kingship of Nemi and with it the legend of the Golden Bough, immortalised by Virgil, which the voice of antiquity associated with the priesthood," Frazer claimed in his third-edition preface. "[S]tep by step I was lured on into far-spreading fields of primitive thought which had been but little explored by my predecessors" (1966, vii), he continued, disarmingly, explaining the serendipitous process by which the project grew into a twelve-volume compendium of primitive rituals and beliefs. The priest who was King of the Wood, associated with the vegetation cycle and with the godhead, who had to be killed to fulfill his role, was a figure of dramatic emotional consequence for Frazer. This figure was also a suggestive correlative to beliefs and rituals of sacrifice, fertility, kingship, magic, spirit-worship, the life cycle, rebirth, and so forth of all the peoples of what he conceived of as the precivilized, prescientific world. And the drama and the emotion were far from being incidental to Frazer's presentation of this complex of material:

> By discarding the austere form, without, I hope, sacrificing the solid substance, of a scientific treatise, I thought to cast my materials into a more artistic mould and so perhaps to attract readers, who might have been re-

pelled by a more strictly logical and systematic arrangement of the facts. Thus I put the mysterious priest of Nemi, so to say, in the forefront of the picture, grouping the other sombre figures of the same sort behind him in the background, not certainly because I deemed them of less moment but because the picturesque natural surroundings of the priest of Nemi among the wooded hills of Italy, the very mystery which enshrouds him, and not least the haunting magic of Virgil's verse, all combine to shed a glamour on the tragic figure with the Golden Bough, which fits him to stand as the centre of a gloomy canvas. (1966, viii–ix)

There is no doubt that in some passages of this very unusual work Frazer is deliberately using an evocative novelistic language of mood and setting—"we picture to ourselves the scene as it may have been witnessed by a belated wayfarer on one of those wild autumn nights when the dead leaves are falling thick, and the winds seem to sing the dirge of the dying year" (1966, 9)—trying to control the attention and emotional involvement of the reader. But there is also no mistaking the extremely rationalistic language by which Frazer means to frame and interpret the profusion of strange and barbaric phenomena that make up the contents of his disquisition:

> If we analyse the principles of thought on which magic is based, they will probably be found to resolve themselves into two: first, that like produces like, or that an effect resembles its cause; and second, that things which have once been in contact with each other continue to act on each other at a distance after the physical contact has been severed. The former principle may be called the Law of Similarity, the latter, the Law of Contact or Contagion. (1966, 52)

Thus he tries to specify and control the range of possible meanings of the diverse and certainly unsettling phenomena he presents with such relish and concreteness. The language of a fascinated spectator and the language of an authority invoking appropriate scientific Laws: both imply absolute distance between cultures, self-reassuring difference between observer and observed.

Viewing this contrast in terms of *The Golden Bough*'s content and impact, a number of critics have cited a disparity between its framework of explanation—rationalistic, even simplistic—and its rich and suggestive diversity of detail and example, as if, in the words of Steven Connor, the work "fluctuates between the centripetal desire to consolidate, organise and simplify, and the centrifugal force of the data, which keep threatening to spin out of conceptual control." As Robert

Fraser observes, the work "would not possess [its] power did it not stir forces far deeper than those its thesis admits."[*]

The framing theses of the work are the progressive ideas, general and anthropological, of the late nineteenth century. Ideas like those of Herbert Spencer about the evolution of societies, cultures, and individuals are clearly recognizable throughout Frazer's discourse, and the then-recently consensual interpretations of primitive peoples in terms of their animism, totemism, and progress toward exogamy (growing out of the work of Tylor, Lang, Morgan, McLennan, Robertson Smith, and others) are applied throughout. Frazer's discovery of the work of German folklorist Wilhelm Mannhardt, who detailedly traced the vegetation rituals of European peasantry, added conceptually to his borrowed repertoire as well as providing a great deal of specific information (Ackerman 1987, 80–82). Growing out of the approaches and anthropological theories of these nineteenth-century experts, *The Golden Bough* could not but embody their unconscious reflexiveness and, as another evolutionist document, project the same assumptions of cultural superiority.

The originality of *The Golden Bough* comes from its specificity and its particular focus. As Frazer's project grew to vastness over the years, it accumulated accounts of myths and rituals, legends and beliefs, practices and mores of virtually every people of the world. Frazer scoured literature, anthropology, archeology, travel accounts, missionaries' reports, and so forth, and in this single work presented their wealth of fascinating specific detail, a kind of master compendium of belief systems.

Furthermore, via its version of the comparative method, it developed a number of new insights through its system of thematic juxtapositions. For example, as Ackerman has pointed out, "no one had ever before focused so intensively on the 'primitive' elements of the religions of Greece, Rome, and the eastern Mediterranean and had juxtaposed these on so large a scale with the religious activity of 'savages'" (1987, 63). Its wealth of materials and means carried Frazer's method well beyond that of many of his predecessors: as James Boon has said, "[The] contrast between Tylor and Frazer suggests a development from one-dimensional reportage to multidimensional representation" (1982, 11).

An important (though generally implicit) insight embedded in *The Golden Bough*'s multidimensionality is the connection it makes be-

---

[*]Connor, "The Birth of Humility," 78, and Fraser, "The Face Beneath the Text," 13, in Robert Fraser, ed. 1990. *Sir James Frazer and the Literary Imagination.* See also the essays of Gillian Beer and Lionel Kelly in that collection.

tween primitive religions, fertility worship, and sex. In culling so much recondite material and presenting it with such lavish descriptiveness, it linked religion and sexuality in a way not customary in the scholarly writing of the time. It was a way that the burgeoningly modernist, psychologically-preoccupied twentieth century would find fascinating. In Ackerman's judgment "it seems likely that he thought of psychology as the queen of the human sciences, and certainly the mother of anthropology and the study of religion" (1987, 51). Frazer's framework psychologizing is nothing like the depth psychology of Freud, however. What interests him most (after the march of evolutionary progress) is primitive peoples' sense of cause and effect: their fundamentally faulty sense of why things happen and how they can be made to happen. As he explicitly psychologizes the evolutionist paradigm, he does so in old-fashioned terms. The modernist fascination with deeper, darker, sexually-linked motives would feed solely on his details of the primitive rituals and beliefs and the suggestiveness of their contextualization.

Conceiving of primitive man—whether in the South Sea Isles, darkest Africa, prehistoric Europe, or wherever—as living, believing, and behaving principally according to his position on the scale of monolinear evolution, Frazer's interpretation of the process of psychoreligious evolution is a matter of considerable simplicity. It involves three major phases: magic, religion, and science. Each phase is essentially a different approach to utilitarian cause and effect; of the prior, inferior stages Frazer says:

> magic is nothing but a mistaken application of the very simplest and most elementary processes of the mind, namely the association of ideas by virtue of resemblance or contiguity; and . . . on the other hand religion assumes the operation of conscious or personal agents, superior to man, behind the visible screen of nature. (1966, 233)

In coming into the scientific phase, recognizing the unique value of empirical knowledge and the absolute reign of immutable physical Law, mankind finally has attained a direct and authoritative sense of causality. "By myths I understand mistaken explanations of phenomena," Frazer says (in another context: his edition of Apollodorus's *The Library*, quoted in Ackerman 1987, 234), and he invests totally in a literalist scientific rationalism as the engine of progress toward civilization. Cultures evolve from magic to religion and from religion to science in the interests of efficacy. The magician learns to give up his attempts to manipulate the world by symbolic means because he experiences the rain not falling or the invalid not recovering in response to his manipulative craft, and the priest likewise learns to see prayer and supplication as futile in many circumstances. Those approaches simply haven't been found reliable for making things happen. Pragmatic trial-and-error and mankind's ability to learn by experience determine the course and rate of human evolution.

Frazer seems to have no sense of alternative explanations: as he conceived of it, evolutionary progress was simply the triumph of scientific rationalism over the stifling influence of tradition and superstition. Interpreting the myths and rites of other cultures solely as attempts to understand and control nature and life's processes, he virtually left out of consideration the aspects of celebration, grief, appreciation, play, spectacle, and so forth that well might have been crucial in their formation. Mightn't some ritualized activities be expressive rather than utilitarian? William James, in meeting Frazer and being impressed with the simplicity of his psychological theory, tried to persuade him to "put in big loads of work in the morbid psychology direction" (Ackerman 1987, 175), in an attempt to get him to enlarge his sense of the possibilities in human behavior, but apparently to no avail. Frazer persisted in that mode of anthropologists' nearsightedness that Johannes Fabian has recently inveighed against as "their fixation on goal-oriented behavior and adaptive functionality" (1983, 113).

Within Frazer's narrow range of psychological and sociological theory, it was easy for him to point up the moral of primitive outrages and atrocities. (Or was it a case of an *a priori* moral dictating the psychological and sociological simplification?) Of the vast number of human sacrifices by the ancient Mexicans, the "bleeding hearts of men and animals . . . presented to the sun to maintain him in vigour and enable him to run his course across the sky," Frazer points out that "the ceaseless wars of the Mexicans and their cruel system of human sacrifices, the most monstrous on record, sprang in great measure from a mistaken theory of the solar system. No more striking illustration could be given of the disastrous consequences that may flow in practice from a purely speculative error" (1966, 315).

Human evolution had a moral for his contemporary culture, and Frazer was determined that it should not be missed. In what amounts to his version of psycho-intellectual imperialism, all of that revealed and interpreted primitivism served to drive home the message that "the hope of progress—moral and intellectual as well as material—in the future is bound up with the fortunes of science, and that every obstacle placed in the way of scientific discovery is a wrong to humanity" (1922, 712). As he accumulates instances of slain vegetation gods and the irrational (and frequently obscenely bizarre) forms of ritual performed on their behalves, he leaves no doubt about their close relation to the religion of his own culture, nor about from whence come the obstacles placed in the way of scientific discovery. Frazer's attacks on Christianity are characteristically oblique but unmistakable; in his preface to *The Golden Bough*'s second edition he declines to mention Christianity *per se*, and he couches his attack in metaphor and tones of sympathetic nostalgia:

> the comparative study of the beliefs and institutions of mankind . . .well handled . . . may become a powerful instrument to expedite progress if it lays bare certain weak spots in the foundations on which modern society is built—if it shews that much which we are wont to regard as solid rests on the sands of superstition rather than on the rock of nature. It is indeed a melancholy and in some respects thankless task to strike at the foundations of beliefs in which, as in a strong tower, the hopes and aspirations of humanity through long ages have sought a refuge from the storm and stress of life. Yet sooner or later it is inevitable that the battery of the comparative method should breach these venerable walls, mantled over with the ivy and mosses and wild flowers of a thousand tender and sacred associations. (1966, xxv–xxvi)

(Incidentally, don't such passages rife with trite figures and artsy elaboration challenge the customarily tossed-off judgment that Frazer was a great prose stylist?) Following the guiding star of truth meant, in terms of Frazer's project, canvassing ethnography and philology, archaeology and literature, travelers' and missionaries' accounts for appropriatable descriptions of the rituals and beliefs of precivilized peoples. Inasmuch as these descriptions came preinterpreted, the selectivity, focus, and judgmental implications all came with them. *The Golden Bough* is not actually a catalogue of primitive customs but an anthology of interpretations. The assumptions behind those interpretations were like Frazer's own: procivilization, antipagan, and conveying the same sense of the primitive as radically other. But Frazer, in aiming his polemical artillery at the Christian "survivals" in his society, went a step beyond a great many of his sources and many of his anthropological predecessors in his repudiation of heritage, his attempt to extirpate his civilization's satyr-traces.

In his use of his thousand-or-so sources, Frazer most often simply transcribed the material into his format by paraphrasing and quoting, counting on his thematic superstructure to focus his interpretation and/or modify the judgments along his own lines. But at times he found it necessary (or perhaps just more likely or more interesting?) to manipulate, change or even invent evidence. For example, he spends a great deal of effort to establish that the golden bough was really mistletoe. His chain of reasoning is baroque—mistletoe looks golden in certain seasons; it's green in the branches of the oak during the winter when the oak is barren; primitive man thus might have viewed the mistletoe as the spirit of the oak and thought it endowed with magic powers for preserving or healing human life; it is an element in many European peasant celebrations, and so forth (1922, 701–5). In some cases, in his enthusiasm to complete a circuit of supposition Frazer will not only invent mythological connections, but he will blur the boundaries between myth and historical reality, so that we cannot be sure whether the personages he talks about were mythic/literary characters or real people to whose lives he has intuitional access beyond any textual authority. Despite his disdain for myth in the context of its juxtaposition to science, he is fascinated by it in other contexts, even in some sense believing in it and, like a detective believing the evidence, contributing his own inferences and extensions.

In one instance he claims, "we shall probably be doing no injustice either to Hippolytus or to Artemis if we suppose that the relation between them was once of a tenderer nature than appears in classical literature. We may conjecture that if he spurned the love of women, it was because he enjoyed the love of a goddess." Frazer supports his supposition with references to other episodes in the accounts of the career of Hippolytus in the works of Herodotus and Pausanias, and to those authorities' commentators, and the statement that "in the story of the tragic death of the youthful Hippolytus we may discern an analogy with similar tales of other fair but mortal youths who paid with their lives for the brief rapture of the love of an immortal goddess" (1966, 38–39). What level of interpretation is this? Is there a real historical situation that all such tales quite truthfully though variously point toward? Frazer's rhetoric would indicate that he was assuming that there was.

There is finally some mystery about how Frazer means us to take his monumental opus. The evidential burden certainly seems quite convincing in terms of its sheer breadth and density, and the judgments and the rationalized structure are anything but indefinite. But by logical standards the entire demonstration is more like a very rich brainstorm than a sound argument—and Frazer acknowledges this freely and frequently in his text, although this aspect of his presentation is quite commonly overlooked. Typically, Frazer's hypotheses, like those of Hippolytus and the mistletoe, are illustrated profusely with details and analogues from any and every sort of textual source. Typically, too, they are enmeshed in a network of preliminary or ancillary hypotheses, which he often admits are unproved or unprovable, or otherwise weakens in his mode of presentation:

> The foregoing evidence *may satisfy us* that in many lands and many races magic has claimed to control the great forces of nature for the good of man. *If that has been so*, the practitioners of the art must necessarily be personages of importance and influence in any society which puts faith in their extravagant pretensions, and *it would be no matter for surprise if . . .* some of them should attain to the highest position of authority over their credulous fellows. In point of fact, magicians *appear to have often* developed into chiefs and kings. (1966, 332; my italics)
>
> [O]ur hypotheses at best are but partial, not universal, solutions of the manifold problems which confront us, and . . . in science as in daily life it is vain to look for one key to open all locks. (1966, 334)

And so on, throughout the work. Even his principal point at issue, the origin and operation of the priesthood at Nemi, based as it is on what Frazer regards as unassailable assumptions about the unitary nature of primitive man and anthropology's comparative method, carries a substantial burden of uncertainty:

> The strange rule of this priesthood has no parallel in classical antiquity, and cannot be explained from it. To find an explanation we must go farther afield. No one will probably deny that such a custom savours of a barbarous age, and, surviving into imperial times, stands out in striking isolation from the polished Italian society of the day, like a primaeval rock rising from a smooth-shaven lawn. It is the very rudeness and barbarity of the custom which allow us a hope of explaining it. For recent researches into the early history of man have revealed the essential similarity with which, under many superficial differences, the human mind has elaborated its first crude philosophy of life. Accordingly, if we can shew that a barbarous custom, like that of the priesthood of Nemi, has existed elsewhere; if we can detect the motives which led to its institution; if we can prove that these motives have operated widely, perhaps universally, in human society, producing in varied circumstances a variety of institutions specifically different but generically alike; if we can shew, lastly, that these very motives, with some of their derivative institutions, were actually at work in classical antiquity; then we may fairly infer that at a remoter age the same motives gave birth to the priesthood of Nemi. Such an inference, in default of direct evidence as to how the priesthood did actually arise, can never amount to demonstration. But it will be more or less probable according to the degree of completeness with which it fulfils the conditions I have indicated. The object of this book is, by meeting these conditions, to offer a fairly probable explanation of the priesthood of Nemi. (1966, 10)

Thus a language of tentativeness pervades the text. Frazer undoubt-edly intended it to frankly acknowledge the lack of sufficient scien-tific proof, but it also might raise in our minds the suggestion that his presumably highly rationalized scientific study in fact is instead a rather personal demonstration of broad erudition and ingenious sup-position.

For Frazer virtually everything compares via the comparative method: complex cultural habits of very distant peoples translated into the terminology and categories of Western intellectuality can eas-ily be seen to manifest very striking uniformities. In his discussion, for instance, of "Absence and Recall of the Soul," what he chooses to regard as "soul," and what behaviors he chooses to regard as attempts to confine the soul within the body, or recall it when it presumably has escaped or roamed, are matters of considerable interpretive lati-tude. Frazer can cite a Dutch authority who claims that in the practice of the Minangkabauers, "a skein of thread or a string is sometimes fastened round the wrist or loins of a woman in childbed, so that when her soul seeks to depart in her hour of travail it may find the egress barred." Three example-loaded pages later, he cites the report of another authority that "In southern Celebes they think that a bridegroom's soul is apt to fly away at marriage, so coloured rice is scattered over him to induce it to stay." And two pages later, still on the same general subject, he launches an example-salvo on dreaming, claiming generically that "The soul of a sleeper is supposed to wander away from his body and actually to visit the places, to see the persons, and to perform the acts of which he dreams" (1911, 32, 35, 36). Thus all recorded beliefs and behaviors that can possibly remind an intel-lectualized, cultured Westerner of his notion of soul and body, of an escaping soul, of the means he could imagine to restrain an escaping soul or recall a wandering soul or such, come out, in the wash of Western religio-philosophical terminology, as correlatable phenom-ena attesting to the existence of a uniform primitive humankind. The comparative method, thus employed, allows no more recognition of individuality, cultural uniqueness, or intracultural differentiation than does the paradigm of monolinear evolution.

And this normalizing, generalizing tendency plays out in the lan-guage Frazer uses in novelistically elaborating and specifying situa-tions in which he apparently means to increase his readers' sense of presence. Still basically the anthropologist, he is novelistic only in dic-tion and description. Very different from the ways that Faulkner or Hurston, say, often focus their fiction on a unique individual in some kind of conflictual relationship with his or her society, Frazer concen-trates imaginatively on the generic situation of the precivilized type.

At one point, for example, he concludes "In this, or some such way as this, the deeper minds may be conceived to have made the great transition from magic to religion," immediately following this intensely particular description of the hypothetical, generic "deeper mind" in the hypothetical moment of its realization of the great paradigm shift:

> All things went on as before, yet all seemed different to him from whose eyes the old scales had fallen. For he could no longer cherish the pleasing illusion that it was he who guided the earth and the heaven in their courses, and that they would cease to perform their great revolutions were he to take his feeble hand from the wheel. In the death of his enemies and his friends he no longer saw a proof of the resistless potency of his own or of hostile enchantments; he now knew that friends and foes alike had succumbed to a force stronger than any that he could wield, and in obedience to a destiny which he was powerless to control.
>
> Thus cut adrift from his ancient moorings and left to toss on a troubled sea of doubt and uncertainty, his old happy confidence in himself and his powers rudely shaken, our primitive philosopher must have been sadly perplexed and agitated till he came to rest, as in a quiet haven after a tempestuous voyage, in a new system of faith and practice. . . . If the great world went on its way without the help of him or his fellows, it must surely be because there were other beings, like himself, but far stronger, who, unseen themselves, directed its course and brought about all the varied series of events which he had hitherto believed to be dependent on his own magic. . . . To these mighty beings, whose handiwork he traced in all the gorgeous and varied pageantry of nature, man now addressed himself, humbly confessing his dependence on their invisible power, and beseeching them of their mercy to furnish him with all good things, to defend him from the perils and dangers by which our mortal life is compassed about on every hand. (1966, 238–39)

Thus primitive man supposedly lived out his equivalent of a nineteenth-century *bildungsroman* (again, much of it in trite metaphor). In presentation it is ambivalent: both cautiously tentative and, in terms of the philosophical emotionality of the nineteenth century, convincingly detailed. But the implied message of the story is absolute cultural distance, as we witness the gropings of this very naive intelligence through the veils of superstition toward our own very solid understandings of things. Frazer's empathy is liberally laced with condescension.

Such distancing and condescension are also evident when he offers expanded descriptions of certain ritual celebrations (usually the more sensational of them, and those for which he has several usable sources). In this example (certainly one of the more sensational, from the description of the fertility rites for the Western Asian god Attis), note the attempt to make the scene come alive by means of highly charged modifiers, and the hypothetical addition of detail to endow the scene with what Frazer regards as its full significance:

> The third day, the twenty-fourth of March, was known as the Day of Blood: the Archigallus or high-priest drew blood from his arms and presented it as an offering. Nor was he alone in making this bloody sacrifice. Stirred by the wild barbaric music of clashing cymbals, rumbling drums, droning horns and screaming flutes, the inferior clergy whirled about in the dance with waggling heads and streaming hair, until, rapt into a frenzy of excitement and insensible to pain, they gashed their bodies with potsherds or slashed them with knives in order to bespatter the altar and the sacred tree with their flowing blood. The ghastly rite probably formed part of the mourning for Attis and may have been intended to strengthen him for the resurrection. The Australian aborigines cut themselves in like manner over the graves of their friends for the purpose, perhaps, of enabling them to be born again. Further, we may conjecture, though we are not expressly told, that it was on the same Day of Blood and for the same purpose that the novices sacrificed their virility. Wrought up to the highest pitch of religious excitement they dashed the severed portions of themselves against the image of the cruel goddess. These broken instruments of fertility were afterwards reverently wrapt up and buried in the earth or in subterranean chambers sacred to Cybele, where, like the offering of blood, they may have been deemed instrumental in recalling Attis to life and hastening the general resurrection of nature, which was then bursting into leaf and blossom in the vernal sunshine. (1914, 268–69)

Frazer's language and rhetoric here make the scene eminently picturable: a "ghastly rite" indeed, with the audience present as voyeurs, horrified at the appalling behavior of these strange primitive Others. The gratuitous though quite scholarly inclusion of the Australian aborigines affirms again the worldwide uniformity as well as the absolute cultural distance of these Others.

It is not at all unusual for the language of nineteenth- and early twentieth-century scientists to be freighted with moral or esthetic judgment (even Darwin's has such moments), but Frazer's polemical purposes and strongly normative sense of civilized belief and behavior frequently impel his statements into strong expressions of Victorian disapproval. Of the natural tendency to believe in the efficacy of the principles of sympathetic magic, he states that "they are familiar in the concrete, though certainly not in the abstract, to the crude intelligence not only of the savage, but of ignorant and dull-witted people everywhere," and, by contrast to the savage's straightforward pseudo-manipulations of nature by magic ("the bastard sister of science"), under the influence of religion mankind "strove to coax and mollify a coy, capricious, or irascible deity by the soft insinuation of prayer and sacrifice" (1966, 54, 222, 234).

Classification was explanation for Frazer, and this indeed seems to have been one of the primary linguistic characteristics of his brand of comparative-method evolutionism. For any given behavior, institution, rite or belief, one located its presumed cognates in other cultures, historical or contemporary, and placed it particularly on the universal scale of evolutionary progress, and one could legitimately feel that he understood it. Classify behaviors of a certain range, no matter how wide, as applications of "homeopathic magic," and those diverse behaviors were by that act things we knew about. Correlatively then, linguistic connections and relationships are assumed to be reliable signifiers of actual connections and relationships. Note in this passage, for example, how the language Frazer uses in defining religion preforms an ethnocentric schema for what one can expect to find in the teeming actual world:

> By religion, then, I understand a propitiation or conciliation of powers superior to man which are believed to direct and control the course of nature and of human life. Thus defined, religion consists of two elements, a theoretical and a practical, namely, a belief in powers higher than man and an attempt to propitiate or please them. Of the two, belief clearly comes first, since we must believe in the existence of a divine being before we can attempt to please him. But unless the belief leads to a corresponding practice, it is not a religion but merely a theology; in the language of St. James, "faith, if it hath not works, is dead, being alone." (1966, 222–23)

Thus Frazer's language of difference, whatever *The Golden Bough*'s effect in stimulating the modernist interest in primitive rites and primitive psychology, is grounded in the cultural attitudes and the intellectual and linguistic practices of the late nineteenth century. He waxes tritely eloquent about science ("Here at last, after groping about in the dark for countless ages, man has hit upon a clue to the labyrinth, a golden key that opens many locks in the treasury of nature" [1922, 712]). He celebrates colonialism, both implicitly throughout his discourse, and explicitly at certain moments ("Intellectual progress . . . cannot be dissociated from industrial or economic progress, and that in its turn receives an immense impulse from conquest and empire. . . . [T]he great conquering races of the world have commonly done most to advance and spread civilisation, thus healing in peace the wounds they inflicted in war" [1966, 218]). He historically deplores influence of Oriental religions in the West ("which in the later days of paganism spread over the Roman Empire, and by saturating the European peoples with alien ideals of life gradually undermined the whole fabric of ancient civilisation" [1922, 357]). And he gives condescending credit to the savage, our forbear ("Our gratitude is due to the nameless and forgotten toilers, whose patient thought and active exertions have largely made us what we are" [1922, 263]). But we can't help wondering at *The Golden Bough*'s fascinating strangeness, the tremendous richness and plenitude of its examples, well in excess of the theses they were supposed to illustrate and the civilized attitudes they were supposed to counterpoint, as if in some part of his mind Frazer felt that there was something more here than could be dreamt of in his rationalist's philosophy.

Sigmund Freud's approach to theorizing about human difference and the primitive, brought to public prominence in 1912, engendered some very different results. Coming to the insights and issues of anthropology as an internationally recognized theorist and practitioner of psychoanalysis, the new science of the disfunction of the individual mind, he was positioned to discover striking similarities between primitive and neurotic beliefs and behaviors, and to inquire into mankind's earliest origins in a search for the essential sources of psychological dysfunction. William James's objection about Frazer's lack of a sense of psychological morbidity was ultimately (and posthumously) answered here, though in some bizarre ways.

Freud's broadly anthropological books, *Totem and Taboo* (1912, American translation by A. A. Brill, 1918), *The Future of an Illusion* (1927, trans. 1928), and *Civilization and Its Discontents* (1930, trans. 1930), were basically applications of psychoanalytic theory to turn-of-the-century anthropology. Ostensibly, Freud saw himself as identifying the psychological mechanisms behind the phenomena social scientists were studying. Not incidentally, he was at the same time promoting psychoanalysis by introducing its language and concepts into anthropological discourse. However questionable his success in either venture, there is no doubt that he was instrumental in turning the focus of anthropological studies more toward the situation of the individual and his psychic needs and complex relation to society. And certainly this conjunction of explanatory systems, anthropological and psychoanalytical, led to a new sense of the primitive and of the primitive-civilized difference.

Freud steeped himself in the writings of the evolutionist anthropologists, fascinated by many of their ideas and finding much in them to supplement and confirm his vision of the human psyche. Edwin Wallace, in *Freud and Anthropology*, states that "There is direct evidence . . . that before 1900 he had read at least three of them (Lubbock, Spencer, Tylor) and a strong probability that he was familiar with at least three others (Morgan, McLennan, Bachofen)." Wallace goes on to cite ideas of these evolutionists that Freud found very congenial: the notions of unilinear evolution, of the "psychic unity" of mankind, of "survivals," of the "comparative method," and of the Lamarckian inheritance of culturally acquired traits (1983, 18–19). Of course Darwinian evolution was also important to Freud, at least in his ideas about primal man (Wallace 1983, 94–95), but that very questionable notion of Lamarckian inheritance is one that Philip Rieff worried over in his thoughtful exoneration, *Freud: the Mind of the Moralist*, allowing that "the connection between psychoanalysis and Lamarckianism cannot be overemphasized" (1979, 200). Frazer's influence on Freud is also one that cannot be overemphasized. John Vickery's *The Literary Impact of The Golden Bough* stresses Frazer's profound influence on *Totem and Taboo*, quoting Freud's own statement that "the chief literary sources of my studies in this field were the well-known works of J. G. Frazer ('Totemism and Exogamy' and 'The Golden Bough'), a mine of valuable facts and opinions" (Vickery 1973, 94; quoted from *The Problem of Lay-Analysis*, trans. J. Strachey, 1927, 308).

All of these adoptions and borrowings from the evolutionists would have put Freud pretty much over the borderline of ethnological obsolescence by the time *Totem and Taboo* was published in America in 1918, and well beyond it for the studies he published in the twenties and thirties, but this seems not to have bothered him, even when it was pointed out. For example, Wallace establishes that Freud in 1909 heard a lecture by Franz Boas attacking the notion that totemism was a universal evolutionary stage. The various phenomena the evolutionists had grouped together under the "totemism" rubric had widely different origins and different meanings in different cultures, Boas pointed out, and "consequently *psychological laws covering all of them cannot be deduced from them*" (Wallace 1983, 177; his italics). But Freud went right on with his particular program of adoptions and adaptations.

He was picking his way through the anthropological writings toward a particular vision of the evolution of the human psyche, and it mattered less that accounts might be apocryphal or theories questionable than that they led him further toward his master paradigm. Feeling that his knowledge of the essential human psyche was sufficient for theorizing about the mentality of people far distant in time, place or culture (shades of Herbert Spencer!), Freud worked an elaborate reciprocity between conceptions of civilized and primitive minds. His clinical experience in turn-of-century Europe and the theory he derived from it provided insight into the primitive mind, and his resulting model of the primitive mind provided insight into the minds of the moderns.

As Rieff puts it, "Freud used the data of anthropology as a source book for studying the irrational. The prehistoric crises of the race illuminate, for him, the meaning of neurotic crises among historical men. At the same time, the neurotic crises of historical men reveal the original prehistoric crises" (1979, 192). Wallace goes a step farther in impugning Freud's version of the primitive:

> Freud never analyzed a single primitive individual; he thus did not even use the most powerful tool (the clinical method of psychoanalysis) that he possessed. Nor was he, so far as I know, acquainted with the detailed culture history of a specific primitive group. He picked and chose his data from authors who had in turn picked and chosen their data from a welter of cultures, without regard to temporal, geographical, or institutional context. (1983, 189)

The abstractness and circularity of his method clearly indicates that Freud's real concern, whatever the ostensible focus of his works, was with civilized contemporary minds. His uncivilized Other was part negative reflection and part intellectually exploitable resource. There is no wonder that Freud's notion of the primitive was so popular and widely influential with moderns: it was custom-made out of the materials of their own minds and world.

Freud thus extended the "comparative method" to include civilized people in the mix with all the culturally undifferentiated primitives, and proposed a "psychic unity" of humankind on a new, deeper and more instrumental level. His interpretation of dreams, symbols and myth, that very essential technique in the practice of psychoanalysis, demonstrates this tendency to homogenize difference. In interpreting the imagery of dreams he often quite carefully focuses on the symbolism in the mind and life of the individual dreamer: "The content of the dream is thus the fulfillment of a wish; its motive is a wish," he insists in explaining the first of his examples in *The Interpretation of Dreams* (1950, 30).

But on other occasions he sees the symbolism as not individually, not even culturally, specific (although he might show some trepidation in evoking a kind of species-memory that inclines toward becoming what Jung would term "the collective unconscious"). The following passage from *The Interpretation of Dreams* is especially interesting, both for the terms in which Freud suggests a kind of universal psyche, and for the traces of tentativeness with which (on this particular occasion) he approaches the possibility:

> [D]reaming is on the whole an act of regression to the earliest relationships of the dreamer, a resuscitation of his childhood, of the impulses which were then dominant and the modes of expression which were then available. Behind this childhood of the individual we are then promised an insight into the phylogenetic childhood, into the evolution of the human race, of which the development of the individual is only an abridged repetition influenced by the fortuitous circumstances of life. We begin to suspect that Friedrich Nietzsche was right when he said that in a dream "there persists a primordial part of humanity which we can no longer reach by a direct path," and we are encouraged to expect, from the analysis of dreams, a knowledge of the archaic inheritance of man, a knowledge of psychical things in him that are innate. It would seem that dreams and neuroses have preserved for us more of the psychical antiquities than we suspected; so that psychoanalysis may claim a high rank among those sciences which endeavor to reconstruct the oldest and darkest phases of the beginnings of mankind. (1950, 404)

Freud again and again bases his theorizing on the underlying notion that the essence of a psychic function or pattern is in its origin, that the identification of its origin is its explanation. Myths, symbols, and dreamed or imagined images he conceived of not as legitimate modes of thought like reason and analogy but as symptoms, and by following such symptomatic markers back to their sources he felt he could discover the universal determinant psychic essences. He was fascinated with the notion that the development of an individual could be conceived of as repeating the stages of the evolutionary development of the species—"ontogeny recapitulates phylogeny" in the embryologists' then current and catchy phrase; thus the symbolism of neurotics' dreams, children's imaginings, primitives' myths, and poets' inventions could be analyzed for what they could reveal about archaic (essential) man. At the same time, he also was taken with the idea that myths were a kind of racial memory, "the idea," to borrow Philip Rieff's words, "that all myths record historic events or figures (e.g., Moses, Jesus) that can eventually be traced back to an actual proto-mythic person, the primal father, and a literal proto-mythic event, his murder by the sons" (1979, 209). Thus symbolism in any mode, from any source—primitive or civilized, dreamed or created, infantile or mature, normal or neurotic—was revelatory of the universal, historical, essential human psyche. All it needed was a psychoanalytically sophisticated act of interpretation.

In part, that interpretation produced some brilliantly unprece-dented and highly stimulating ideas, especially for the production and interpretation of works of art and literature, as well as for the involve-ment of a wide popular audience in the psychological interpretation of many aspects of experience. But in terms of our inquiry, it acted to homogenize difference, as the template of Western psychological interpretation was placed over all manifestations of otherness. The civilized language of interpretation identified and fixed the meanings of those symbols, regardless of whatever various aspects of meaning or ritual or institutions they might have evoked in their original con-texts. As Paul Ricoeur emphasizes, in studying psychoanalytic theory "we are constantly led back to interpretation, to the act of interpret-ing, to the work of interpretation . . . Psychoanalysis is interpretation from beginning to end." He insists, too, on the textual nature of the empirical data of psychoanalysis: "it is not the dream as dreamed that can be interpreted, but rather the text of the dream account. . . . [I]t is not desires as such that are placed at the center of the analysis, but rather their language" (1970, 66, 5–6).

And if in the case of the patient-dreamer we recognize a twofold screen of interpretation in both the dreamer's language and the ana-lyst's, what relation to reality do our notions have when the analyst/ theorist is interpreting an anthropologist's interpretation of the inter-pretation of an eyewitness missionary or of a classical text? Freud's unquestioning acceptance of Frazer's "mine of valuable facts and opinions" thus seems to give us the primitive Other behind interpre-tive screens to the third power, each with its own peculiar proclivity for distortion. Was science necessarily so naively uncritical in those times? Was this even science?

Freud was steeped in the science of his time, and his writings often clearly represent and sometimes even express the desire to be positiv-istic, to be empirical, to find the scientifically provable determinants, especially from the basis of his own clinical experience. The qualifiers in the preceding quotation hypothesizing about dreams and archaic inheritance at times show a kind of canny caution, even about a con-clusion that he very much wants to obtain. He even at times voices questions about the very status of his whole endeavor: in a published letter to Einstein entitled "Why War?" (1932) after explaining his the-ory of the death instinct, he goes on,

It may perhaps seem to you as though our theories are a kind of mythol-ogy and, in the present case, not even an agreeable one. But does not every science come in the end to a kind of mythology like this? Cannot the same be said to-day of your own physics? (1949, 283)

In a very general sense he knows he's producing a myth of the human mind, while trying to build and support it as empirically as possible.

Yet he has a strong tendency, as his critics have frequently recognized, to go off into extrapolation, analogy, and metaphor, to hypothesize nonobservables, to trust purely anecdotal examples, and to draw absolutistic conclusions on questionable grounds. This of course is not at all unlike the nineteenth century dream of the universal theory: the scientific statement that finally fixes an overarching Law of Nature, the attainment of which always involved some liberties taken with semantics and strict logic, some reflexive compromises with perspective and data. Freudianism's vast influence on twentieth-century thought preserved this holdover metaphysical habit beyond the tenure of other nineteenth-century universal theories of human cultures, but made it a vulnerable target for subsequent anthropological critics; here is Marvin Harris:

> The entire idiom of the Freudian synthesis with its instinctual drives, its ontogenetic recapitulations, its energy flows and its energy blockages, and its epiphenomenal symptoms and subterfuges is a physicalist and materialist tour de force. But Freud's system could only generate the universals of culture and a few crude stages of a unilinear evolution. Specific cultural differences and similarities were beyond his grasp and interest. (1967, 457)

Totem and Taboo is Freud's text most focused on anthropological matters and the notions of difference and the primitive. "*Resemblances between the Psychic Lives of Savages and Neurotics*," runs his subtitle; it signals to us the comparative nature of the whole project, but it also modestly understates the purpose of the book, as though identifying resemblances were going to be the whole project. Actually, he is going to explain a whole range of behaviors and institutions in terms of their psychodynamic origins, which level of explanation Freud regards as ultimate. Similarly, his preface seems to be disclaiming authoritative status for the essays that make up the study. "It is hoped that they may serve as a bond between students of ethnology, philology, folklore and of the allied sciences, and psychoanalysts," he states. He claims only that his contribution to the notion of totemism (the anthropologists' home subject) can be "modestly expressed"; and he almost apologetically allows that in his book "the attempt is ventured to find the original meaning of totemism through its infantile traces."

Of his principal theory, he concludes his Preface, "although this hypothesis leads to somewhat improbable conclusions, there is no reason for rejecting the possibility that it comes more or less near to the reality which is so hard to reconstruct" (iv–v; to maintain the historical locus of my study I am using the 1918 A. A. Brill translation). He certainly shows a caginess toward his audience—which he fully (and quite correctly) expected would include experts in anthropology and other social sciences in which his own credentials were not established,—but from the very structure of his argument we might surmise that he is quite intentionally proposing what he feels is a brilliant solution to the problematic relationship between totemism and exogamy in the anthropological discourse of that day. Repeatedly throughout the study he refers to anthropologists' uncertainty and disagreement about the connection between the primitive peoples' beliefs in totemism and their institution of exogamy: which factor came first, which was cause of the other? (See, for example, specific references on pp. 6, 174, 178–79, 198, and the whole discussion on 180–206.) He then produces, after a careful series of increments, the Oedipus complex and the primal act of parricide and its psychic consequences as the grand solution, and "Thus psychoanalysis . . . bids us argue for an intimate connection between totemism and exogamy as well as for their simultaneous origin" (241). Could Freud have a great deal more invested in this study than he as novice anthropologist was willing to display?

Totemism and exogamy were of course specialties of Frazer, and Freud's borrowing from him—all but Frazer's rather simple rationalistic explanations of the causes and relationships of things—was extensive and very thoroughly acknowledged. As if he had come along to find in the material what Frazer himself couldn't, Freud mined *The Golden Bough* and *Totemism and Exogamy* for examples of subrational behavior interpretable in terms of instinct and obsession rather than in terms of superstition and simple ignorance. In his picking-and-choosing research Freud also depended heavily on Wilhelm Wundt, on Tylor and Lubbock, Spencer, McLennan, Robertson Smith, and other evolutionists. And therein is an enormous drawback: Edwin Wallace clearly explains the devastating effect of this dependency, quoting as an example of the anthropologists' critical response Clyde Kluckhohn's judgment "that Freud's sources 'had been rejected by the anthropological profession before *Totem and Taboo* reached it'" (Wallace 1983, 113).

Freud's translations of the language of that ethnology into the (purportedly more fundamental) language of psychoanalysis begin simply and plausibly, but as they gradually develop toward the grand and all-embracing synthesis they become increasingly ingenious and arbitrary. To begin with, totemism and exogamy are seen as institutional expressions of "the savage's dread of incest." Freud's "savages" are thus endowed with a strong and instinctual moral sense—they do not differ from civilized people by being devoid or weak of moral compunction, as so many evolutionists assumed in their retrograde visions of the precivilized world. The function of totemism that interested Freud was its supposed capacity to bond the members of a given tribe or phratry with a particular ancestor- or guardian-spirit and impose on them a sacred prohibition against marriage or cohabitation within the group. And adopting the idea of several anthropologists that the earliest societies were matrilineal, he saw the sexual encounter of son and mother as thus institutionally forbidden virtually from the beginning of human time (although the father-daughter relationship, he has to admit in a footnote, is not thus prohibited).

In citing a number of examples of how "these savages reveal to us an unusually high grade of incest dread or incest sensitiveness, combined with the peculiarity, which we do not very well understand, of substituting the totem relationship for the real blood relationship" (9), Freud involves some rather conventional markers of difference. The belief in totemism is one: the reason that we do not understand it very well is because our civilization has grown past that stage. Our instinctual incest urges and sensitiveness are quite differently controlled, and that is one of the ways we know we are civilized. Another marker of difference is the "savages'" propensity to have little or no mediation between their sexual appetite and its physical gratification. Of Australian aborigines he states, "We must say that these savages are even more sensitive to incest than we, perhaps because they are more subject to temptations than we are, and hence require more extensive protection against it" (15). Referring to the gender restrictions of a Sumatran people reported on by a Dutch missionary quoted by Frazer, he says, "It is assumed without question by these races that a man and a woman left alone together will indulge in the most extreme intimacy, and as they expect all kinds of punishments and evil consequences from consanguinous intercourse they do quite right to avoid all temptations by means of such prohibitions" (18).

Although throughout *Totem and Taboo* he follows the interpretations, projections and questionable data of a number of evolutionist theorists, Freud still recognizes, at least on several notable occasions, that the knowledge about cultures long defunct or peoples far distant is not nearly direct or reliable enough. The subject of totemism especially evokes some very sophisticated epistemological caution on his part. At one point he introduces a long footnote explaining his interpretation of totemism via his sources, Frazer, Lang, and McLennan. But Freud follows with a paragraph on the uncertainty of all such interpretations and the impenetrability of totemist cultures long gone or much altered by time, saying "Not only is the theory of totemism controversial, but the very facts concerning it are hardly to be expressed in such general statements as were attempted above" (5n). At another point (in another footnote) he gives a long (almost a full-page) discussion of the fallibility of the evidences of totemism and the hazards of reflexiveness in the interpreters of that questionable data, saying

> those who collect the observations are not identical with those who digest and discuss them; the first are travelers and missionaries, while the others are scientific men who perhaps have never seen the objects of their research.—It is not easy to establish an understanding with savages. Not all the observers were familiar with the languages. . . . Finally, it is not easy to adapt oneself to the ways of thinking of primitive races. (169n)

And so forth. Freud was apparently quite aware of scientific method in its strictest early twentieth-century sense, anticipating in his own questions and misgivings about the status of the notion of totemism the very kinds of criticisms that would be legitimately brought against his whole project. The problem of the coexistence of his unquestionable epistemological insight and his extreme carelessness of it has not to my knowledge been solved.

Taboo he approaches with a whole lot more single-minded confidence: "[T]aboo still exists in our midst" (v), he states, and for one acquainted with psychoanalysis, "[T]hese phenomena are by no means foreign" (43). "The ambivalence of the emotions" is the larger category by which he translates taboo into psychiatry, an ambivalence generated by the existence of "a forbidden action for which there exists a strong inclination in the unconscious" (54). "The taboo prohibitions lack all justification and are of unknown origin," and "it is generally assumed that taboo is older than the gods and goes back to the pre-religious age" (31). For the "savage," "taboo is a command of conscience" (114), and Freud speculates that it was probably the origin of our civilized conscience as well. Thus taboo is another concept by which the difference between civilized and "primitive" becomes redefined:

> It may be surmised that the taboo of Polynesian savages is after all not so remote from us as we were at first inclined to believe; the moral and customary prohibitions which we ourselves obey may have some essential relation to this primitive taboo the explanation of which may in the end throw light upon the dark origin of our own "categorical imperative." (38)

Freud conceives of the difference in morality as a matter of the development of abstract thought. Instinctually the civilized and the "primitive" are morally equivalent; the moral difference is intellectual, the development of the ability to abstractly view our own inner processes:

> Only with the development of the language of abstract thought through the association of sensory remnants of word representations with inner processes, did the latter gradually become capable of perception. Before this took place primitive man had developed a picture of the outer world through the outward projection of inner perceptions, which we, with our reenforced conscious perception, must now translate back into psychology. (108)

And another taboo-related marker of difference is suggested by Freud as he offers as an assumption

> *that the psychic impulses of primitive man possessed a higher degree of ambivalence than is found at present among civilized human beings. With the decline of this ambivalence the taboo, as the compromise symptom of the ambivalent conflict, also slowly disappeared.* (111; his italics)

His framework of assumptions about "primitives" corresponds very neatly to his psychiatric interpretation of neurotics; in continuing the preceding passage he can state: "Neurotics who are compelled to reproduce this [ambivalent] conflict, together with the taboo resulting from it, may be said to have brought with them an atavistic remnant in the form of an archaic constitution" (111). Not that neuroticism and "savagery" are equivalent: Freud is careful to stipulate that "the neuroses are asocial formations; they seek to accomplish by private means what arose in society through collective labor" (122). Taboo is thus defined as a collective, communal phenomenon, and not an alienating factor like neuroticism.

In his ingenious process of correlating the "primitive" and the neurotic, Freud continually inserts psychoanalytical language into the discourse on peoples and difference. All those archaic and contemporarily "primitive" people manifest this *ambivalence of emotion* involving a *latent hostility* in *the unconscious*, which is controlled by a process of *displacement*, a *defense process* which is referred to as a *projection* (102–3). And then the game is afoot in earnest: all the counters and symbols and systems can take on typical psychoanalytical characteristics. The animism fundamental to the "primitive's" beliefs (and the defining characteristic of his stage of mental evolution) is another version of *the omnipotence of thought*, which is also characteristic of the infant's all-consuming subjectivity during the stage of *narcism*, and of the neurotic lost in his mental projections. The totem animal (and by this point in the argument all totems seem to be animals) is correlatable with the animal fears of children, which are essentially transferences of unconscious parental fears. Ultimately the totem animal signifies father, and its taboo status and the ceremonies wherein it is worshipped and yet killed and eaten are expressions of the very most basic universal emotional ambivalence. Thus the "primitive's" totemism does what religion would do in the next stage of cultural evolution: provide a symbolic fulfillment of the deepest and most forbidden urges. "Primitive" or civilized, behaviors and belief systems are all at root Oedipal.

This is the key to the Frazerian rituals of "the theanthropic god sacrifice" that Frazer himself had never recognized: "[T]he object of the sacrificial action has always been the same, being identical with what is now revered as a god, namely the father" (249). And in his passion for ultimate origins, Freud saw a pattern emerging from the whole complex that he felt *had* to be based on some actual historical event. He introduces it modestly enough, as "another attempt to explain the origin of incest dread. . . . It might be called a historic explanation," and saying "[T]his attempt is associated with a hypothesis of Charles Darwin about the primal social state of man" (206–7).

In Freud's version of Darwin's imagined reconstruction of the original human social order, "[T]here is only a violent, jealous father who keeps all the females for himself and drives away the growing sons." The event that Freud hypothesizes occurs when "the expelled brothers joined forces, slew and ate the father, and thus put an end to the father horde." Since they both hated and loved their father, after their hate had been satisfied by his murder, a "sense of guilt" overtook them, and with it an act of renouncement of the "liberated women." "Thus they created the two fundamental taboos of totemism out of the *sense of guilt of the son*, and for this very reason these had to correspond with the two repressed wishes of the Oedipus complex" (233–36; Freud's italics). Psychoanalysis is thus able to solve the problem of the relation of totemism and exogamy by discovering their common origin and essential connection.

Freud's seeming to posit the primal parricide as an actual historical event has been embarrassing to his subsequent proponents; indeed, it does seem to employ the same spuriously expansive reasoning that Frazer showed in inferring an actual sexual relationship between Hippolytus and Artemis. The caution Freud exercises in proposing his "historic explanation" involves two specific aspects of the "primitive's" difference. One is the heightened psychic reality of "primitive man's" world: "We must beware of introducing the contempt for what is merely thought or wished which characterizes our sober world where there are only material values, into the world of primitive man and the neurotic, which is full of inner riches only" (264). But could the wish for the killing of the father, and its accompanying guilt, have served for the act? Perhaps, Freud allows, but a second aspect of "primitive" difference argues against that more morally acceptable supposition:

> Primitive man is not inhibited, the thought is directly converted into the deed, the deed is for him so to speak rather a substitute for the thought, and for that reason I think we may well assume in the case we are discussing, though without vouching for the absolute certainty of the decision, that, "In the beginning was the deed." (265)

The biblical language is entirely appropriate, since Freud conceives that "the beginnings of religion, ethics, society, and art meet in the Oedipus complex"; and even more fundamentally, he goes on to consider that possibly "ambivalence, originally foreign to our emotional life, was acquired by mankind from the father complex" (258–59). "In the beginning" indeed—even of the pattern of human emotion.

Entirely dismissive of cultural differences, Freud thus projected the emotions and impulses of turn-of-century European families, illuminated by a deeply conflictual sense of sonhood, into societies and peoples he knew little or nothing about. The whole endeavor is a combination of brilliant insight and eccentricity; of studiously correlated research, gullibility, and highly selected supporting evidence; of broad perspective and pervasive ego- and ethnocentricity. Whatever his assumptions of factuality and universality, his product is, as he in some moments realized, a new myth, remythologizing the sacrificial gods and reconceptualizing mankind's essence and the bases of human difference.

His myth certainly contributed to altering the notions of self-and-society and the primitive Other then regnant in American intellectual society. The very comfortable view of cultural evolution—that it was an inevitable progress through the stages of animism, religion, and science—Freud would modify to correspond with the stages of individual growth (another application of his much-favored recapitulation phenomenon)—from infantile narcissism to parent-dependence to the mature state where one "seeks his object in the outer world" (149). But, in the words of Philip Rieff, "nothing was more foreign to his mind than the optimistic temper in which the three-stage positivist theory was regularly set forth" (1979, 191). In the Freudian paradigm, guilt—individual and social—has a history and is an essential, inescapable part of the human future. We live in the presence of our ultimate ancestors' urges and deeds and we always will. Our understandings and institutions might differ from those of primitive peoples, but our psychological and moral makeup is a continuing heritage.

Civilization has come about not, as so many evolutionists imagined, simply by the triumph of knowledge over ignorance, of reason over superstition, but by a combination of the development of abstract thought, the suppression of instincts, and the changing, increasingly indirect means of managing guilt. As Freud says in *The Future of an Illusion*, "It is in keeping with the course of human development that external coercion gradually becomes internalized; for a special mental agency, man's super-ego, takes it over and includes it among its commandments" (1961b, 11). "Generally speaking, our civilization is built up on the suppression of instincts," he claims in his essay "'Civilized' Sexual Morality and Modern Nervous Illness" (1961a, 186). "[T]he price we pay for our advance in civilization," he claims in *Civilization and Its Discontents*, "is a loss of happiness through the heightening of the sense of guilt" (1961a, 134). The civilized self is involved in conflict both inner and outer: id against superego, and personal desire against societal restraint and coercion.

Freud thus deconstructs the sentimentalized optimism of the progress-oriented society and its vision of the primitive Other: images of the poor savage, the simple savage, the noble savage cannot, he insists, serve as the forerunner of the modern psyche. And if civilized society is fraught with "discontents" because of the restrictions and coercions with which it inhibits individual satisfaction, primitive life cannot be imagined as a freer and happier alternative: "As regards the primitive peoples who exist to-day, careful researches have shown that their instinctual life is by no means to be envied for its freedom. It is subject to restrictions of a different kind but perhaps of greater severity than those attaching to modern civilized man" (1961a, 115).

In attempting to absorb, reconstruct, or supplant the old myths with his new one, Freud thus provided the culture with a language and a set of concepts that could redefine their sense of their own instinctuality and of the primitive not-so-other.

Carl Jung took pathways somewhat different from those developed by Frazer and Freud, and established some new senses of difference and similarity of primitive and civilized. His greatest contribution to the culture's discourse on human difference was his enfranchisement of the irrational. The language of difference that he strove to create was one that would legitimate intuition, myth, and dream as accesses to psychic wholeness and truth. His methods were eccentric, unabashedly reflexive, and improvised; and his theoretical findings were metaphor-studded, continually undergoing modification, and seemingly based on whatever tended to confirm them. Yet his vast project of mapping the human mind and correlating all peoples and cultures was framed by the systemics of scientific rationalism. Scientific rationalism was a deep determinant of his thought and approach, although in many ways he broke through its reductionist, mechanistic constraints.

He adopted several aspects of Frazer's basic theory and approach, including the assumptions that rationality was the defining characteristic of civilization and that the mythologies of the world could be systematically correlated. He also relied on Frazer's writings for a good deal of basic information about specific myths and myth motifs (J. Vickery 1973, 95). (His *Symbols of Transformation* has a great deal in common with *The Golden Bough*, being a vast compendium of myths and symbol-systems based on a relatively slender initial problematic.) Freud's influence is of course everywhere apparent in Jung's work. A disciple and heir-apparent of Freud early in his career, he broke with him on some basic issues, evident in this 1931 acknowledgment/condemnation:

> *Totem and Taboo* was one of the first direct contributions of the new psychology of the primitive mind. It matters little that his attempt is nothing more than an application of his sex-theory, originally gleaned from morbid minds. His essay nevertheless demonstrates the possibility of a "rapprochement" between psychology and the problem of the primitive mind. (Quoted in Aldrich 1931, xvii)

Nevertheless, even after the break he had been reliant on Freudian conceptions of the unconscious, of the basic premises and techniques of psychoanalysis, and of the correlation of neurotic and primitive behavior. He worked, too, within the framework of the evolutionists, basing much of his thinking on their theories and preconceptions, such as: the notion of developmental hierarchies of cultures; the comparative method; the doctrine of "survivals"; the concepts of primitive animism and totemism; and, almost conversely, a sense of "the psychic unity of mankind." But even though he developed his ideas within the categorical frameworks of these borrowings, Jung tended to define himself oppositionally toward them. He was a highly individualistic thinker who redefined whatever he adopted according to his own very personal promptings. Thus his system of thought gives a new status to the irrational and to "survivals"; finds (as did Freud) a new basis in the depths of the human psyche for "psychic unity"; and develops an original, superbly timely, but somewhat unstable psychosocial definition of human difference.

It was his idea of the "collective unconscious"—the universal, inherited area of the mind, distinct from the personal conscious and unconscious, repository of the "archetypes" that determined the pathways of instincts and concepts, and powerful motivator—that is at the heart of his system, of his legitimization of the irrational, and of his vast influence (and incidentally, of one of his crucial differences with Freud). His conception of the existence of the collective unconscious, and its archetypes and of their persistence into present-day civilized psyches, posited not only that there was a fundamental psychic component that warranted such widespread myth-collocation as Frazer had carried out but, beyond that, that the myths and symbols of all times and peoples had powerful potential for helping us to understand contemporary civilized minds. By a method termed "amplification," the analyst could, Jung proposed, reintegrate a contemporary psyche by aligning an individual's dream images, fears, and formless phobias with archetypal myth motifs from whatever culture or time, and thereby enable the patient to understand and creatively employ the irrational unconscious that had been a source of disorientation. Symbol and myth thus became in Jung's system important means of accessing the unconscious motivators and meaning-determiners, serving as substantially more than mere rudimentary precursors of science or symptom signifiers. And in the process, the collective unconscious became a psychic bridge across the vast chasms of manifest human difference.

There are a number of problems, though, in identifying the essential Jung. He was a voluminous writer whose thought was always in a state of process. Throughout his career he continued to elaborate, alter, reconcoct, and refocus his ideas. Many of his works exist in two or more versions, and often there are two or more translations. Since Jung's written opinions sometimes vary a great deal, what he said is often significantly dependent on when he said it. For my purposes, focusing as I do historically, I mean to consider only the pre-1940 Jung material. Even observing that limitation, there is a great deal of unresolvable variation and inconsistency, and this is due also to the way he arrived at his ideas. He enfranchised the intuitional, the irrational in his method as well as in his theory.

Often his theory is an extremely various blending: categories or data from Lang or Tylor or Frazer, ideas from Freud or Nietzsche, and references to characters or situations from Western myth or literature, mixed in with original inductions from his psychiatric practice, from his experience with primitive Africans or Amerindians, from his own psychological crises, and from his dreams and his imaginary discussions with various mythic gurus, like Salome and Elijah. As Paul Homans has pointed out, "his personal struggle, with all its achievements and failures, became the paradigm of what he would teach during the rest of his life" (1979, 81–82, 110). Not only assertive about projecting his own visions as absolutes of human mentality, he often confidently pronounced his intuitions of others' perceptions, such as how a primitive man would make sense of the world. He is colossally, unabashedly reflexive in redesigning the canons of scientific method.

In formulating theory Jung had a strong proclivity to think in terms of bipolar oppositions. Rational versus irrational, conscious versus unconscious, personal unconscious versus collective unconscious, civilized versus primitive, white versus Negro, male versus female, and so forth—each formulation begins with an oppositional duality, some of purely conventional elements and some definitely not, with the oppositional interactions or the spaces in between providing the sites of new psychological understanding. The whole structure doesn't line up into a macro-duality, with, say, the right-hand terms—irrational, collective unconscious, primitive, Negro, female—constituting some larger entity, although they do influence and infect each other, as we shall see. And Jung's language of difference owes a good deal of its originality as well as a good deal of its slipperiness to his method of imbricating bipolarities.

The rationality-irrationality bipolarity is elemental in human mentality and its instability is endemic in contemporary culture, as Jung conceived of it: "We should never identify ourselves with reason, for man is not and never will be a creature of reason alone, a fact to be noted by all pedantic culture-mongers. The irrational cannot and must not be extirpated. The gods cannot and must not die" (1953, 71). The swipe at "pedantic culture mongers" is of course one of Jung's many means of separating himself from the whole of the rationalistic culture, and "the gods must not die" a hyperbolic affirmation of the irrational that so many of his scientific colleagues routinely treated as anathema.

For Jung, rationality and irrationality functioned principally in the conscious and the unconscious respectively, the parts of the mind conceptualized by Freud and himself for that specific purpose. Jung conceives of the unconscious, much as did Freud, as the mental source and repository of the instincts—"it is just the instinctual processes

which make the supplementary concept of the unconscious necessary" he claims. And he similarly (and problematically) defines it as a
negative nonobservable: "I define the unconscious as the totality of
all psychic phenomena that lack the quality of consciousness" (1961,
133). That the notion of the unconscious evokes fear and distrust in
contemporary thinkers is not only inevitable but appropriate, in
Jung's view:

> There is, however, something to be said for this characteristically Western
> fear of the other side. It is not entirely without justification, quite apart
> from the fact that it is real. We can understand at once the fear that the
> child and the primitive have of the great unknown. We have the same
> childish fear of our inner side, where we likewise touch upon a great un-
> known world. All we have is the affect, the fear, without knowing that this
> is a world-fear—for the world of affects is invisible. We have either purely
> theoretical prejudices against it, or superstitious ideas. One cannot even
> talk about the unconscious before many educated people without being
> accused of mysticism. The fear is legitimate in so far as our rational *Welt-
> anschauung* with its scientific and moral certitudes—so hotly believed in
> because so deeply questionable—is shattered by the facts of the other side.
> (1953, 201)

There are indeed dark and disturbing things in the unconscious—and,
as we shall see, not only for rationalists and pedantic culture-mongers.
  The unconscious is itself the site of another bipolarity, of the personal and the collective. The personal is "the receptacle of all lost
memories and of all contents that are still too weak to become
conscious . . ." as well as of "all the more or less intentional repres-
sions of painful thoughts and feelings" (1961, 133). The collective unconscious is the dynamic repository of "the history of the brain-
structure, . . . the story of mankind: the unending myth of death and
rebirth, and of the multitudinous figures who weave in and out of this
mystery" (1964, 10). Along with the bipolar tendency of Jung's
thought was a fascination like Freud's with the notion of ultimate
human origins—not only as generic inheritances but as essence-
definers and primary motivators. The quasi-biological theory represented as "ontogeny recapitulates phylogeny" even affected Jung's
language:

> Indeed, in accordance with phylogenetic law, we still recapitulate in child-
> hood reminiscences of the prehistory of the race and of mankind in gen-
> eral. Phylogenetically as well as ontogenetically we have grown up out of
> the dark confines of the earth; hence the factors that affected us most
> closely became archetypes, and it is these primordial images which influ-

ence us most directly, and therefore seem to be the most powerful. (1964, 32)

Jung's language of explanation of the human psyche thus veered toward ur-forms and origins: the "collective unconscious" was a "racial unconscious," meaning of the human race; "primordial" was a key term, as in the "primordial images" which at times were synonymous with the "archetypes," perhaps the most notable of his coinages. The "archaic man" was within us all and always had been: "every civilized human being, however high his conscious development, is still an archaic man at the deeper levels of his psyche" (1964, 51). Thus at one pole of Jung's bilateral analysis of human mentality—where the strange and hauntingly unfamiliar stuff lurked—a new sense of "the psychic unity of mankind" took shape: the notion that at the deepest psychic levels there were no human differences.

As Jung conceived it, the collective unconscious was unexplored territory. As the psychic zone closest to human essence and causally implicated in so much psychological imbalance, its exploration was enormously important. As a nonobservable, it could be studied only indirectly, in terms of its traces and effects—all images and verbal descriptions; so, in this very substantial phase of his work, analysis became something very like textual hermeneutics. The interpretation of symbols became a primary task. As Jolande Jacobi points out, for Jung "the symbol is a kind of mediator between the incompatibles of consciousness and the unconscious, between the hidden and the manifest" (1959, 98). Jung posited a *"symbol-creating function"* of the mind that produced the kind of holistic signifiers that required the analyst's interpretation, since indeed, "the union of rational and irrational truth is to be found ... in the symbol *per se*; for it is the essence of the symbol to contain both the rational and the irrational. It always expresses the one through the other; it comprises both without being either" (1964, 18).

Symbols, and especially mythic motifs, sprang from the archetypes of the collective unconscious, which proposition had enormous significance for the anthropological and literary as well as the psychoanalytic communities. In Jung's framework classical mythology was no longer immature science, nor were the myths of primitive peoples mere barbaric superstition. Literature was given significance at the deepest and most universal level:

> Whoever speaks in primordial images speaks with a thousand voices; he enthralls and overpowers, while at the same time he lifts the idea he is seeking to express out of the occasional and the transitory into the realm

of the ever-enduring. He transmutes our personal destiny into the destiny of mankind. . . .

That is the secret of great art, and of its effect upon us. The creative process, so far as we are able to follow it at all, consists in the unconscious activation of an archetypal image, and in elaborating and shaping this image into the finished work. By giving it shape, the artist translates it into the language of the present, and so makes it possible for us to find our way back to the deepest springs of life. Therein lies the social significance of art. (1971a, 321)

Psychiatric patients could presumably find their way to mental health by having their dreams and fantasies focused, in the words of Joseph Campbell, "by comparison outward with the analogous mythic forms . . . so that the disturbed individual may learn to see himself depersonalized in the mirror of the human spirit and discover by analogy the way to his own larger fulfillment" (Jung 1971a, xxii). To discover the unconscious is for Jung to recover the very spring of creative energy, since, in his own words,

the unconscious . . . contains the dark springs of instinct and intuition, it contains all those forces which mere reasonableness, propriety, and the orderly course of bourgeois existence could never call awake, all those creative forces which lead man onwards to new developments, new forms, new goals. . . . [I]t adds to consciousness everything that has been excluded by the drying up of the springs of intuition and by the pursuit of a single goal. (1964, 18–19)

New accesses of creativity indeed: discovering shared archetypes with even the most distant, most different peoples, and reawakening the irrational to induce such discovery so that even one's feelings and dreams held deep and universal meaning—these were notions that could give the civilized world a fresh view of the self and the Other. ("In all probability the most important mythological motifs are common to all times and races; I have, in fact, been able to demonstrate a whole series of motifs from Greek mythology in the dreams and fantasies of pure-bred Negroes suffering from mental disorders," he claimed late in his career [1971b, 443].) Recent critics finding postmodernist tendencies in Jung's work have appropriately enough been attracted to his hermeneutic theory and practice. Pelligrino D'Acierno and Karin Barnaby give this interpretation of his contribution:

a properly Jungian hermeneutics involves the deployment of a flexible (pluralistic), comparative, and interdisciplinary "exegesis" that seeks out interpretative possibilities—not conclusions—and whose canonic procedures *amplify* the symbol-text by adding to it a wealth of personal and collective, historical and cultural analogies, correspondences, and parallels. . . . This constructive process is clearly set out by Jung in one of his infrequent methodological formulations of his hermeneutic approach:

"The essential character of hermeneutics . . . consists in making successive additions of other analogies to the analogy given in the symbol. . . . This procedure widens and enriches the initial symbol, and the final outcome is an infinitely complex and varied picture, in which certain 'lines' of psychological development stand out as possibilities that are at once individual and collective." (1990, xii; Jung quote from 1953, 287)

I am less than convinced by the postmodernist relativism of the "flexible (pluralistic)" aspects of Jung's "exegesis," acknowledging that the procedure genuinely is "amplification" rather than interpretation, but still wondering, from an anthropological perspective, for whom is a symbol a symbol, and of what? But the effect of Jung's hermaneutic method in neutralizing difference as his age knew it was considerable.

Jung's applications of the new notions certainly involved questionable elements: a good deal of mystical intuition of the sort that might be regarded the self-projection of a very literarily educated psychoanalyst; a naive trust in the verbalization of images, feelings, and the components of the mind; and an ambiguous status for the mythic motifs (could one assume they had absolute meanings, or did their interpretation necessarily involve taking into account specific personal or cultural determinants?). But his general theoretical vision had great potential for stimulating idealistic, holistic cultural change.

For Jung, "primitive"—in most contexts conceived of as the polar opposite of "civilized"—stands for a complex and problematical category. It is much used in his discourse, highly significant and deeply evocative. On the one hand, connected with the idea of the collective unconscious it connotes universal human instinct, intuition, and the archetypes; on the other, dark-skinned races. In one typical context, it designates the creative elements of irrationality that modern man has repudiated in his vain attempt to live wholly rationally. In another, it represents the darker psychic forces that threaten to pull him down and utterly destroy his individuality and his cultural existence.

The characteristic problem of modern civilized man is produced by his thoroughgoing rationalism. Jung traces the problem historically (although somewhat murkily) in *The Psychology of the Unconscious*: with the beginning of the modern era,

mankind had achieved that *independence of the idea* which could resist the aesthetic impression, so that thought was no longer fettered by the emotional effects of the impression, but could rise to reflective observation. Thus man entered into a new and independent relation to nature whereby the foundation was laid for natural science and technique . . . which has reached its greatest development in our time. Materialistic interest has everywhere become paramount. Therefore, the realms of the spirit, where earlier the greatest conflicts and developments took place, lie deserted and fallow; the world has not only lost its God as the sentimentalists of the nineteenth century bewail, but also to some extent it has lost its soul as well. (1916, 84)

I take that to mean that the separation of thought and emotion has separated man from nature and from his own deep inner nature, and brought about an age of science and rampant materialism. Primitive man, in identifying quite concretely with natural phenomena or animal characteristics, "create(s) a world in which man is completely contained psychically as well as physically. . . . Man is still dovetailed into nature. . . . It never occurs to him that he might be able to rule her" (1964, 66). One corollary to this particular primitive/civilized polarity that had considerable social impact was its application to the realm of Eros:

Eros is a questionable fellow and will always remain so, whatever the legislation of the future may have to say about it. He belongs on one side to man's primordial animal nature which will endure as long as man has an animal body. On the other side he is related to the highest forms of the spirit. But he only thrives when spirit and instinct are in right harmony. If one or the other aspect is lacking to him, the result is injury or at least a lopsidedness that may easily veer towards the pathological. Too much of the animal distorts the civilized man, too much civilization makes sick animals. This dilemma reveals the vast uncertainty that Eros holds for man. For, at bottom, Eros is a superhuman power which, like nature herself, allows itself to be overpowered and exploited as though it were impotent. But triumph over nature is dearly paid for. Nature requires no explanations of principle, but asks only for tolerance and wise measure. (1953, 26)

Jung's prescription not only for certain obsessed neurotics, but for others as well, is to return to the "primitive":

besides these neurotics there are many more normal people—and precisely people of the higher type—who feel restricted and discontented. For all these reduction to the sexual elements should be undertaken, in order that they may be reinstated into the possession of their primitive self, and thereby learn to know and value its relation to the entire personality. In this way alone can certain requirements be fulfilled and others be repudiated as unfit because of their infantile character. (1916, 260)

In many passages and various ways Jung asserts that studying primitive man is of special value to the civilized (and here again we can see psychic imperialism in the assumptions and purposes that structure the inquiry and its terms). At one point he insists, as part of his own continuing argument with his society's rationalism, that primitive man's superstitions are superior to our own: "Primitive man simply has a different theory—the theory of witchcraft and spirits. I find this theory very interesting and very sensible—actually more sensible than the academic views of modern science" (1964, 11). The dreams and myths of primitive man can offer substantial clues to our own psyches, and his intentional acts grow out of a more elemental reaction to things than our own. All this follows from his greater closeness to the collective unconscious:

[As] for the primitive, whose personal differentiation is, as we know, still in its infancy, . . . his psyche is essentially collective and therefore for the most part unconscious. He is still more or less identical with the collective psyche, and accordingly has all the collective virtues and vices without any personal attribution and without inner contradiction. The contradiction arises only when the personal development of the psyche begins, and when reason discovers the irreconcilable nature of the opposites. The consequence of this discovery is the conflict of repression. (1953, 146–47)

In the process of correlating analytical psychology and anthropology—of hypothesizing external figurations of unconscious motives and vice versa—Jung slid into the assumption that "primitive" is a unitary defining characteristic, that the remarkable diversity of non-European peoples is purely superficial. The assumption is of course part of the superstructure of evolutionism, but Jung's more immediate source is the French anthro-philosopher Lucien Levy-Bruhl. And insofar as Jung relied on Levy-Bruhl's defining characteristics of primitive mentality—its pervasive "mysticism" (nondiscrimination in regard to the boundaries of physical and spiritual, verifiable and magical, actual and metaphoric), its susceptibility to its culture's "collective representations" (those notions regarded as self-evident), and its sense of "participating relations" (totemic and related senses of oneness with environment, legends, and so forth)—Jung also accepted Levy-Bruhl's stereotyping of primitive difference.

In several contexts Jung's idea of the primitive entailed conventional connotations of inferiority, unbridled animality, and dark skin. And such connotative viruses served to infect his notion of the collective unconscious. The primitive is indeed in us all, but it has a color (it is dark or black) and a direction (it can pull us "downward"). In explaining the necessity of our maintaining an interactive balance between our conscious and collective unconscious, he theorizes that once we recognize the collective unconscious

> we have an entirely new task before us: the question of how the ego is to come to terms with this psychological non-ego. Can we rest content with the constatation of the real existence of the archetypes and simply let things take care of themselves?
>
> That would be to create a permanent state of dissociation, a split between the individual and the collective psyche. On the one side we should have the differentiated modern ego, and on the other a sort of negroid culture, a very primitive state of affairs. We should have, in fact, what actually exists—namely, a veneer of civilization over a dark-skinned brute; and the cleavage would be clearly demonstrated before our eyes. (1953, 95)

The racist language here (in this authoritative English language text) is no mere one-time accident, either. Jung's conception of the white/Negro polarity not only imports the infamous white Western stereotypes, but it carries them into his theorizing about the heretofore universal collective unconscious. "Racial" unconscious in the sense of the human race becomes, at some indeterminate intermediate level, "racial" in the polygenist sense, and difference is difference after all: "In so far as differentiations exist that correspond to race, tribe, or even family, there exists also a collective psyche limited to race, tribe, or family over and above the 'universal' collective psyche" (1953, 145). Racial essentialism is evident in many of Jung's statements, such as his characterization of "lower races, like the negroes" as childlike in their naturally animistic ideas of their environment (1916, 26), as well as in his silence on some relevant issues, as seen in the almost total lack in his *Collected Works* of any discussion of racial mixing: their general index notes two minor references to "miscegenation" and none at all to "mulatto," "intermarriage," or "racial mixing."

But running counter to this essentialism is the sense he gives in a number of passages of the dangers of racial infection. This of course is another element of racist, colonialist folk wisdom that is admitted to Jung's theory by his casual intuitive method. At different points in his theorizing, racial characteristics seem to be both essential and culturally determined:

> At the beginning of our era, three-fifths of the population of Italy consisted of slaves—human chattels without rights. Every Roman was sur-

rounded by slaves. The slave and his psychology flooded ancient Italy, and every Roman became inwardly a slave. Living constantly in the atmosphere of slaves, he became infected with their psychology. No one can shield himself from this unconscious influence. Even today the European, however highly developed, cannot live with impunity among the Negroes in Africa: their psychology gets into him unnoticed and unconsciously he becomes a Negro. There is no fighting against it. In Africa there is a well-known technical expression for this: "going black." It is no mere snobbery that the English should consider anyone born in the colonies, even though the best blood may run in his veins, "slightly inferior." There are facts to support this view. (1964, 121)

Bypassing Jung's confusion of the categories of race and social status here, we can see that whatever he might assume in other frames of reference about the separateness and essentialness of racial characteristics, they certainly have the potential to be overridden, presumably by way of counter-resonance in the collective unconscious. Jung says little of substance about the effects on Negroes or primitive people living in proximity of civilized whites—the influence is somehow principally a one-way affair? The larger paradigm works better if the dark races are presumed to be immutably primitive? Whatever the reason, the pattern seems peculiar, and what Jung perceives (and imagines) by it shows that ignoring difference has deleterious effects. As he says in "The Complications of American Psychology,"

[R]acial infection is a most serious mental and moral problem. . . . The white man is a most terrific problem to the Negro, and whenever you affect somebody so profoundly, then, in a mysterious way, something comes back from him to yourself. The Negro by his mere presence is a source of temperamental and mimetic infection, which the European can't help noticing just as much as he sees the hopeless gap between the American and the African Negro. Racial infection is a most serious mental and moral problem where the primitive outnumbers the white man. America has this problem only in a relative degree, because the whites far outnumber the coloured. Apparently he can assimilate the primitive influence with little risk to himself. What would happen if there were a considerable increase in the coloured population is another matter. (1964, 509)

Jung was very much interested in the United States, its mix of peoples white and red and black, their influence on each other, and the direction of its civilization. "Racial infection" was one of the things he was most attuned to find: "It would be difficult not to see that the coloured man, with his primitive motility, his expressive emotionality, his childlike directness, his sense of music and rhythm, his funny and picturesque language, has infected the American 'behaviour'" (1964, 508).

There is just too little methodological discipline in Jung's theorizing: the way things seemed to him at a given point in time was the way they were. And the problem with this state of affairs is not merely one of deciding whether or not it is good science. There is a great deal of fascinating insight and speculation in Jung's writing, but in reading it we continually come up against such confidence-destroying cliches, such indiscriminate crossing and confusing of the terminology of psychology and anthropology (as "primitive" becomes dark-skinned and "collective unconscious," either or both)! He leaves us with no middle ground. His insights open new understandings of the human psyche; they legitimate mental functions like intuition, dream and symbolization; and they deepen our understanding of literature and art and religion and their psychological functions. His ideas stimulated the production of a good deal of literature and art and religious thought, too.

But he was largely an intuitive, metaphoric, associative thinker who was nevertheless strongly influenced by the very scientific rationalism he attempted to repudiate in so many ways. Metaphors became entities, analogies became identities, intuitions became theoretical constructs, and the whole framework, in all its hypotheticalness and genius and inconsistency, assumed the status of scientific truth. To a scientist Jung might well seem a literary figure, and to a literary writer, a scientist. But considering his impact on twentieth-century culture and its sense of human nature and human difference, there is no respectfully disowning him. In the imaginations of Jung and his fellow psychological theorists of the early twentieth century the primitive became internalized, revised, reanimated, and sent on its way into a welcoming modernist world.

5

Dramas of Primitive Difference: Eugene O'Neill and *The Emperor Jones, The Fountain,* and *All God's Chillun Got Wings*

THE PSYCHOLOGICAL ETHNOLOGIES OF THE EARLY TWENTIETH CEN-
tury fed a complex mixture of new conceptual possibilities into the
discourse on the primitive and primitive difference. This discourse
was already complicated by the evolutionist alternatives to polygenist,
creationist, and other systems of defining and discriminating. Eugene
O'Neill, when he came to getting down to cases on the deepest
human problems, inherited a wide range of general intellectual constructions. But in his world the serious dramatist was a dealer in fictive particularities, striving to present individuals on the stage who
seemed to have their own individual drives and desires, conflicts and
capacities. The process of creation was intuitive, unrepeatable, and its
product was of course unverifiable by any scientific canons. But the
what-was-represented was nuanced and holistic beyond (or beneath)
the level of ethnographic generalization or psychological paradigm.
What self-image would such-and-such a character have? How would
he or she relate to a naively hopeful mother? To an unattainable or
an unreasonable lover? To someone of a presumably inferior race or
culture? How would he or she handle situations in times of depres-
sion? Handle hostility from society? Injustice? And so on and on.
Difference then would not be a subject the dramatist would directly
theorize about but would be a condition of the lives of a number of
invented characters, imbuing or implying significance within the ful-
ler framework of their lives and fates.

This chapter will look into *The Emperor Jones, The Fountain,* and
All God's Chillun Got Wings—three plays of O'Neill's early middle
period, written as he was coming into his real power and maturity
as an artist—and focus on their representations of racial and cultural
difference as a factor in the human drama. I am interested in the way
that his elaborated, nuanced treatments of difference move beyond

the standard categories of evolutionism, colonialism, racism, and depth psychology and constitute original (and genuinely drama-based) insights into those matters and the human condition generally.

It is interesting first to see just how he came into his ideas on racial and cultural difference, since that process involved a series of discoveries and revisions, original deductions and recombinations, and also since, like Henry Adams, he had some real experience, as anthropologists would say, "in the field."

Eugene O'Neill was just twenty-one years old—unsettled, feckless, and showing neither incentive nor promise to become a writer or anything else productive—when he had his "field experience" with the primitive Other. Actually, his journey into the heart of Honduras was both an attempt to seek his fortune (or perhaps his family's fortune), and a scheme of distinguished actor James O'Neill to get his son out of the dangerous proximity of an amorous woman James regarded as a gold-digger. Eugene went at his father's urging on a mini-expedition to investigate a mining claim in which his mother had some stock, and otherwise to look to the main chance. According to O'Neill biographers Arthur and Barbara Gelb, James had a good deal of confidence in mining engineer Earl C. Stevens, and possibly thought his influence and example (and likelihood of discovering gold in Honduras's undeveloped wilderness) would be helpful in getting his son into some practical, unencumbered, preferably nontheatrical, path of life. For 'Gene, having secretly married and made an honest woman of Kathleen before he left (Black 1999, 101), the trip promised both escape and adventure—at least until he got into the back country.

Honduras in 1909 (as represented in the 1910 eleventh edition of the *Encyclopedia Brittanica*) was a country characterized by difficult terrain, mixed population and low population density, unequal distribution of wealth, widespread poverty, a daunting level of national debt, a history of governmental instability, and considerable natural resources. Reading the human story between *Britannica*'s lines we discover the familiar drama of primitive difference—the narrative of the working-out of human happenstance in Civilization's encounter with those indigenous people so different from Civilized selves—in the colonialist context. The indigenous population had been decimated by the Spanish discoverer/conquerors, and the lure of those natural resources had brought continued episodes of immigration, depredation and exploitation. There were still some native peoples living relatively unevolved in remote regions, but most of the population were of mixed or wholly foreign origin. Wealth had become concentrated in the hands of European ex-colonials. The silver mining was controlled by British interests, and gold by the Americans; the timber and other resources were still largely undeveloped. The rather recently improvised national government had not evolved into a stable force, and the most recent revolution had seen American intervention to help establish what (it was hoped in 1910) would be a peaceful nation able to discharge its international debts. For enterprising American mining engineers and fortune seekers, Honduras loomed enormous in its potential for wealth, but formidable in the obstacles of its mountainous terrain, dense forests, scarcely navigable rivers, harsh living conditions, and backward peoples.

The Stevens/O'Neill expedition was a total flop. The Hondurans' information about the location of gold was unreliable, and they were casual and unhurried as paid guides and porters. The terrain and jungle were difficult, and the insects were incessantly tormenting. Finally, the river that was to have taken them to their El Dorado was totally blocked by fallen trees, and the surrounding jungle impenetrable. According to the Gelbs, when "after about five months" of torment and frustration he "was stricken with malaria" . . . "Eugene was almost joyful" (1962, 135). When he broke from the expedition the only profit seems to have been reaped by the insects; in distant retrospect the whole escapade seems a comically frustrating *Heart of Darkness*.

The young O'Neill's reactions are recorded in a couple of letters to his parents, written along the way. We should keep the parental audience in mind, and the complex purposes he might have had in writing these things to them. (Did he want to draw their admiration by exaggerating the difficulties? Was he consciously or unconsciously preparing them for his abandoning what he wanted them to see as a hopeless cause?) But he sounds simply frustrated, depressed, and radically intolerant. On 9 November 1909, there is a great deal to disgust him, but he still expresses high hopes, both for his own achievement and for the future success of American venture capitalism:

[E]verything would be O.K. if it were not for the fleas that infest the native huts and eat you alive at night. I am a mass of bites and itch all over. . . . The native villages are the most squalid and dirty it has ever been my misfortune to see. Pigs, buzzard, dogs, chickens and children all live in the same room and the sanitary conditions of the huts are beyond belief. However the cities—like Tegucigalpa—are fine and the climate wonderful. . . . Down here they are in no hurry. If we don't do it today why we can tomorrow—that is the way they seem to feel about it. Taking it all in all I like the country and the people and think there is every chance in the world for making good. . . .

Tell Papa that there are lots of mining lands down here that can be taken up for a song and they are laying loose because no one has the capital to hold them or develop them. Holding some of them as an investment for the future would not be a bad idea. All the Americans claim that Honduras has more gold than all the States combined but on account of the difficulties of transportation etc. it has to wait until people with capital take it up. (1988b, 18–19)

A little over a decade later, in his play *The Fountain*, he would represent Spanish adventurers with that imperialistic gold-grabbing attitude as deplorable, but in this early stage, living out his father's and his country's values, he seems not only seduced by the lure of success-through-wealth but, like *The Fountain*'s Spaniards, quick to condemn the local peoples for their lack of cooperation in the achievement of his goals. On Christmas Day 1909 Eugene wrote to his parents in a more exasperated vein: inveighing vigorously against the fried and soggy local food and the fierceness of the insects, his diatribe soon turns to a focus on his human environment:

From a two months experience, and after having been in all the different zones of this country, I give it as my candid opinion and fixed belief that God got his inspiration for Hell after creating Honduras. The country as far as climate and natural advantages goes is fine but the natives are the lowest, laziest, most ignorant bunch of brainless bipeds that ever polluted a land and retarded its future. Until some just Fate grows weary of watching the gropings in the dark of these human maggots and exterminates them, until the Universe shakes these human lice from its sides, Honduras has no future, no hopes of being anything but what it is at present—a Siberia of the tropics. As long as the yearly revolutions keep up foreign capital and foreigners will steer clear of the whole outfit. Even granting that the revolutions cease it will take an awful lot to get an American (who has not previously slept in a cowshed and eaten out of a trough) to live here any amount of time. (1988b, 19–20)

Thus in the mind of the frustrated twenty-one-year-old, the personal discomfort and disappointment is identified with a primitive country's resistance to imperialist development, to the kind of progress represented by the intervention of American capital and American settlement, and turns to fantasies of genocide. "Exterminate all the brutes" the young O'Neill urges in not so few words, as his own journey up the river ends in a despair not so profound or self-realizing as Kurtz's.

It was only five years later, when O'Neill had been trying for just a year to be a playwright, that he showed a much different understanding of the significance of difference in the colonial situation. An interesting article by Paul Voelker (1992, 99–109) shows how two very early works, the satirical one-act play *The Movie Man* and the long polemical poem, "Fratricide," treat American relations with Mexico and show a new social consciousness. The play is O'Neill's first comedy and is a send-up of a real situation in the Mexican revolution in which Pancho Villa had made a contract with an American film company. The play shows a pair of wiseguy film makers essentially controlling much of the revolutionary strategy by controlling the flow of American guns and liquor to the rebels to insure that they would cooperate by setting up their attacks and executions during the daylight when the filming was good.

The poem, published in the Socialist newspaper *The Call*, was a fervent protest against the landing of a force of U.S. Marines at Vera Cruz in an apparent attempt to control the actions of the Mexican government. O'Neill, focusing on the soldiers involved, represented the conflict of American and Mexican as brother killing brother, and all for the benefit of American capitalist interests:

> What cause could be more asinine
>   Than yours, ye slaves of bloody toil?
> Is not your bravery sublime
>   Beneath a tropic sun to broil
> And bleed and groan—for Guggenheim!
>   And give your lives for—Standard Oil!
>
> . . . For every peon that you shoot
> A brother's death will stain your soul. (O'Neill 1965, 116)

Of course O'Neill's Greenwich Village milieu was teeming with all brands of liberated, radical and deconstructive ideas about art, society, and politics, but what we have in his developing vision is more than just some attitudes that had rubbed off on him. As Voelker shows, O'Neill was not, in these early forays, simply echoing the position of his politically radical friend John Reed (1992, 100). At this point he was feeling his own way into radicalism: absorbing Marxian class consciousness, to be sure, but with a vision of something larger about oppression too. Despite the staginess and forced comic diction of *The Movie Man* and the potted rhetoric of "Fratricide," we can see O'Neill beginning to trace the relationship of difference and dominance.

As O'Neill got ever further into twentieth-century culture he developed an increasingly complex grasp of human motivation, interrelationship, and fate. He read widely and inquiringly—Nietzsche, Aeschylus, Dostoyevsky, Strindberg, Schopenhauer, Freud, Jung, and others—as if questing, groping for some notion of the significance of human life and human suffering. And the search for broader, deeper insights turned increasingly in the direction of primal, elemental motifs that could be seen as the determinants, the universal fate-factors. Along with a goodly number of other twentieth-century thinkers and artists, O'Neill was reconfiguring the primitive and modern humankind's relationship to it. "It seems to me that, as far as we can judge, man is much the same creature, with the same primal emotions and ambitions and motives, the same powers and the same weaknesses, as in the time when the Aryan race started toward Europe from the slopes of the Himalayas" (Sayler 1922, 358–59). Such was the opinion he offered in an interview in 1921, between the writing of *Emperor Jones* and *The Fountain*. He repeatedly represented his art in terms of that philosophical quest for the primal basis of human significance. In a letter to literary scholar Arthur Hobson Quinn in 1925, just after the composition of *All God's Chillun*, he states that he has tried

> to see the transfiguring nobility of tragedy, in as near the Greek sense as one can grasp it, in seemingly the most ignoble, debased lives. And just here is where I am a most confirmed mystic, too, for I'm always, always trying to interpret Life in terms of lives, never just lives in terms of character. I'm always acutely conscious of the Force behind—(Fate, God, our biological past creating our present, whatever one calls it—Mystery, certainly)—and of the one eternal tragedy of Man in his glorious, self-destructive struggle to make the Force express him instead of being, as an animal is, an infinitesimal incident in its expression.

He repeatedly refers the ultimate aims of his art to Greek tragedy—"the Greek dream in tragedy is the noblest ever!" (1988b, 195)—which is probably why he rejects so testily the assertions by critics that his work is inspired and informed by Freud.

But the modernist who was searching for that deeper, elemental "Force behind" had the full impetus of the psychoanalytic movement impelling and directing him/her.* Where the Greeks had their gods, modernists (especially Greenwich Village modernists) had their ids, superegos, and collective unconsciousnesses. Kenneth Macgowan, friend of O'Neill and collaborator with him on so many theatrical projects in these formative stages of his art, brought the elemental forces, the primitive, and the psychoanalytical together in the framework of Greek drama in his 1921 booklength manifesto, *The Theatre of Tomorrow*:

---

*A great deal of interpretation of O'Neill has of course focused on his relationship to psychoanalytic theory. See, for example, the books by Falk, the Gelbs, Raleigh, Bogard, Sheaffer, Chabrowe, Floyd, and others.

The drama must seek to make us recognize the thing that, since Greek days, we had forgotten—the eternal identity of you and me with the vast and unmanageable forces which have played through every atom of life since the beginning. Psychoanalysis, tracing back our thoughts and actions into fundamental impulses, has done more than any one factor to make us recover the sense of our unity with the dumb, mysterious processes of nature. We know now through science what the Greeks and all primitive peoples knew through instinct. The task is to apply it to art and, in our case, to the drama. (1923, 264)

O'Neill saw it the same way: the theater, he wrote in 1925, "should give us what the church no longer gives us—a meaning. In brief, it should return to the spirit of Greek grandeur. And if we have no Gods, or heroes to portray we have the subconscious, the mother of all gods and heroes" (Quoted in Chabrowe 1976, 113).

The fusion of the primal, the psychoanalytical, and the ancient Greek had another dimension for O'Neill, one I would suggest had its origin in the metaphysic of theatre. In the phenomena of act and reenactment, of lives seemingly self-determined and yet scripted (determined not just by the forces represented in the play but by the very fact that the action had in a way already been completed in the playwright's mind and script, had been performed just this way before and would be performed just this way again), O'Neill had an intuitive basis for his perception that that "Force behind" worked by overriding our autonomy with fixed, generic roles inherent in certain basic human situations, and by forcing our behavior and its outcomes into generic recapitulation, fated ritual reenactment. The theater itself, I feel, could thus have provided a diagnostic for O'Neill's analysis of the human condition. In that sense the world's indeed a stage, and vice versa.

Such ideas of generic roles and ritual recapitulation fit nicely with Jungian notions too—the collective unconscious preserving and continually reviving the inherited myths of the ages; the timeless archetypes channeling the instincts and behavior—and O'Neill admitted to preferring Jung's *Psychology of the Unconscious* to the few other psychoanalytical works he read. (*Totem and Taboo*, for example, with its far more prescriptive suggestion of the universal Oedipal recapitulation of the primal parricide seems not to have been as broadly applicable a myth for him.)*

There were several powerful cultural figurations that O'Neill might

---

*For a greatly expanded interpretation of O'Neill in terms of religious ritual and psychoanalysis, see Leonard Chabrowe's 1976 book, *Ritual and Pathos—The Theatre of O'Neill*.

have used in his dramatic inquiry into the human predicament but didn't: Christianity, Shakespearean drama, and the American notion of democracy could each have offered a plausible and widely acceptable framework. But in his major plays O'Neill presents a darker vision than any of these, of a human universe where suffering brings no redemption, where there is no justly hierarchical order to be threatened and restored, and where there are no human relationships that do not involve power differentials and conflict. O'Neill chose to ignore these traditional figurations of higher significance, concentrating on the pagan, the elemental, and the deconstructive.

The individualistic modernist education O'Neill put himself through in the late teens and early twenties certainly deepened his art as it complicated his vision. His characters became more interesting and their relationships more revealing. The stagey characterizations and conflicts of the early plays—the dreamer vs. the doer, the restless vs. the stable, the selfish materialist vs. the humanist, and so forth—gave way to subtler, deeper, more problematical delineations. In the matter of human difference, the increased complexity of his developing perspective enabled him to relativize race and culture and evolutionary level. The Other—even the primitive, racially different, or culturally alien Other—could be presented as fully human and legitimately motivated. O'Neill is thus able to show how the colonial situation translates difference into dominance and how an interracial relationship tends to do likewise, how individuals in contended or ambiguous situations or relationships are impelled into certain fixed roles, and how certain outcomes then become inevitable, regardless of the individual's "glorious, self-destructive struggle to make the Force express him instead of being . . . an infinitesimal incident in its expression" (1988b, 195).

With the deep impressions of his Honduran experience as a part of his consciousness, O'Neill the emerging playwright was intrigued by a story-germ of a Haitian dictator, Guillaume Sam, who, in O'Neill's own words, "said they'd never get him with a lead bullet; that he would get himself first with a silver one." A bit later he read of religious feasts in the Congo and their use of a drum beat starting at the rate of a normal pulse and slowly accelerating. With those elements, then, he had the initial materials for *The Emperor Jones* (Gelb 1962, 438–39). At least so goes the story of that play's origination.

But there was another drama that he incorporated in it as well, the tragicomedy of the Caribbean republics. The postcolonial/neocolonial history of the Caribbean region was widely known to the American public in an official, simplified, rationalized version that O'Neill in his maturing social consciousness saw negatively, deconstructively. The officially sanctioned view of "the horrors which have so darkened the history of the Black and Brown republics" (the rhetoric is that of Rear Admiral Colby M. Chester, in "Haiti: a Degenerating Island" in the 1908 *National Geographic*, p. 217) itself constitutes a drama of primitive difference, part history and part racial fear myth.

If we take the drama of Haiti, for example (since that half-island provided the source of one part of O'Neill's myth), and conflate several officially sanctioned presentations (especially the unsigned 1920 *National Geographic* article "Haiti and Its Regeneration by the United States," pp. 497–511, and the "Haiti" entry in the 1910 eleventh edition of *The Encyclopedia Britannica*), the drama plays out in this way: the first act saw the arrival of Columbus and the Spanish who claimed the island and named it "Hispaniola" ["Little Spain"] and shortly did away with the native population. Some accounts express strong misgivings at the behavior of the Spanish, but *Britannica* only characterizes the primitives and their fate in its most detached prose:

> At the time of its discovery, the island was inhabited by about 2,000,000 Indians, who are described by the Spaniards as feeble in intellect and physically defective. They were, however, soon exterminated, and their place was supplied (as early as 1512) by slaves imported from Africa, the descendants of whom now possess the land. (826)

The Spanish had a good deal of trouble with buccaneers and depredators, and ultimately in a colonial struggle with the French, to whom, in the drama's second act, they ceded the island. Under the French, times were good for a while: "Under the French rule, civilization and prosperity on the island rose to a high pitch. Roads gridironing the agricultural districts were constructed and magnificent chateaux, the homes of landed proprietors, dotted the hills and valleys." When the French Revolution and other European conflicts weakened the whites' hold on the island, "the negro slaves arose and with indescribable atrocities wiped out almost the entire white population" (*National Geog.* 1920, 499).

All of the accounts attribute the Negroes' "indescribable atrocities" to their primitive Africanness, especially their religion. As Rear Admiral Chester had put it, "the inhabitants themselves are naturally ... gentle, except when overcome by the barbarous religious customs handed down from their African ancestors" (1908, 214). The unsigned authority represents the postcolonial behavior as "unthinking animalism, swayed only by fear of local bandit chiefs and the black magic of voodoo witch doctors" (*National Geog.* 1920, 497). Voodoo and its tendency to call up an innate response in dark-skinned people was especially repulsive and frightening to these commentators. One recounted a "carnival of barbarism," as "cannibalism and the black rites of voodoo magic of the African jungles were revived in all their horror, and the sacrifice of children and of animals to the mumbo jumbos of the local wizards was practiced" (*National Geog.* 1920, 500). Even the contemporary United States may not be exempt from such primitive reversion, Rear Admiral Chester warned in 1908: "It is well for us to consider whether we too may not expect some such acts of savagery to break out in our country if our own colored people are not educated for better things" (216).

If the drama's third-act climax was the rampage of voodoo and banditry, the extermination of whites, and the sacrifice of children, what followed was "an abandoned civilization" (*National Geog.* 1920, 499), characterized by unrule and crumbling chateaux, prompting the *Britannica* to soberly observe, "On the whole it must be owned that, after a century of independence and self-government, the Haitian people have made no progress, if they have not actually shown signs of retrogression" (826). With "Haiti . . . getting blacker and blacker," it was "degenerating to a condition of barbarism" (Chester 1908, 214). Referring to the series of revolutions and upheavals since the throwing off of white rule, the unsigned authority says, "from that time, retrogression to the present followed *in natural steps*" (*National Geog.* 1920, 499; my italics).

One lesson of the drama seems to be that the dark peoples are childlike, nonrational, and prone to regressive, animalistic behavior. Another is that they need the strong civilizing influence of an enlightened white culture. That comes out in the fifth-act resolution of the Haitian drama: an incident in which the Haitians violated the French embassy and prompted U.S. intervention in 1915. The marines landed, and soon the *National Geographic* authority could boast that "peace and security of life and property have been given to this island republic" (510), redeeming Rear Admiral Chester's 1908 admonition that "they are our neighbors, and that we owe it to ourselves as a Christian nation to help them over the many pitfalls of popular government" (217).

O'Neill's contribution to this officially promulgated drama of primitive difference is wholly ironic. Of the setting of *The Emperor Jones* he says, sarcastically, "The action of the play takes place on an island in the West Indies as yet not self-determined by White Marines.

The form of native government is, for the time being, an Empire" (1988a, 1030). And the color symbolism of the opening set conveys its own ironic message, with the unremitting whiteness of the walls, pillars and floor tiles contrasted with the "dazzling, eye-smiting scarlet" of the throne and the strips of matting leading from the throne to each of the two entrances (1031).

But then on that stage the only white character is "pasty . . . a sickly yellow," and the exploiting emperor, when he arrives, himself is black, "typically negroid" (1031,1033). Thus the play invokes the Caribbean colonial background of white-on-black, civilized-on-primitive exploitation, but with an unexpected displacement in the person of the black American emperor. By establishing Brutus Jones as of African descent O'Neill shifts the burden of difference from race to class. And visually, in the beginning his is the gaudy richness of garb, the imperiousness of manner, while the "native negro woman" who "sneaks in cautiously" in the opening scene is "dressed in cheap calico, bare-footed, a red bandana handkerchief covering all but a few stray wisps of white hair" (1031). The native revolutionary leader Lem, when he appears in the final scene, is "a heavy-set, ape-faced old savage of the extreme African type, dressed only in a loin cloth," and his soldiers "are in different degrees of rag-concealed nakedness" and wearing simple palm-leaf hats (1060). Brutus defines the difference (which he himself has done much to establish and perpetuate) in terms of a notion of the primitive similar in all but diction to that of the officially rationalized view. He sees "all dem fool bush niggers" (1036) as childishly irrational, gullible and superstitious—without the intellectual capacity either to understand his open exploitation of them or to stop his carefully thought-out plan of escaping with all their wealth. As O'Neill draws him, Brutus will never come to understand their motives or powers, the shallowness of his own self-understanding, or the fate-ritual they are together reenacting.

Difference is the key to dominance for Brutus, and with his imitative facility he reproduces (quite intentionally) the characteristics of exploiting classes everywhere:

> For de little stealin' dey gits you in jail soon or late. For de big stealin' dey makes you Emperor and puts you in de Hall o' Fame when you croaks. (*reminiscently*) If dey's one thing I learns in ten years on de Pullman ca's listenin' to de white quality talk, it's dat same fact. And when I gits a chance to use it I winds up Emperor in two years. (1035)

In his attempt to control and enhance his fate Brutus takes on the role of exploiter, and manifests the standard markers: the external symbols and trappings of power and authority, the promotion of a superiority myth, the unremitting greed, the rationalistic plotting and finagling, the use of intimidation (and of deals and alliances where intimidation won't work), the intentional putting down of the lower classes, the dehumanization and then the distrusting of them, and so forth. Thus the revolt and revenge of the natives (the exploited proletariat) is entirely within the role-system of this quasi-Marxist colonial framework.

But O'Neill, drawing on his deep involvement with ancient Greek drama, casts Brutus in the role of hubristic tyrant too. The play's first scene is full of his intimidation of the white man Smithers—"Talk polite, white man! Talk polite, you heah me! I'm boss heah now, is you fergettin'?" (1034)—and of his boasting about his superiority not only over the natives his subjects, but over the hazards of his situation and of the forest, the dark, the ghosts, of whatever might stand in his way:

"Ain't I de Emperor? De laws don't go for him." (1035)
"I got brains and I uses 'em quick. Dat ain't luck." (1036)
"I'se gone out in dat big forest, pretendin' to hunt, so many times dat I knows it high an' low like a book. I could go through on dem trails wid my eyes shut. (*with great contempt*) Think dese ign'rent bush niggers dat ain't got brains enuff to know deir own names even can catch Brutus Jones? . . . It's a shame to fool dese black trash around heah, dey're so easy." (1040)
"I kin outguess, outrun, outfight an' outplay de whole lot o' dem all ovah de board any time o' de day er night! You watch me!" (1041)
"Does yo' s'pect I'se silly enuff to b'lieve in ghosts an' ha'nts an' all dat ole woman's talk? G'long white man! You ain't talkin' to me." (1042)

The Emperor's boundless confidence in his own powers, in his silver bullet luck charm, and in the protection of the Baptist Church (although he admits "I 'se after de coin, an' I lays my Jesus on de shelf for de time bein'" [1042]) seems like overdone parody of first-scene hubris of heroes of Aeschylus or Sophocles. And even in a purely modern framework it seems forebodingly naive. We know in advance what scenarios such attitudes let one in for.

There is no doubt that Brutus is created with a number of characteristics that are drawn from insulting black stereotypes—his diction and pronunciation, gaudy costuming, simpleminded materialism, naive faith in lucky charms and the physical protection of the Baptist Church, association with crap games and chain gangs, and later, his susceptibility to atavistic regression, and so forth—and his naive and overdrawn hubris seems a part of this pattern. John Cooley even observes that "in the context of the Harlem Renaissance and the 'New Negro' movement . . . O'Neill's portrait of Brutus Jones will be seen as a combination of several white stereotypes of black character, each of them well established in earlier white literature" (1986, 53). There is considerable critical discussion of what Brutus represents and how this relates to O'Neill's views on race, but—and here is where I see a serious antioppression message coming through the play—Brutus has, and employs, a strong sense of the superiority of his civilization over the primitive culture of the Others. His principal tools of survival and dominance are his rationality, his utilitarian ingenuity, and his gun, while his sole motive is monetary gain: his methods, means and intentions clearly reflect a radical view of those of the United States in its role in the Caribbean.

Thus on one level, O'Neill can be seen as implying that Brutus in all his crudities and naiveté is a representation of neocolonial domination, and that his shortsightedness and his inevitable fate should be a lesson for us all. Furthermore—and here is another respect in which I see the play as an effective attack on the problem of difference and dominance—since the play offers the audience only characters different from their white selves, they have no choice but to relive these situations, the exploitation and the slavery, the arrogance and the fear, as members of the other race. Too little has been made of the likely ulterior effects on a white audience in 1920 experiencing this very peculiar emotional placement, crossing the boundary of racial difference for the first time in the theatre, even if it be somewhat stereotypically concocted. Implicitly the play is indeed about race, and about transcending race.

O'Neill explained his strategy of overriding the audience's conventional notions with more profound, more universally human truth in a 1922 interview. His interviewer, Mary B. Mullett, perceptively suggested that it was amazing that *The Emperor Jones*, *Anna Christie*, and *The Hairy Ape* each was essentially "a rough slap in the face to people accustomed to the conventions of society and the traditions of the theatre. Yet crowds of these people . . . applauded enthusiastically when their faces were metaphorically slapped." That elicited O'Neill's explanation that

> the audiences sat there and listened to ideas absolutely opposed to their ordinary habits of thought—and applauded these ideas . . . [b]ecause they had been appealed to through their emotions, . . . and our emotions are a better guide than our thoughts. They are the result not only of our individual experiences but of the experiences of the whole human race, back through all the ages. They are the deep undercurrent, whereas our

thoughts are often only the small individual surface reactions. Truth usually goes deep. So it reaches you through your emotions. (Estrin 1990, 26–27)

That response sounds quasi-Jungian in its primal, collective referent, but it also sounds deeply and personally absorbed—and it sounds like it comes from a thoughtful sense of what theatre can do in this psychological, ritual vein.

O'Neill stimulates the audience's emotional undercurrent in this play by theatrical means, some of them rather innovative. He admits to being interested in "the effect of the tropical forest on the human imagination" in writing the play, an interest that he refers back to his Honduran experience (Gelb 1962, 438–39), and of course the setting of the major part of the play is contrived to capitalize on that effect. The steadily intensifying drum beat not only achieves a kinesthetic/emotional effect on the audience, but evokes the aura of the drum's very alien and primitive connotations for the civilized culture. As is observed in a 1920 *National Geographic* article on Haiti by Major G. H. Osterhout, U.S.M.C., "the tom-tom is one of the weirdest of musical instruments. It sounds far away when close at hand, and close at hand when far away. The voodoo worshipers make great use of it in their frenzied orgies" (482). The apparitions Brutus encounters in each of the clearings are speechless, mechanical in their actions, and powerfully affecting, like ritual reenactments in dreams. C.W.E. Bigsby has recently and very interestingly interpreted this as "the collapse of language" and claimed that O'Neill's use of it "creates rather than destroys meaning." It is "a theatrical assertion of the primacy of nonverbal communication. At the level of language lies are possible; at the level of instinctual behavior, of gesture, and of unconscious impulse there is an available truth" (1987, 138). It is interesting that O'Neill would use this (very theatrical) means, too, to carry his audience beneath the level of the "small individual surface reactions" of their conscious and culturally determined thoughts.

In an increasingly futile struggle Brutus tries desperately to rely on his "small individual surface reactions," and to maintain his faith in his ability to master his circumstances by means of his egocentric utilitarian rationality. The escape plan in which he had so much confidence meets with unexpected obstacles when the "ign'rent bush niggers" have had the foresight to confiscate all the horses; the Emperor will have to convey himself by foot. Then his carefully hidden-away food supply is unlocatable; instead of one white rock, there are (unaccountably) many, and his food cache is under none of them, so the Emperor will trek through the forest with an empty stomach.

(Was Brutus simply mistaken about the location of his food, or were the natives on to that part of his plot and able to confound him in that too?) After he encounters the first of the apparitions, the Little Formless Fears, reacts "with a yell of terror" and fires his gun at them, he forces a very rational explanation: "Dey was only little animals—little wild pigs, I reckon. Dey've maybe rooted out yo' grub an' eat it. Sho', you fool nigger, what you think dey is—ha'nts?" Then, realizing the irrationality of having fired a shot that gave away his location to his pursuers, *"[h]e plunges boldly into the forest,"* but not before struggling with rising fear, and trying to bolster his confidence with (again) rational, materialistic explanation: *"(He starts for the forest—hesitates before the plunge—then urging himself in with manful resolution)* Git in, nigger! What you skeered at? Ain't nothin' dere but de trees" (1046).

Brutus's ability to explain and control things rationally fails him more pathetically with each new apparition he experiences, although he never allows himself to admit that the things he is struggling against are not combatable on the level of logical cause-and-effect and purposeful action. He can only resort to shooting his way out, the expression of physical force somehow symbolically producing his release from each psychospiritual entanglement—at least until his bullets are gone and he, unarmed and nearly naked, unwittingly delivers himself to his executors, his formerly oppressed subjects. In a general thematic sense, whatever Force is acting here, playing out its fate-ritual, completely overrides Brutus's intentions and autonomy; he's playing a role he had blindly chosen by his past actions, and one he cannot escape. And each of his encounters in the clearings develops with a similar ritualistic necessity. Each of the apparitions incorporates him in a role—defines him, actually—in such a way that his actions are controlled, nightmarelike, until he can recover his present-time self, recall his precarious situation, and destroy the apparition.

All of the apparitions are fate-controlled, ritually narrative, and all of them are about dominance and its costs. When Brutus's crap game with Jeff and his loaded dice—a crap game itself being a model of a struggle for dominance of one player over another—turns into a razor fight in which Brutus kills him, the result is the chain gang for Brutus, where he is subject to domination by a brutal white prison guard. Race difference is increasingly important in defining the roles in dominance situations, O'Neill shows. The assertion of dominance breeds resentment and rebellion, and in this fourth scene Brutus, motivated by his resentment, turns from victim to perpetrator. He kills the guard, this time not with the ritualized shovel-blow the scenario leads up to, but with the gunshot that disperses the whole apparition, another desperate reassertion of dominance that attempts to cancel the past and its demands on him.

O'Neill leaves no doubt that Brutus is haunted by guilt for these two murders: He had prevailed in those episodes of his life and in the apparitional reencounters too, but in the processes he has become vulnerable internally. O'Neill shows him realizing guilt too for his exploitive domination of the natives: "[D]own heah whar dese fool bush niggers raises me up to the seat o' de mighty, I steals all I could grab. Lawd, I done wrong! I knows it! I'se sorry! . . . Forgive dis po' sinner! *(then beseeching terrifiedly)* And keep dem away, Lawd. . . . And stop dat drum soundin' in my ears!" (1052). Brutus is having no Learlike realization of the nature of suffering humanity, but having been repositioned into a situation of inferiority he is feeling the feelings of the dominated, the victimized.

Victimization succeeds guilt as a destabilizing element in Brutus's mind as subsequently the narrative elements are drawn (Jungianly) out of the collective rather than his personal unconscious, as the terror of the situation drives his mind ever deeper toward inherited primal fears and perceptions. Can O'Neill be intuitively suggesting some deeply buried primal link in the human emotional makeup between feelings of guilt and the emotional residue of victimization? Both have the same effect on Brutus, making him subconsciously, unwillingly acquiesce in his own surrender, his own loss of self. Here then is another of O'Neill's challenges to the definitions of difference and of primitive: dominator or dominated, his protagonist is not only guilty for being Brutus, but guilty for *being*.

As he suddenly finds himself in the midst of a nineteenth-century slave auction, and then, fleeing that, in *"the dark, noisome hold of some ancient vessel"* (1055) in the Middle Passage, Brutus is forced to play increasingly dominated, increasingly anonymous roles in ritually reenacting the history of his race. He is selfless as well as virtually helpless in the zones of the racial unconscious, and his escapes are made without rationalization, without words even, articulated with nothing but primal utterance: from the slave auction he flees *"crying with fear,"* and from the Middle Passage with a wail that *"reaches the highest pitch of sorrow, of desolation."* And as the scene with the crocodile god and the witch doctor dematerializes he *"lies with his face to the ground, his arms outstretched, whimpering with fear"* (1054, 1056, 1059). In this play the primally motivated human being has no causal explanations and no language but a cry, a wail, or a whimper.

That final apparition, with its heavy reliance on the material of pseudo-anthropological fantasy and popculture primitivism—the totemically decorated, bright-red-painted *"Congo witch-doctor"*; his wildly barbaric dance, gibberish incantations, and *"shrill cries"*; the pantomimed narrative of *"the fierceness of some implacable deity demanding sacrifice"*; the appointing of Brutus himself as the human sacrifice; and the appearance of the huge crocodile deity—all make the scene seem more expressionistic, more purely just a mental construct of Brutus's than were the preceding slavery scenes. Such elements might have passed muster with a 1920 theatre audience as an archetypical reenactment of an actual primitive African ceremony, especially given its visual power and *"the beating of the tom-tom,* [which] *grows to a fierce, exultant boom whose throbs seem to fill the air with vibrating rhythm"* (1058). But in trying to move his audience emotionally at their deepest levels by laying on with such intensity all the popular cliches of primitive difference, O'Neill risks not only misinformation but bathos or unintentional humor as well. Certainly this scene would be difficult to bring off for a latter-day audience, except as a projected psychological aberration.

The ideas of deep unconscious memory, self-assumed guilt, ritual recapitulation, and loss of autonomy are all emphasized by O'Neill in the scene directions. As Brutus enters this clearing, *"[t]he expression of his face is fixed and stony, his eyes have an obsessed glare, he moves with a strange deliberation like a sleep-walker or one in a trance,"* and *"as if in obedience to some obscure impulse, he sinks into a kneeling, devotional posture before the altar"* (1057). Momentarily coming to himself again he wonders (evoking in the process the idea of a racial memory): "What—what is I doin'? What is—dis place? Seems like I know dat tree—an' dem stones—an' de river. I remember—seems like I been heah befo'" (1057). And then when the witch doctor's frantic dance imposes sympathetic movement on Brutus and at the touch of his wand *"Jones squirms on his belly, nearer and nearer* [the crocodile], *moaning continually,"* for a long interval Brutus's body and instincts seem controlled by the primeval ritual, with only his voice pleading "Mercy, Lawd! Mercy!" and his desperately unwilling conscious mind trying to hold back—until he remembers the silver bullet, symbol of his luck and mastery and control of his own fate, and firing it he shatters this scene, too (1058–59).

As Lem and his revolutionaries enter at the beginning of the final scene, they appear to us (as they must have all along to Brutus) primitive, ragged, and definitively underclass. But they proceed systematically and with absolute confidence. "We cotch him," Lem pronounces, *"gutturally . . . calmly"* (1060). And of course they do, just the way they thought they would. The class-struggle drama, the civilized-versus-primitive drama, the hubristic tyrant drama has played itself out, like a ritual enactment, to its inevitable end. In the process, the primitive underclass has been shown to have a new weapon—the unconscious. As their quite inevitable threat and their nightmarish night jungle impinged on the exploiter's consciousness, the very mental capacities that initiated and supported the exploitation broke down, and he was reduced to a poor naked fearful human animal. His rationality, his materialist's sense of utilitarian cause and effect that enabled him to dominate in the short run was finally too narrow a psychological base to sustain his mastery.

What he forgot in his purely utilitarian approach to the difference of these primitives was that at a deeper psychological level we are all primitive, all carrying in our unconscious minds those certain images of our origins and our common fears and fates. The proletarian natives' reaching Brutus at a level he was too self- and gain-involved to recognize reversed the power relationship and gained their dominance over him. Societally, difference is a matter of class and power. But those are human contrivances, assumed and imposed by certain specific and limited psychological processes. This, at any rate (along with that sense of the necessitous, virtually ritualistic course of events precipitated by the exercise of dominance) seems to be the psychopolitical message of this play.

It is important to note how the paradigms of neocolonialism and depth psychology are brought together and deconstructed in this play. In the drama of primitive difference envisioned in evolutionist anthropology and U.S. intervention in the Caribbean (even in the *National Geographic* titles:1908, "Haiti: a Degenerating Island," and 1920, "Haiti and Its Regeneration by the United States"), we can imagine the psychoanalytical model of a well-balanced psyche providing the trope for the sociopolitical structuring of difference: the rational in control, the potentially valuable energies coming from below and needing control. The more the Other societies are identified with nonrationality and instinct, the more civilization is seen as a progressive overlayering of control, of willed purpose and inhibition; and the more politically relevant will seem that psychoanalytical template. Whether the psychological paradigm itself seems right because we're used to perceiving the world as being thus structured, whether we're projecting our psyches into the intercultural world, whether there is some ur-trope at the basis of both paradigms, or whether their similarity is just a striking, self-confirming analogue, it's a subtly persuasive conjunction, both terms of which O'Neill deconstructs in *The Emperor Jones*.

Colonialism of the Other or colonialism of the inner self, there is a cost for dominance, O'Neill's play proposes—in the resentment and rebellion of the oppressed and in the loss of contact with the deeper self by the oppressor. Dominance dehumanizes, de-individualizes at both ends of its harsh transaction. Reprisal is foreordained, and the forests are dark and deep—and within.

In a crucial moment in *The Fountain*, O'Neill has his protagonist, Juan Ponce de Leon, speak these words to Nano, a Caribbean Indian chief believed by Ponce de Leon to know the secret location of the fabled fountain of youth:

> Why do you look at me? I can never read your eyes. They see in another world. What are you? Flesh, but not our flesh. Earth. I come after—or before—but lost, blind in a world where my eyes deflect on surfaces. What values give you your loan of life? Answer! I must know the terms in which to make appeal! (1955, 202)

The scene is set during the Spanish colonization of Puerto Rico, and Juan Ponce de Leon is governor of the colony. He has tried to be a humane governor and tried (although with little success) to protect the natives from brutal plunder and repression by his fellow country-men. Here he is trying desperately to cross chasms of cultural and racial difference to achieve a deep empathetic understanding of his opposite Other. Juan will never achieve it: his motive is egocentric—to satisfy his obsession with recovering youth—and Nano is hanging in chains.

The Fountain is a more ambitious play than *The Emperor Jones*. *The Fountain* covers Western colonial history from the initiation of Columbus's second voyage to the Caribbean to Ponce de Leon's ambush in Florida and subsequent death, and involves several real events and historical characters. The play was not particularly successful in any sense, and O'Neill went from a high level of enthusiasm about it to nearly total repudiation. While he was writing it, he was confident he was using the unusual subject matter to express "truth as I know it—or better still *feel* it," and when its production was forthcoming, he called it "my best play, I think—and a stab in a new direction." Just eight years later he characterized it and *Gold* as "two of my worst" (1988b, 160, 166, 325). Its critique of colonialism is more direct than *The Emperor*'s, although colonialism's drama of difference is less focal in this play, more a matter of pervasive and determining background. The protagonist's inner conflicts and the roles he is forced to play in living out the demands of the difference-dominance dyad are again prominent, although here not in any way suggestive of psychoanalytical theoretics.

In Juan Ponce de Leon, O'Neill attempted to draw a protagonist who was intelligent, sensitive, skeptical, self-aware—quite different from Yank or Brutus Jones. Juan is tragic hero material: fearless soldier-conqueror; romantic lover; idealistic patriot; campaigner against cupidity, vice, and even mortality. He is freely individual and outspoken, even against the powerful and the holy. But love and power, high position and renown in their earthly manifestations come to pall for him in his later life (twenty years later, according to the play's chronology), and he finally fastens all his aspirations on an idealization of his beautiful young ward, the daughter of a former mistress, for whom his desire to recover his youth drives him to extraordinary lengths of credulousness and exertion. Yes, it is in the protagonist's motivation that the play seriously falters. Fitzgerald would do better concocting a whole social and psychological narrative framing Gatsby's similar yearning, but the twenties writers' strange fascination with this yearning for a dream-fabricated Beatrice hardly served to produce psychological profundity for O'Neill. He used it to try for a religiously mystical, difference-transcending conclusion to Juan's quest and to the tragedy of misdirected colonial aspiration—but more of that later.

No Brutus Jones, O'Neill's Ponce de Leon sees through the passionately materialistic motives of his fellow colonialists and is contemptuous of them. At the time of his first landing on the shores of the New World, although he is buoyed by ideals of discovery and settlement and Spanish glory—"I have my vision, too," he tells Columbus, "Spain can become mistress of the world, greater than ancient Rome"—he also quite accurately forsees the corruption of the colonial venture and condemns it in advance:

> Look at the men of this fleet—now when the East dawns for them! . . .
> Adventurers lusting for loot to be had by a murder or two; nobles of Spain
> dreaming greedy visions of wealth to be theirs by birthright; monks itching for the rack to torture useful subjects of the Crown into slaves of the
> Church! . . . Looters of the land, one and all! There is not one who will
> see it as an end to build upon! We will loot and loot and, weakened by
> looting, be easy prey for stronger looters. God pity this land until all looters perish from the earth! (1955, 184–85)

The play's minor characters speak and act out this disastrous scenario quite directly, even the churchmen disgracing and morally weakening themselves in brutalizing and exploiting the natives. After twenty

years Juan, now the colonial governor (*"His expression and attitude
are full of great weariness"*) exasperatedly condemns a colonialist no-
bleman's plan for indenturing natives to extract tithes from them: "It
means slavery. It defeats its purpose. The Indians die under the lash—
and your labor dies with them." And of the Church's efforts of con-
version: "Whether you convert by clemency or . . . by cruelty, the
result is the same. All this baptizing of Indians, this cramming the
cross down their throats has proved a ruinous error. It crushes their
spirits and weakens their bodies. They become burdens for Spain instead of valuable servitors" (189, 187). O'Neill quite clearly shows
that the colonists perceive the natives' difference callously, demeanin-
gly: for them, the Indians are exploitable resources or disobedient
children. Either way, difference is the opportunity—and the justification—for dominance.

Interestingly, O'Neill gives his audience a sympathetic look at difference from what he conceives would be the Indian point of view.
Individual native characters are introduced into the drama in entirely
conventional terms, glaring with suppressed hatred or bearing up
with *"aloof, stoical dignity,"* expressing conventional awe at the white
man's winged boats, and manifesting stereotypically primitive religious beliefs in the "Great Father . . . Maker of Days. Ripener of the
Corn" (188, 214, 217).* But their interpretation of the white man's
actions, motives, and faith are both clear-sighted and bizarre. Nano,
wholly at the mercy of Juan, rejects not only Juan's interpretation of
their previous encounter, but his present avowals of friendship as well:

JUAN. Are you not Nano, chief of the last tribe I conquered? . . .
NANO. The devils were with you. Our villages were burned. Women and
children were killed—my wives, my children!
JUAN, *frowning.* Contrary to my command. But again, what use? The
dead are dead. It is too late. (189)

What was for Juan a personal triumph, a military victory that regret-
tably went too far, let bygones be bygones, was for Nano quite under-
standably an unforgivable atrocity. Thus when Juan attempts to enlist
Nano's aid in locating the fountain of youth, promising home and
protection and happiness,

NANO. . . . The tongues of the white devils are false. How can I trust
your word?

---

*While writing the play O'Neill had requested a friend to supply him with Fra-
zer's *The Golden Bough*, (O'Neill 1982, 19, 21) although there is no clear evidence
that he used any of it in portraying these primitives.

JUAN. I take my sacred oath! (*He raises his hand.*)
NANO. Your God is a God of lies. (203)

Seeing an opportunity both to return to his home and to get revenge on his oppressor, Nano relents and agrees to guide Juan. So eager is O'Neill to maintain a sense of this native's integrity and purposes, he has Nano ask his God's forgiveness to do so: "(*. . . with religious fervor*) Great Spirit, forgive my lie. His blood shall atone!" (204). And in explaining the Spaniards, their beliefs and actions, to his fellow Indians who have not yet had contact with them, Nano reveals to the audience just how strange and barbarous these "civilized" beings would seem from the "primitive" side of the chasm of cultural difference:

NANO. These are no Gods. They are men who die from wounds. Their faces are white, but they are evil. They wear shirts that arrows cannot pierce. They have strange sticks that spit fire and kill. Their devils make them strong. But they are not true warriors. They are thieves and rapers of women.
CHIEF. Have they no God?
NANO. (*with scorn*) Their God is a thing of earth! It is this! (*He touches a gold ornament that the chief wears.*)
MEDICINE MAN. (*mystified*) Gold? Gold is sacred to the Sun. It can be no God itself.
NANO. (*contemptuously*) They see only things, not the spirit behind things. Their hearts are muddy as a pool in which deer have trampled. Listen. Their Medicine Men tell of a God who came to them long ago in the form of a man. He taught them to scorn things. He taught them to look for the spirit behind things. In revenge, they killed him. They tortured him as a sacrifice to their Gold Devil. They crossed two big sticks. They drove little sticks through his hands and feet and pinned him on the others—thus. (*He illustrates. A murmur of horror and indignation goes up among them.*)
MEDICINE MAN. To torture a God! How did they dare?
NANO. Their devils protected them. And now each place they go, they carry that figure of a dying God. They do this to strike fear. They command you to submit when you see how even a God who fought their evil was tortured. . . . They would lay waste your land as they did mine. They killed my wives and children. They burned. They tortured. They chained warriors neck to neck. They beat them with a whip to dig in the fields like squaws. (214–15)

Being beaten and tortured and forced to work is a singular message for the natives. Under that regimen they draw no fine moral distinctions between the raw greed of the gold-hungry nobles, the sadistic

persecution of heresy by the self-righteous churchmen, and the idealism of a would-be benevolent governor living on his past military
glory and searching for love and eternal youth. In this play, absolutely whatever it is that the colonialists want from the "primitive"
peoples, they serve the same function of callous, self-interested ex-
ploiters. Thus Juan, however noble his motives (and there's even room
for debate about that), is forced to enact the role of tyrant, attempting
to use his dominance over Nano, first to coerce, then (when that is
ineffectual) to entreat his cooperation. For Nano this situation is an
opportunity to exploit the dominator's weakness—and his motives
for doing so, although not apparent to Juan, are plainly so for the audience: As he explains in concluding that foregoing indictment, "This
old chief led them. My heart is fire. Until he dies, it will know no
peace." Thus Juan, whatever his personal motives and vision, will re-
enact the ritual of the deposed tyrant, with Nano and his fellow natives as the underclass in revolt.

But in this play O'Neill attempts to go beyond the deterministic
ritual of "the Force behind," crushing "Man in his glorious, self-
destructive struggle" (1988b, 195). In working on *The Fountain* he
wrote that "I feel that I'm getting back, as far as it is possible in modern times to get back, to the religious in the theatre. The only way we
can get religion back is through an exultance over the truth, through
an exultant acceptance of life. . . . And it is a difficult thing to get
exultance from modern life" (Gelb 1962, 520–21). *The Fountain's* religious "exultance" comes (as another innovation in modernist theatre, with echoes of Strindberg) in a series of dream-visions Juan (and
the audience) see after he has been misled by Nano, ambushed, and
fatally wounded. In the tenth of the play's eleven scenes, O'Neill attempts to transcend the themes of difference and colonial dominance
and offer a metaphysical dream of human unity and eternal renewal.

The forest spring beside which Juan had been ambushed transmutes
into "*a gigantic fountain, whose waters, arched with rainbows, seem
to join earth and sky,*" accompanied by the singing of his beloved
Beatriz ("Love is a flower/ Forever blooming") (223). Four figures
from his former life appear therein—Chinese poet, Moorish minstrel,
Indian Medicine Man and Dominican monk—and join hands, leading
Juan to exclaim, "All faiths—they vanish—are one and equal—within.
. . . What are you, Fountain? That from which all life springs and to
which it must return—God! Are all dreams of you but the one
dream?" (225).

Then when he takes the hands of a hag and she becomes the young
beauty Beatriz, Juan realizes "Age—Youth—They are the same
rhythm of eternal life!" (225). In a delirium of exultance, Juan has dis-

covered the essence of all life and all religion, and it only remains for him to survive a little longer to see his living Beatriz about to be united with his young nephew, the very image of his virile and ambitious earlier self, to seal the message that essences live eternally although individuals die and are succeeded, like the flower in the song. This play's ending is like a prayer: that differences of race and culture and age be only temporary, transcendable illusions, and that all life and all gods be one.

With *All God's Chillun Got Wings* O'Neill turned to dramatizing difference in a domestic, rather than a colonial situation—in the particular domestic situation he seems to have regarded as an archetypal site of conflict and dominance, of role-enacting and fated unhappiness—a marriage. From the beginning his idea involved domestic conflict complicated by racial difference—between a black man and a white woman—and if there is transcendence in the conclusion of this vision, it is almost certainly sardonic. A somewhat cryptic (to us) entry in his notebook of ideas first signals his intent to dramatize difference: "Play of Johnny T—negro who married white woman—base play on his experience *as I have seen it intimately*—but no reproduction, see it only as man's" (Floyd 1981, 258). Its writing was then "undertaken in response to critic and editor George Jean Nathan's invitation to contribute to the inaugural issue of the *American Mercury*, due to appear in January 1924" (Editors' note, O'Neill 1982, 49).

The staging of a marriage of a black man and a white woman, both contemporary urbanites uninsulated from the audience by antique or distant settings or Shakespearean rhetoric, was an outrageous idea to consider for public presentation in the 1920s United States—another "rough slap in the face to people accustomed to the conventions of society and the traditions of the theatre" (Estrin 1990, 26). The controversies it incited—the racist prepublicity in the newspapers, O'Neill's and the Provincetown Players' staunch defense of their production, the New York mayor's ban on the child actors and the Players' easy accommodation of that, the lack of riots or obstruction of the actual performances, and the critical discussions ever since about whether or not the play is really about race—are part of the legend of American theater. But through it all echo O'Neill's own statements of intent and belief, which, however genuine, have largely determined the channels of discourse about the play's significance. Quite obviously he strongly wished to steer interpretation toward meanings more broadly philosophical, more generically inherent than those connected with the race situation in the United States. In a statement to the newspapers responding to the preperformance publicity he said:

> The play itself, as anyone who has read it with intelligence knows, is never a "race problem" play. Its intention is confined to portraying the special lives of individual human beings. It is primarily a study of the two principal characters, and their tragic struggle for happiness. To deduce any general application from "God's Chillun" except in a deep, spiritual sense, is to read a meaning into my play which is not there. . . . Nothing could be farther from my wish than to stir up racial feeling. I hate it. It is because I am certain "God's Chillun" does not do this but, on the contrary, will help toward a more sympathetic understanding between the races, through the sense of mutual tragedy involved, that I will stand by it to the end. (Gelb 1962, 550–51)

And in two separate interviews stimulated by the controversy:

> "But, don't you think there is a difference? Isn't the white race superior to the black?"
> "Spiritually," he replied—"spiritually speaking, there is no superiority between races, any race. We're just a little ahead mentally as a race, though not as individuals.
> "But," Mr. O'Neill continued, "I've no desire to play the exhorter in any racial no-man's land. I am a dramatist. To me every human being is a special case, with his or her own special set of values. True, often those values are just a variant of values shared in common by a great group of people. But it is the manner in which those values have acted on the individual and his reactions to them which make of him a special case." (Estrin 1990, 46)
> "But the Negro question, which, it must be remembered, is not an issue in the play, isn't the only one which can arouse prejudice. We are divided by prejudices. Prejudices racial, social, religious. Tracing it, it all goes back, of course, to economic causes. . . . And these prejudices will exist until we understand the Oneness of Mankind. Life is hard and bitter enough without, in addition, burdening ourselves with prejudices." (Estrin 1990, 54)

In O'Neill's thinking and urging, there seem to be life-determining factors deeper and more primal than racism that he wants to explore and represent. There is that one reference to a Marxian diagnosis: "it all" going back to "economic causes." But as the more frequently urged, more fundamental diagnosis, "life is hard and bitter enough," especially in regard to "the special lives of individual human beings," their psychological needs, and their relationships to each other, to society, and to those "values shared in common"—it is those problems that O'Neill insistently wants *All God's Chillun* to be regarded as addressing.

In a scarcely believable stroke, he gave the two main characters the first names of his own parents. Jim, the young Negro husband, incredibly straightforward would-be lawyer, failure, idealistically carrying into adult life a childhood love for a white girl; and Ella, the fallen woman, crossing the color line to be redeemed in Jim's love, and then unable to handle the anomie of her situation and going psychotic—these characters are named after O'Neill's father and mother? Critic Virginia Floyd suggests that the effect of this naming is to dispose the play to transcend its racial messages and represent the "universal dimensions" of the tragedy inherent in marital incompatibility (1981, 269). Along such lines we can see again, here in the domestic realm, the "Force behind" represented in the operation of a generic and pre-scripted role system, in a doomed struggle of self against a complex system of dominance factors, played out on a field of difference.

Difference is made strikingly visual in the scene directions, especially for the four outdoor scenes in Act One. In each scene the stage is divided down the middle, with all-white population, activities and color-coding on the left and all-black on the right. The activities, attitudes, and simultaneous contrasting songs are all radically stereotypical. However, none of the play's main characters are racially stereotypical in the way that the physical and human settings suggest that all whites and blacks would be. Thus the characters and their context seem to be at odds. Somewhat later in his career, fascinated by the effect that could be achieved with the use of masks, O'Neill decided *post facto* that "In *All God's Chillun Got Wings*, all save the seven leading characters should be masked; for all the secondary figures are part and parcel of the Expressionistic background of the play, a world at first indifferent, then cruelly hostile, against which the tragedy of Jim Harris is outlined" (Gillett 1972, 114). If the *mise-en-scene* is "Expressionistic background" then the stereotypical racial contrasts are not representative of racial essences but of fabricated images from the popular media and the general public imagination. Difference and its significance seem to be social constructs, constituting the context of racism against which the characters must struggle to win their individual happiness.

Here is some of what O'Neill envisions as the nature of the dominant culture's dominance:

Scene One:
In the street leading left, the faces are all white; in the street leading right,
all black. . . . People pass, black and white, the Negroes frankly participants
in the spirit of Spring, the whites laughing constrainedly, awkward in nat-
ural emotion. Their words are lost. One hears only their laughter. It ex-
presses the difference in race. . . . From the street of the whites a high-
pitched, nasal tenor sings the chorus of "Only a Bird in a Gilded Cage."
On the street of the blacks a Negro strikes up the chorus of: "I Guess I'll
Have to Telegraph My Baby." (1934, 279)

Scene two (nine years later) displays the same radically segregated
scene, the same racial contrast in songs and laughter, but a slightly
more hostile and depressing atmosphere, as "[t]*he street noises are*
now more rhythmically mechanical, electricity having taken the place
of horse and steam," and "[w]*ith a spluttering flare the arc-lamp at*
the corner is lit and sheds a pale glare over the street" (283). In scene
three (five years later), again, "[n]*othing has changed much"* in the
physical setting, although it has deteriorated tonally so that "[t]*he*
arc-lamp discovers faces with a favorless cruelty" and the street noises
are *"more intermittent and dulled with a quality of fatigue,"* with no
laughter (289). Scene four—the scene in which Jim and Ella try to
overcome their racist social heritages and their own histories and to
create a new, mutual life in marriage—presents them with the harsh-
est, most explicit racist message:

> *people—men, women, children—pour from the two tenements, whites*
> *from the tenement to the left, blacks from the one to the right. They hurry*
> *to form into two racial lines on each side of the gate, rigid and unyielding,*
> *staring across at each other with bitter hostile eyes. The halves of the big*
> *church door swing open and Jim and Ella step out from the darkness*
> *within into the sunlight. The doors slam behind them like wooden lips of*
> *an idol that has spat them out. Jim is dressed in black. Ella in white, both*
> *with extreme plainness. They stand in the sunlight, shrinking and con-*
> *fused. All the hostile eyes are now concentrated on them* (295).

The visual, expressionistic presentation of society's construction of
race shows that difference will be insisted on; this "Force behind"
will impose racial separation and hierarchism whatever the cost to
straying individuals.

As children, Jim and Ella had seemed virtually exempt from the
dominant social constructions. They had genuinely and naturally
liked each other, each envious of the other's skin color, and their os-
tracism by their cohort of eight-year-olds was brought on more by
their sweetness on each other than by any factor of difference: "Look

at de two softies, will yeh! Mush! Mush!" (280) Epithets that fore-shadow the forces that will later destroy their lives flow freely in the children's' conversation, although seemingly harmlessly: "Jim Crow," "Chocolate," "Painty Face." But as the characters mature, they internalize society's constructions—the racism and role designa-tions—and face internal battles between those constructions and their own more individual affinities and yearnings. Jim, not at all the lan-guorous, sensuous, natural Negro of the expressionistic scene direc-tions, strives hard to become a lawyer and be worthy of his childhood ideal, Ella. His motivation seems another of those twenties' Beatrice-like idealizations, as well as a yearning to cross a line of color and social value that he himself acknowledges, anxious to be "the whitest of the white."

But at every turn he is confronted by, or calls up in himself, defini-tions of his societally predetermined role. When on high school grad-uation night Jim, on his way to get his diploma (and full of ideals about aspiring to his own future and protecting Ella's womanhood), meets Joe's insistence that they're both just niggers, Mickey's "yuh're tryin' to buy yerself white—graduatin' and law, for Christ sake!" and Ella's cold rebuff (286–87), he tries to stand up for his own self-defi-nition until Ella's "You and me've got nothing in common any more" destroys his confidence and he admits to Joe "Yes. I'm a nigger. We're both niggers" (288). Later, his sister Hattie and their mother oppose his love for his wife Ella directly and indirectly, Ella opposes and di-minishes his chance to pass the bar exam, and his own trepidation at sitting in the examination room with all those white, societally legiti-mized potential lawyers alienates and incapacitates him. The roles he is cast in by his racial difference have counteracted all his aspirations and made his effort at self-definition impossibly difficult.

Ella in her adolescence seems to have easily given up the relation-ship with Jim for the more impressive role of favored moll of the neighborhood's most impressive bully, Mickey. She mitigates Mick-ey's racist attitudes a bit in her acceptance of the street's norms, but in rejecting Jim's appeal for friendship she clearly takes the role of the aloof and superior white. What Ella aspires to is never revealed in the play, but her exploitation by Mickey subsequently casts her, intolera-bly, as a white of the lowest class, an abandoned fallen woman whose only options are factory work, prostitution, or the river. Jim's stand-ing by her at that lowest point of her life changes her color sense ("ELLA. You've been white to me, Jim. . . . JIM. White—to you! ELLA. Yes" [293]) and gives her a new sense of mission ("ELLA. I'm alone. I've got to be helped. I've got to help someone—or it's the end—one end or the other" [294]). Is she expressing altruism or a last desperate and subconscious effort to bolster her ego by maintaining some kind of superiority? Whether ambiguous or ambivalent, her motives are far from being as pure and uncomplicated as Jim excitedly takes them to be. His motives likewise are deeply questionable and forebode confusing and self-conflicting times ahead. In response to her acceptance of him he shelves his legal studies at a stroke, sets a new course, and revives, in a frenzy of lover's enthusiasm, a particularly humiliating role inherited from the heritage of racial difference:

> **JIM.** Yes! Yes! We'll go abroad where a man is a man—where it don't make that difference—where people are kind and wise to see the soul under skins. I don't ask you to love me—I don't dare to hope nothing like that! I don't want nothing—only to wait—to know you like me—to be near you—to keep harm away—to make up for the past—to never let you suffer any more—to serve you—to lie at your feet like a dog that loves you—to kneel by your bed like a nurse that watches over you sleeping—to preserve and protect and shield you from evil and sorrow—to give my life and my blood and all the strength that's in me to give you peace and joy—to become your slave!—yes, be your slave—your black slave that adores you as sacred! (*He has sunk to his knees. In a frenzy of self-abnegation, as he says the last words he beats his head on the flagstones.*)
> **ELLA,** *overcome and alarmed.* Jim! Jim! You're crazy! I want to help you, Jim—I want to help—. (294)

On that unstable basis, each of them in a mode of self-contradiction, self-denial or self-delusion, they next must face that hostilely segregated, hotly disapproving crowd outside the church doors.

O'Neill's use in act two of Jim's mother and sister Hattie helps maintain perspective against both the fervency of that expressionistically stereotyped society and the increasingly claustrophobic melodrama of the minds of the newlyweds. Mrs. Harris is portrayed as a worried mother, proud of her son's aspiration to be a lawyer, but, feeling that "Dey's on'y one should. (*solemnly*) De white and de black shouldn't mix dat close" (298). Hattie, as an accomplished and militant young professional, feels that Jim is called to greater things than he is pursuing: "We don't deserve happiness till we've fought the fight of our race and won it!" (299) Each of them has her idea of a role Jim should fill, different from the one that he is so desperately electing, and thus they, too, challenge his self-confidence and complicate his range of choices. As characters themselves, however, Mrs. Harris and Hattie are individuated in their reaction to racial difference, surely typical in some ways but not at all grotesquely stereotypical, legitimately motivated according to the perceptions of their respective generations. Thus they supply a rational and humane context for those radical elements on the one side who attempt to elevate racial difference to the level of an absolute determinant, and those on the other side who would utterly deny it.

In their domestic drama Jim and Ella futilely try to find some set of roles by which they can fit themselves to marriage and fit their marriage to the world—some combination socially acceptable, mutually compatible, and yet ego-preserving for each. As exiles in France, they incur social alienation and self-recrimination. Later as law-student husband and stay-at-home wife in the U.S., they are no less socially alienated, and the incompatibilities of their personal needs begin to emerge. Critic Marcelline Krafchick cites other "roles Jim and Ella play within their marriage to accommodate to their obstacles: brother-sister, buddies, father-daughter, saint-demon, rescuer-lost soul" (1992, 233). Finally comes their endgame regression to childhood playmates and the plantation delusion of Massuh's daughter and "my old kind Uncle Jim who's been with us for years and years" (315). O'Neill's expressionistic interior sets symbolize the domestic drama: *"The walls appear shrunken in still more, the ceiling now seems barely to clear the people's heads, the furniture and the characters appear enormously magnified"* (311). The physical parallels the psychological claustrophobia.

Despite all their good intentions to provide help and support for each other, Jim and Ella's relationship turns (perhaps inevitably, in O'Neill's universe) into a struggle for dominance.* Jim's drive to succeed in becoming a lawyer, thus to be a deserving husband Ella could be proud of, along with his constant solicitude and self-sacrifice for her welfare, both dictate a subordinate role for her, reinforcing an inferiority she finds (subconsciously, certainly, and quite possibly consciously too) loathsome, given the ego-destroying facts of her personal background and the social significance of their racial difference. She can only counter by impeding his progress with the only weapons she has at hand: her illness and extreme dependency and the paralyzing effect on him of racism. Her options are exceedingly narrow and tend to grow out of, and to augment, her instability.

Both their situations are untenable; *All God's Chillun* is another of O'Neill's concoctions of a human-relationship-as-mutual-destruction-machine. Interestingly, in this one the difference/dominance dyad pits gender against race: as society would have it, the husband

---

*Edwin Engel interestingly suggested that the characters' motivations "may also be explained in part by Adler's 'individual psychology,'" which posits a kind of will to power as the elemental force of ego (1953, 119–21).

was naturally superior to the wife, as the white was superior to the black. O'Neill's positing a black husband with a white wife confuses those conventional lines of authority and challenges that whole system of superiorities and inferiorities, as I have no doubt he intended to do.

For Ella, her struggle for an acceptable self-standing in her marriage becomes a drama of primitive difference. Whatever it is that she feels about Jim himself, his race, and her own confusing, deeply compromised situation she attaches symbolically to the Congo mask Hattie had given Jim as a (monitory) wedding present. O'Neill seems to be showing that beneath anomie lies primitive fear. In Ella's case that fear throws her back into believing that the mask has real racial power, hostile to her and her whiteness, and ultimately into reviving the plantation-relationship fantasy that will subdue the power of that blackness.

Ella's sense of the significance of the mask does not seem to be shared by Hattie or Jim. As Hattie explains the mask to Ella, "It's a mask which used to be worn in religious ceremonies by my people in Africa. But, aside from that, it's beautifully made, a work of Art by a real artist—as real in his way as your Michael Angelo. . . . Here. Just notice the workmanship." To Ella's fright at the sight of it, Jim calmly suggests, "Maybe, if it disturbs you, we better put it in some other room" (303).

Later, when Ella plunges a knife through the mask in a laughing frenzy of triumph that Jim failed his exams, he shouts, "You devil! You white devil woman! (*in a terrible roar, raising his fists above her head*) You Devil!" (313) Certainly the violence she has done to the mask is a factor in precipitating his violent response, but so is her exultance in his failure, a very personal kind of disloyalty. That the mask has some kind of primitive power, and that there is abroad some elemental struggle of blackness and whiteness is then purely Ella's psychotic, fear-laden perception. As Peter Gillett has put it, we are "inclined to attribute to Ella's diseased mind the notion of ineradicable primitiveness conveyed in the symbolism" (1972, 118).

Since Ella's psychosis is inflexible and Jim's role of forgiving-rescuer-of-lost-soul must be infinitely accommodating, it is her patterning that finally determines the terms of their relationship. Unable to accept herself as an anomalous adult woman, she regresses into what Freud would certainly regard as infantilism. Jim prays to God for the capacity to accept the final terms of the relationship: "make me worthy of the child You send me for the woman You take away!" (315) Thus he *elects* his particular regression, and the play ends in a devastatingly ironic affirmation of love configured in childish games and plantation-fantasy reenactment.

The characters in *All God's Chillun* want to be individuals, to find their own personal satisfactions and identities, but they are dictated to by their racial and social histories and forced finally into unconsciously parodic reenactments of race-conflict and antebellum servitude. Difference for Jim and Ella is not reinscribable. Their own innately human struggle for dominance carries them willy-nilly into the traditional societal channels of racism—its whole array of presuppositions, oppositions, aversions and escapes—and they are forced to give up even their own identities and their relationship as husband and wife.

In general, the play seems to say that in such an interracial relationship all the inferrings and sayings and blamings—all the generic responses—are *there*, hovering, pressuring to come true (seemingly what we've always known), ready to mold our individualities and quite personal feelings and knowings and behavior into generic reenactments. In a moment of exasperation with his sister Hattie's constant badgering about race, Jim demands, from the very depths of his willed idealism, "Where does the human race get a chance to come in?" (309) The play itself seems to answer that wherever it "comes in" it is structured by difference, dominance, resentment, and preritualization.

In these three plays O'Neill explores the issues of difference and primitiveness variously and originally. He presents readings of colonialism and race quite independent of the majority opinions of his society, and he relies only sporadically, situationally, on ideas from evolutionist anthropology and psychoanalysis. A dramatist to the core, he works from the inside of characters' minds and relationships, following the contours of their particular hopes and experiences, always with an eye for what can be dramatic, what can test the notions and suppositions we live by, and what the theatre can especially do. In trying to develop each of the characters along his or her own lines, he gives even the primitives rather full measures of humanity and capability. The prevailing racial hierarchy and its justifications are thus seen to be false and intolerant. The perception of primitive difference is more a matter of distorted individual or cultural perspective than of actual difference, and it functions for the characters primarily as a facilitator of dominance and exploitation.

For O'Neill the struggle for dominance seems endemic in all

human interactions, morally repulsive in its suppression of individuals' hopes and autonomy, and inevitably tragic in its outcomes. To exercise dominance over another, to thus assume or define that person inferior, breeds either resentment and rebellion, as it does in Nano and the natives of Brutus Jones's empire, or the kind of abject depersonalization elected by Jim Harris. However melodramatically, O'Neill made his audiences thus reflect innovatively on the psychology of primitive difference, on the nature and costs of colonialism and racism, and applaud these new insights almost in spite of themselves.

6

Relativizing Difference: Franz Boas and
The Mind of Primitive Man

FRANZ BOAS DID A GREAT DEAL TO EFFECT FUNDAMENTAL CHANGES in the very language of difference—not just modifying or elaborating the prevailing nomenclatures and conceptual systems, but destroying them. He brought into anthropology a stricter understanding of scientific method, a more sophisticated epistemology, and a keener sense of language, its nature and fallibility. Under his attacks monolinear evolution and a number of other important scientifically authorized concepts joined the ranks of phlogiston, the ether, and the conservation of force as outworn and erroneous notions that had only paved the way (or given way) to more accurate conceptualization. The evidences of a single-track universal human evolution, he maintained, were often only ethnocentric perceptions of surface similarities with no relation to their significances in the societies in which they were found. And the logic of evolutionists was faulty in their assumption—implicit in their comparative method—that similar customs, institutions, or behaviors necessarily were produced by similar causes.

Intending an uncompromising empiricism, Boas insisted that totemism, for example, was not a single universal phenomenon, that its manifestations had very different significances to various peoples. Attacking the naively ethnocentric reflexiveness he saw in the Euro-American experts on primitive societies, he insisted that what they often perceived as indistictness or indefiniteness in the natives' languages was really a consequence of their own culturally-based inability to hear the nuances that the natives easily could hear. In fact, the whole generic and value-laden notion of the primitive was disconfirmed, he asserted, by particular knowledge of the history, social structure, and accomplishments of each particular people. Not at all incidentally, his anthropology decentered race as a primary category of classifying and interpreting human difference, Boas insisting that it was neither precisely definable nor a reliable predictor of individual capacity.

From the late nineteenth century onward, Boas continued the attack, combating such reflexiveness, overambitious generalization, reification, ethnocentricity, and misidentification of beliefs and behaviors—the endemic fallacies of the (mostly library-study) anthropologists of his day. But his was more than an epistemological crusade. In Boas's work, the emerging epistemology of twentieth-century science interfused with the ethics of humanism: his scientific approach—particularist, methodologically and logically strict, keenly aware of the relativity of perspective—directly related to the humane treatment of other peoples. As historian of anthropology Curtis Hinsley has put it, "the basic tenets of Boasian anthropology, the structures he worked to create, and his long crusade against racial, ethnic, and cultural intolerance formed a single fabric of activist, humane social science" (1981, 284).

For all his deconstruction of the absolutisms and ethnocentric intuitive approaches of nineteenth-century anthropology, Boas was certainly indebted and attached to the work of many of its practitioners. Acknowledging the work of forerunners Spencer and Tylor (for whatever effect) in a 1904 address on the history of anthropology, he said they "applied with vigor and unswerving courage the new principles of historical evolution to all the phenomena of civilized life, and in doing so sowed the seeds of the anthropological spirit in the minds of historians and philosophers" (Stocking 1974, 27). And as historian George Stocking points out, "Despite his reaction against evolutionism, Boas' anthropology was deeply rooted in nineteenth-century tradition. As he himself was aware, its goal was essentially that of pre-evolutionary diffusionist ethnology, refashioned in the context of late-nineteenth-century science: 'the genesis of the types of man'" (1992, 122).

Boas never developed full-scale ethnological theory as had the evolutionists (possibly feeling the propensity of such widely general concerns to distort or even preclude the situational particularism he strove for?). But on the basis of scientific epistemology he gave anthropology two powerful concepts, the notions of standpoint and of culture, along with their discipline-defining methodological correlatives. His sense of standpoint established the ethnocentric fallibility, the inescapable relativity of the observer's point of view in any ethnographic study. His concept of culture stressed the particular self-defined internal coherence of any society; in offering an alternative to race and evolutionary stage it provided (in the words of Susan Hegeman), "a nonbiological and nonevolutionist way to think about collective features of human populations" (1999, 205). Typically, Boas never developed either concept into full-blown theory.

His idea of culture, for example, would be fully and somewhat di-

versely developed by his students and grow into the dominant concept of the anthropology of the years between the wars. But for Boas
"culture" certainly had some latitude and ambiguity in its applications: he seems to have been discovering the concept's parameters and
possibilities in the process of using it. Of its function in his new, more
strictly scientific framework (Stocking points out),

> it involved the rejection of simplistic models of biological or racial deter-
> minism, the rejection of ethnocentric standards of cultural evaluation, and
> a new appreciation of the role of unconscious social processes in the deter-
> mination of human behavior. It implied a conception of man not as a *ra-
> tional* so much as a *rationalizing* being. (1968, 232)

For Boas a culture was seemingly incidentally formed, but still determinant:

> On the one hand, culture was simply an accidental accretion of individual
> elements. On the other, culture—despite Boas' renunciation of organic
> growth—was at the same time an integrated spiritual totality which some-
> how conditioned the form of its elements. (Stocking 1968, 214)

There is some mystery about a culture's power of determining, what
that is and how it operates, but

> the general effect of Boas' argument was to show that the behavior of all
> men, regardless of race or cultural stage, was determined by a traditional
> body of habitual behavior patterns passed on through what we would now
> call the enculturative process and buttressed by ethically tainted second-
> ary rationalizations—in other words, by the particular "cultures" in
> which they lived. (Stocking 1968, 222)

Boas's sense of cultural determinism did indeed include the presumably rational thought of civilized man. As Stocking points out, in this
aspect (yes, and in many others, as we shall see) there was no difference between primitive and civilized:

> the behavior of human beings everywhere, primitive or civilized, was de-
> termined, in ways that never came fully to their consciousness, by the par-
> ticular cultural tradition in which they experienced their "early bringing
> up." Boas always remained critical of Freudian theory, and his usage of
> "unconscious" was a far cry from the Freudian unconscious, but . . . Boas,
> too, was a major contributor to the intellectual revolution that destroyed
> the rationalistic Victorian conception of man. (1974, 220–21)

If even a thinker's most sophisticated general categories and judgments were culturally determined, then what earlier anthropologists tended to offer as determining theories of humankind were likely tainted by secondary rationalization. Considering that, one needed to try by whatever means one could contrive to make another start more sensitive to specifics *in situ*, beginning by recognizing the biases of one's own culture's generalizations and judgments and keeping them as much as possible out of the attempt at understanding.

The notions of standpoint and culture so conceived entailed an investigative methodology that could attempt to interpret the subjects' lives and beliefs and social arrangements in their own terms, the kind of ethnographic investigation that would later be termed "emic." Accessing the specifics *in situ* thus involved not only on-site immersion in the society, its routines, its mores and its language, but a kind of imaginative relativism, a conscious projection into the Other's way of understanding.

Epistemological and cultural relativism "came in Boas' work to be a fundamental premise of anthropological method, a necessary basis for accurate observation and sound interpretation," as Stocking points out (1968, 230). Subsequently in the discipline, relativism has been variously defined and variously employed—adopted, adapted, universalized, innovated, radicalized, challenged, derided—a site of enormous stimulation and controversy. But Boas, back at that time, "not a relativist in a consistent sense . . . still found in the general development of human culture at least qualified affirmation of the specific values most central to his personal world view: reason, freedom, and human fellowship" (Stocking 1968, 231).

As scientist, humanist and founder and designer of so much that has been effective and enduring in anthropology, Boas has a unique reputation, both within the discipline and beyond. The progress of anthropology, like the progress of every other science, has been conflictual, and much of Boas's own writing and institutional maneuvering involved him in much vigorous attacking and defending. A number of aspects of his own work and his own theory have been questioned, controverted, and refuted, and the struggles continue even to the present day. Still, Boas is generally regarded as the most important figure in twentieth-century American anthropology, a landmark point of reference for most contemporary approaches.

He was born in 1858, about forty years after Lewis Henry Morgan and Herbert Spencer, those contributors to the founding of anthropology and its evolutionist paradigm, and about twenty years after their followers Daniel Brinton and John Wesley Powell. He was practically of an age with Sir James Frazer and Sigmund Freud, all three of them dying within a three-year period, Boas the last in 1942. Carl Jung was almost twenty years younger. Boas was born into a German Jewish family, his Jewishness frequently cited by commentators as a significant factor in the antiracist sentiments that later stimulated so much of his research on human difference and spurred so much of his activism. His formal education was principally scientific, in the strictly methodological, basically deterministic way that science was promulgated in nineteenth-century German universities; his doctorate from the University of Kiel was with a major in physics and a minor in geography.

Thus in a time when the majority of anthropologists came from outside science *per se* (from law or classical studies or whatever), Boas brought a background steeped in concern for method and the problems of perception and knowledge. Stocking lucidly traces this early epistemological bent (see especially his chapter "From Physics to Ethnology" [1968, 133–60]) showing, for example, how Boas's doctoral dissertation on the color of water raised in his mind crucial issues concerning the relativity of perception (1968, 142). Anthropologist-historian Marvin Harris emphasizes Boas's reading of, and affinity for, Kant's concept of the relation of mind and reality (1968, 266–69).

Boas's living among the Eskimo people of Baffinland, having joined an expedition as geographer, is assumed to have shifted his interest from the physical environment to the people. For scholars tracing the steps by which he came to the profession of anthropologist, it has become standard to quote this passage from his notebook (here taken from Stocking 1968, 148):

> Is it not a beautiful custom that these "savages" suffer all deprivation in common, but in happy times when someone has brought back booty from the hunt, all join in eating and drinking. I often ask myself what advantages our "good society" possesses over that of the "savages." The more I see of their customs, the more I realize that we have no right to look down on them.

Stocking rightly observes that this passage "embodies so much of the emotional dynamic underlying *The Mind of Primitive Man*." It also foreshadows some crucial themes of Boas's ethnology: the ethnocentricity of ordinary "civilized" thinking, the value of living among a people one wishes to understand, and the possibility that individual cultures each have their own values, their own ways.

Subsequently, Boas was a seminal contributor to an amazing variety of anthropological fields. As field researcher and ethnographer he described the Kwakiutls and other indigenous peoples of the Pacific Northwest; as linguist and translator he preserved and disseminated their language and their oral texts; as folklorist he studied their myths and legends, their cross-cultural borrowings, and adaptations; as physical anthropologist he painstakingly measured those peoples and made collections of their skeletal remains, also directing a project to measure the physiques of European immigrants and their children; and as ethnologist he studied and theorized about the concepts of racial and cultural difference.

Over the course of his career he held a number of important posts as investigator, curator, editor, professor, association president, and so forth, inevitably in a flurry of antagonism, controversy, and power politics—with directors and trustees, with the evolutionists and the anthropological establishment, with the Bureau of American Ethnology, the Field Museum, the Smithsonian, and so forth. He also developed a university pedagogy for anthropology, trained most of the important American anthropologists of the next generation, helped to professionalize the field, and wrote and lectured to the American public and their policy-makers on the scientific basis of issues of immigration, race, and human difference. Boas revolutionized American anthropology, made it more scientific, more methodologically and theoretically self-aware, and at the same time had a significant influence on the American people's general understanding.

The year 1911 is especially notable in the history of American anthropology because it marked a kind of culmination in Boas's work, an *annus mirabilis* that saw his publication of three major works: *A Handbook of American Indian Languages* (which established important principles for investigating indigenous languages, as well as detailing a number of them quite specifically); *Changes in the Bodily Form of Descendants of Immigrants* (which presented for both scientific and political policy-making audiences a demonstration of the environmental malleability of human physical types); and the greatly influential *The Mind of Primitive Man* (which challenged the prevalent notions about "primitives" and served as a kind of compendium of Boas's work to that point on race, language and numerous other crucial matters). He had been developing and testing and refining his ideas in the two decades before 1911 and he would continue to refine and modify them in the decades following, but what he presented in that year publicly defined his outlook and approach and poised him for the travails and the very substantial achievements of the years to come.

The characteristics of his basic outlook—his particularism and his resistance to general theory and the comparative method—were evident even in his earliest publications. "Every phenomenon [is] worthy of being studied for its own sake. Its mere existence entitles it to a full share of our attention; and the knowledge of its existence and evolution in space and time fully satisfies the student, without regard to the laws which it corroborates or which may be deduced from it"—thus he proclaimed in an 1887 essay, "The Study of Geography" (Stocking 1968, 644), in which he juxtaposed this principle against the principle of valuing single phenomena only as exemplifications of general laws. When he applied the principle in anthropological contexts he stressed the particular, the holistic, the historical. "In ethnology, all is individuality," Stocking quotes in his useful "Introduction: The Basic Assumptions of Boasian Anthropology," proceeding to point out that "the individuality that most concerned Boas was . . . that of the element in its 'surroundings,' which Boas defined not simply in the present, but as the product of 'the history of the people, the influence of the regions through which it passed in its migrations, and the people with whom it came in contact'" (1974, 4–5).

In one way like Henry Adams trying to reconstruct the history of Tahiti, Boas's particularist, historicist bent would lead to a far subtler sense of human difference than the monolinear theorists and general public knew. In his classic introduction to the *Handbook of American Indian Languages* he emphasizes (feeling he has to do this in 1911) that whereas American Indians were all simply "Indians" to the first explorers, "It was only when our knowledge of the Indian tribes increased, that differences between the various types of man inhabiting our continent became known. . . . Much later came a recognition of the fact that the Indians of our continent differ in type as much among themselves as do the members of other races" (1911, 6). (And of course the publication of that *Handbook* would itself be a factor in the increasingly specific knowledge and respect with which the diverse Indian peoples could be approached.)

But another effect of Boas's particularist approach—especially in its resistance to generalization—was its inconclusiveness. "The student must have a full grasp of all the forms of culture of the people he studies, before he can safely generalize," Boas insisted in 1905 (Stocking 1974, 184). As Stocking points out about Boas's work, "In each area, his emphasis was on the empirical study of the actual distribution of phenomena, and the collection and publication of large masses of data—whether head measurements or the texts of folk-tales and myths—to provide the basis for future inductive study" (1974, 15). Some have found it a flaw in his system that Boas never produced a theoretically definitive study, or that he avoided comparative theoretical constructs (see, for example, "Historical Particularism: Boas," in

Marvin Harris, 1968). Others discover a theoretical stance in Boas's very critiques of the theory of his day (see "The Boasians and the Critique of Evolutionism," in Adam Kuper 1988). And still others see his contribution as perfectly appropriate, as Margaret Mead insisted, in its providing for "the continuous possibilities of illumination from the material," and in "building an exhaustive corpus of materials which could be analyzed for negative as well as for positive points" (1959b, 32).

Boas's field research and his critical examination of fundamental terms, concepts, and techniques of anthropology had actually yielded a good deal of synthesizing general insight about human difference before his publication of *The Mind of Primitive Man*, at least within the several specific anthropological areas in which he had been working. In physical anthropology he had shown that there was a wide spectrum of differences within specific populations, with characteristics that largely overlapped those of other populations. And as Marshall Hyatt has pointed out, "Boas's most important discovery was the instability of the human form, which contradicted all previous knowledge" (1990, 110).

In linguistics he had disconnected language from specific preconceptions about race and evolutionary stage: linguistic difference was no indicator of racial or cultural capability. The languages of "primitive" peoples were no less complex, no less intraculturally functional than "civilized" languages. Furthermore, Boas is credited with importing a new sense of relativity into the study of languages. Marshall Sahlins contrasts Boas's sense of the arbitrariness of all languages with Morgan's implicit sense of the absoluteness of his own ("for Morgan, language is no more than perception articulate" [1976, 64]), an epistemological difference that would liberate Boas to discover a great deal about human difference. And Roman Jakobson considers Boas's notion that "each language may be arbitrary, but solely 'from the point of view of another language' in space and time," and decides that "Boas' task in the development of linguistics could be compared with the historic role of a Lobschevsky, an Einstein and other fighters against self-centered tradition," and that "ethnology and particularly linguistics was for Boas first and foremost a means to understand the other and perceive oneself from without" (1966, 133, 132, 131).

In folklore Boas had demonstrated that although certain myths and stories were shared by different peoples, their significances were adapted to the specific culture. They were not simply matters of racial propensity or geographic effects, nor were they a kind of pre-science, a directly symbolic interpretation of natural phenomena. He insisted that the issue of the existence of similar tales in different cultures was an extremely complex one, affected by specific historical forces and intercultural dissemination as well as by some elements of independent creation.

In ethnography his early relativism, his propensity to give priority to the category of culture as the most significant manifestation of difference, is even more obvious. He would become the American champion of the emic study of cultures, of the attempt to understand the others essentially in their own terms. In defining the purposes of his most ambitious early research foray, the 1897–1900 Jesup Expedition, he had set forth his historicist, culturally centered, linguistically relativistic, emic program in these terms:

> It seemed to me well to make the leading point of view . . . on the one hand an investigation of the historical relations of the tribes to their neighbors, on the other hand a presentation of the culture as it appears to the Indian himself. For this reason I have spared no trouble to collect the descriptions of customs and beliefs in the language of the Indians, because in these the points that seem important to him are emphasized, and the almost unavoidable distortion contained in the description given by the casual visitor and student is eliminated. (Quoted in Rohner 1966, 190–91)

Boas was not by any measure the sole practitioner of such studies of Amerindian peoples by American anthropologists: there were a number of turn-of-the-century studies along similar lines (as Melville Herskovits points out in explaining why British anthropologist Bronislaw Malinowski, who is often cited as one of the founders of the in-the-field participant-observer method for his 1922 *Argonauts of the Western Pacific*, is given somewhat less credit in the U.S. [1953]). But of the Americans' work Boas's would become the most concentrated, extensive, and methodologically informed. According to the very detailed accounting of Ronald Rohner, Boas ultimately was to make thirteen field trips to the Pacific Northwest, spending a total of twenty-nine months among the people (1966, 152), and according to Helen Codere, he published 8,978 pages of interpretation and texts of tales and such (1959, 62).

Such were his attempts—specific as well as general—to understand and to bridge human difference. In the framework of his interpretation truly significant difference between peoples inhered only in cultural particularity, not in categories, stages, races, or types. All general conceptualizations were relative, suspect. As he concluded in the introduction to his *Handbook of American Indian Languages*, after demonstrating the lack of correlation of physical type, language and culture within the earth's various populations, "we recognize thus that every classification of mankind must be more or less artificial, according to the point of view selected" (1911, 14).

The Mind of Primitive Man* actually presented a compendium of much of Boas's work up to that time, along with a good deal of interpretation of its intellectual and ethical implications. His language and rhetoric are aimed at a general audience in this book (more so than in most of his other writings), and in this consideration the title "The Mind of Primitive Man" is both an understatement of the book's rather more expansive content and a lure for readers of that time into deeper and more challenging waters than their surface expectations would warrant. According to their general knowledge (unless they were familiar with particular Indian people or were careful readers of any of the several empirically scrupulous studies of American Indians then available), the mind of primitive man was mainly a matter of strange superstitions, rudimentary technology, and brutish instinct. The representations in museum and world's fair exhibits, in popular magazines, newspapers, romance and adventure novels, and even in evolutionist theory reinforced such a condescending view of "primitives" as fascinating, somewhat awesome curiosities—observably inferior and needing the guidance and governance of well-meaning civilized people. What Boas would offer under this rubric, virtually rendering it ironic, was a challenge to his audience's whole understanding of human difference, an undermining not only of the regnant notions of race, of the primitive and of human evolution, but of their own sense of cultural superiority as well.

His approach was that of a rational persuader, his persona authoritative but patient, nonabrasive, only a touch condescending, not as touristy and specular as was Frazer's, not as presumptive as Morgan's or Freud's. His language is literal, logical, pedestrian; word choices are the obvious ones, presumably the most communicative but with a hedge of skepticism around many of the audience's favored abstractions. In his writing as in his ethnography Boas knew there were always strong emotional, largely unconscious motivations for beliefs and actions, and the rhetoric of *The Mind* shows his attempts to deal with them in his audience while explaining them in the people who were his subjects. Counteracting his audience's ethnocentricity—especially that emotional allegiance to cultural mores that becomes an

---

*The text I use in this discussion is the 1931 (New York: Macmillan) reprinting of the original 1911 edition based on "A Course of Lectures Delivered Before the Lowell Institute . . . and the National University of Mexico" and using material that Boas admits he "at various times dealt with . . . in brief essays," (v).

absolute of perception—is perhaps his biggest challenge. The anthropologist, Boas knew, could make people able to understand human difference only by making them able to perceive differently, to perceive with imagination, to make some change in their standpoint. At one point in his fourth chapter he makes a rather direct appeal to them, trying to get them to see as the anthropologist must see (and it is notable how much like a novelist's seeing is the kind of perception he is advocating):

> [T]he activities of the human mind exhibit an infinite variety of form among the peoples of the world. In order to understand these clearly, the student must endeavor to divest himself entirely of opinions and emotions based upon the peculiar social environment into which he is born. He must adapt his own mind, so far as feasible, to that of the people whom he is studying. The more successful he is in freeing himself from the bias based on the group of ideas that constitute the civilization in which he lives, the more successful he will be in interpreting the beliefs and actions of man. He must follow lines of thought that are new to him. He must participate in new emotions, and understand how, under unwonted conditions, both lead to actions. (98)

Boas begins *The Mind* tellingly enough with a chapter entitled "Racial Prejudices," but in its opening discussion of the relationship of civilized to primitive man (which he would delete from the text in a 1938 revision), he attempts to stand at a point near to the preconceptions of the audience. "Proud of his wonderful achievements, civilized man looks down upon the humbler members of mankind," he begins, risking condescension toward both his subject and his audience. "With pity he looks down upon those members of the human race who have not succeeded in subduing nature," Boas goes on, at least feigning understanding for the "civilized" attitude: "[w]hat wonder if civilized man considers himself a being of higher order as compared to primitive man" (1–2).

But, he goes on, "[b]efore accepting this conclusion which places the stamp of eternal inferiority upon whole races of man, we may well pause, and subject the basis of our opinions regarding the aptitude of different peoples and races to a searching analysis" (2). His next step is to question the assumption that superior achievements of a culture indicate superiority of its peoples' aptitudes. Thus he has attempted to get inside the confidence of the readers by temporarily taking their part, and then begun very logically and systematically to dismantle the infrastructure of their presumed biases. There's no great subtlety or skill to this opening gambit, but it makes Boas's intents and general strategy quite clear.

His assault is quite systematic. The first chapter tackles several obvious markers of difference and reinterprets their significance. Using a good deal of historical evidence he shows that superior or inferior levels of cultural achievement are largely attributable to historical causes, to patterns of war and peace, of commerce and communication, of conquest and colonialism. Another powerful marker of difference being the physiology and physical appearance of various peoples, the notion was then current—reinforced at least superficially by the Darwinian perspective—that those whose characteristics more nearly resembled those of the apes were lower on the scale of humanity. Boas insists that "the gap between man and animal is a wide one, and the variations between the races are slight as compared to it" (21). Additionally, although the Negro and the Mongol have physiognomic dimensions closer to those of the apes,

> the European shares lower characteristics with the Australian, both retaining in the strongest degree the hairiness of the animal ancestor, while the specifically human development of the red lip is developed most markedly in the negro. The proportions of the limbs of the negro are also more markedly distinct from the corresponding proportions in the higher apes than are those of the European. (22)

Thus, Boas concludes in relativizing this particular marker of difference/inferiority that "when we interpret these data in the light of modern biological concepts, we may say that the specifically human features appear with varying intensity in various races, and that the divergence from the animal ancestor has developed in varying directions" (22).

He does his best to undermine the notion that physical characteristics are indicators of mental ability. Theories concerning relative brain weight and skull capacity were especially prominent at that time, and several statistical studies attempted to identify the averages for the various races—the object being, of course, to rank them. There is, Boas acknowledges, "a decided difference in favor of the white race" in the extant studies, and although he raises crucial questions about how these data can be interpreted, he is unable to overcome the biological likelihood that "the greater the central nervous system, the higher the faculty of the race, and the greater its aptitude to mental achievements," or to deny the white race a modicum of superiority (25). There have been men of great genius who have had smaller than average brains, he notes; one study even showed that murderers as well as men of eminence had brains larger than average; poor nutrition could certainly account for smaller brain size; and the brains of women were, in keeping with their smaller structural size, ordinarily smaller than those of men. Such are his challenges to a simple racist interpretation, but finally the farthest his deconstruction of this line of thought can go is to recognize that there are "fundamental facts" of biology which "make it more than probable that increased size of the brain causes increased faculty, although the relation is not quite as immediate as is often assumed" (28). It is increasingly apparent in the course of this book that it is at least as concerned with racism and the treatment of American Negroes as it is with the mind of primitive man, and that this brain-size consideration, which Boas seems to feel might be an undeniable marker of racial inferiority, persists as an unignorable part of that concern.

In a pair of chapters on the influence of heredity and environment on human types, Boas interestingly begins with environment—there, of course, is where much of his previous work has focused, and there is where he wants the emphasis to fall. One of his main purposes is to dissociate the notions of race and the primitive (this despite his own occasional linguistic slips, like those on pages 12 and 39, in using "white" as the antonym of "primitive"). He insists that there is a great amount of variation within each "racial or social type," that every type has its own range from primitive to civilized, and that social status has a great deal to do with the placement within that range. Correlatively, the different races share a great many characteristics: statistically the vast midrange in the distribution of stature or skull capacity of any race will substantially overlap the midrange of the other races. As he concludes, "the differences between different types of man are, on the whole, small as compared to the range of variation in each type" (94).

In posing the question, "In how far are human types stable, in how far variable under the circumstances of environment?" (40) Boas can bring in his rather surprising study of the bodily characteristics of immigrant children while working toward an understanding of the primitive/civilized difference. "It has been my good fortune to be able to demonstrate the existence of a direct influence of environment upon the bodily form of man by a comparison of immigrants born in Europe and their descendants born in New York City," he boasts (53). The study itself involved parent-to-child comparisons of groups of South Italians, Central and Northern Europeans, and East European Jews, and it focused on head measurements, stature, weight, and hair color.

"The results," Boas claims, "have led to the unexpected result that the American-born descendants of these types differ from their parents. . . . It is furthermore remarkable that each type changes in a peculiar way. The head of the American-born Sicilian becomes rounder than that of the foreign-born. . . . The head of the . . . Central European . . . becomes more elongated," and so forth (54–55). Boas uses this material in this context to show that "[w]e are thus led to the conclusion that environment has an important effect upon the anatomical structure and physiological functions of man; and that for this reason differences of type and action between primitive and civilized groups of the same race must be expected" (75). Thus he works at reconstructing the concepts of race and primitive and civilized, at the same time establishing the importance of environment, of specific culture, as a determinant of human difference.

Environment surely influences human bodily form, Boas insists, but still admits that "these influences are of a quite secondary character when compared to the far-reaching influence of heredity. . . . The descendants of the negro will always be negroes; the descendants of whites, whites" (76). His chapter on heredity affirms the Mendelian doctrine (at that time still a somewhat controversial alternative to the Galtonian characteristic-averaging scheme) and employs it in emphasizing his idea of the variability within types. His theory of primitive difference then follows from the idea that the size of the group influences the range of variability: a small, relatively isolated group would have relatively few hereditary lines and a narrower range of characteristics, some of them possibly quite different from the species's norms, while a large and broadly connected group would have a much wider and more generically typical range available. (Theoretically, Boas calculates, over the past twenty generations one could conceivably have had over a million ancestors.)

Boas's fourth chapter shifts the focus of his argument from physical to mental differences, and in it he continues to maintain the focus on race. The question he means to confront is "Do differences exist in the organization of the human mind?" (104) He insists that "in the domain of psychology a confusion prevails still greater than in anatomy," as notions of race are confused with those of evolutionary stage and sociocultural development (101). Consistent with his schema for the preceding two chapters he intends to establish a clear distinction between elements of heredity and environment. As a preliminary, he attacks the prominent racist theorists of his day (Klemm, Wuttke, Nott, Gliddon, Carus, and DeGobineau). Each of their essentially white supremacist characterizations of the races of mankind he finds unsupportable and transparently self-aggrandizing:

> The belief in the higher hereditary powers of the white race has gained a new life with the modern doctrine of the prerogatives of the master-mind, which have found their boldest expression in Nietzsche's writings.

All such views are generalizations which either do not sufficiently take into account the social conditions of races, and thus confound cause and effect, or were dictated by scientific or humanitarian bias, by the desire to justify the institution of slavery, or to give the greatest freedom to the most highly gifted. (100–101)

Boas argues universal similarity in "the organization of the human mind" principally by analyzing three apparently uncivilized characteristics commonly attributed to "primitive" peoples: their inability to inhibit their impulses, their lack of power of attention, and their lack of capacity for original thought. His approach is cleverly effective: to undermine the ethnocentricity of his readers by positing a typical situation and reversing the perspective. An example is well worth quoting in full:

> the traveler or student measures the fickleness of the people by the importance which he attributes to the actions or purposes in which they do not persevere, and he weighs the impulse for outbursts of passion by his standard. Let me give an example. A traveler desirous of reaching his goal as soon as possible engages men to start on a journey at a certain time. To him time is exceedingly valuable. But what is time to primitive man, who does not feel the compulsion of completing a definite work at a definite time? While the traveler is fuming and raging over the delay, his men keep up their merry chatter and laughter, and cannot be induced to exert themselves except to please their master. Would not they be right in stigmatizing many a traveler for his impulsiveness and lack of control when irritated by a trifling cause like loss of time? Instead of this, the traveler complains of the fickleness of the natives, who quickly lose interest in the objects which the traveler has at heart. (106–7)

The lesson the emic anthropologist means to drive home along with the point about similar organization of the human mind is one about the relativity of emotions and values: "The proper way to compare the fickleness of the savage and that of the white is to compare their behavior in undertakings which are equally important to each" (107). And Boas does go on to cite a number of situations in which "savages" have been documented demonstrating extraordinary patience and self-control. Likewise he cites his own experience of natives' intense and extended powers of attention, claiming that the opposite experience of so many observers results because "[t]he questions put by the traveler seem mostly trifling to the Indian, and he naturally soon tires of a conversation carried on in a foreign language, and one in which he finds nothing to interest him" (111).

The notion of natives' lack of original thought Boas treats by allowing that for them "more customs are binding than in civilized society," but partially countering with examples from his own fieldwork (and that of others) of "the great frequency of the appearance of prophets," the frequent incidence of specific local reinterpretation of borrowed myths and beliefs, and "the increasing complexity of esoteric doctrines intrusted to the care of a priesthood" (112). Is there then essential difference in mentality between primitive and civilized man?

> I think these considerations illustrate that the differences between civilized man and primitive man are in many cases more apparent than real; that the social conditions, on account of their peculiar characteristics, easily convey the impression that the mind of primitive man acts in a way quite different from ours, while in reality the fundamental traits of the mind are the same. (114)

But still the ideas of similarity of mind and equality of capacity are darkened by the recollection that "differences of structure must be accompanied by differences of function," that given the "clear evidence of difference in structure between the races," and the fact that "a smaller size or lesser number of nervous elements would probably entail loss of mental energy, and paucity of connections in the central nervous system would produce sluggishness of the mind" (115), the best we can conclude with respect to universal human parity is that

> the average faculty of the white race is found to the same degree in a large proportion of individuals of all other races, and, although it is probable that some of these races may not produce as large a proportion of great men as our own race, there is no reason to suppose that they are unable to reach the level of civilization represented by the bulk of our own people. (123)

Convinced by those brain-size findings, Boas repeatedly qualifies his ideas about the equality of human mental capacity, at least in its upper reaches, thereby reintroducing race as a fundamental, determining factor in his analyses.

Boas concludes his consideration of primitive versus civilized mental traits by addressing the question "Has the organic basis for the faculty of man been improved by civilization, and particularly may that of primitive races be improved by this agency?" (118). His answer is necessarily and admittedly inconclusive. The anatomical changes produced by changed environment may certainly involve mental changes, but whether these are "progressive changes, or such as are transmitted by heredity" is "doubtful." Directly confronting his readers' likely bias, he declares that "It seems to me that the probable effect of civilization upon an evolution of human faculty has been much overestimated" (119). So much for that cultural myth, so important as an underlying assumption of the evolutionist-colonialists.

In taking on the subject of the relation of language to race and difference Boas uses much of the material from his *Handbook of the American Indian Languages*, especially its demonstration that the classification of peoples by race or physical type does not coincide with classifications by culture, and that classification by language is not congruent with either. People of different races or types often share common cultures or languages, people of the same type often have different languages or cultures, any of the three aspects can change at a different rate than the others, and so forth. Race, culture, and language simply do not coincide in any useful way, he insists, and he demonstrates in detail that "It is obvious . . . that attempts to classify mankind, based on the present distribution of type, language, and culture, must lead to different results, according to the point of view taken" (133). He points this demonstration directly against racist thought, embedding within it a summary-discussion of the radical disagreements among race theorists as to what constitutes a race and how many races there are, and specifically attacking the notion of a superior Aryan race: "Aryan" is a purely linguistic category, he insists, and

the assumption that a certain definite people whose members have always been related by blood must have been the carriers of this language throughout history, and the other assumption, that a certain cultural type must have always belonged to this people—are purely arbitrary ones, and not in accord with the observed facts. (134)

But his demonstration also destroys the intricate universal patterning of the monolinear evolutionists, although Boas does not mention this fact. The master interpretation of the development of mankind through the stages of savagery, barbarism, and civilization, so fervently initiated by Morgan and championed by Powell and the Bureau of American Ethnology, was absolutely dependent on precisely such cross-correlations as Boas was denying. The whole point of the three-stage evolutionists' model was that barbarism was barbarism in all respects, that a culture that had reached whatever level of evolution in social organization would be at a corresponding level in religion, technology, language, and all. And Boas here removes the foundation of such ethnology, still official in many quarters, without even making a point of so doing. The full attack will come a bit later in the book, but the audience has already been subliminally prepared.

Continuing his assault on the prevailing notions of difference via linguistics, Boas turns to the question of language ranking, "whether the languages developed by any one stock bear marks of superiority or inferiority" (140). To the common ethnocentric judgment that the languages of primitives lack distinctness he invokes the aforementioned idea that the perception of distinctness is a culture-specific endeavor. To the notion that primitive languages "lack the power of classification and abstraction" (142) he likewise shows first of all that classification is itself culture-specific. For the Eskimo, "the seal in different conditions is expressed by a variety of terms. One word is the general term for "seal"; another one signifies the "seal basking in the sun"; a third one, a "seal floating on a piece of ice"; not to mention the many names for the seals of different ages and for male and female" (146). Then he goes on to show that classification itself and the degree and kind of abstraction are also relative to the needs and habits of the daily living of the particular people. Thus, by implication, every people has more or less the language that is sufficient and appropriate for it. "[T]hus we have found that language does not furnish the much-looked-for means of discovering differences in the mental status of different races" (154).

Setting aside a chapter for "The Evolutionary Viewpoint," Boas begins his assault on it in the same (rather beguiling) way he began the book, agreeing with the audience's preconceptions. He describes a number of human phenomena—the development of social organizations, of inventions, of agriculture and animal domestication, of realistic artistic depiction, of religion—that certainly manifest a course of evolution that must be apparent to all. But having acknowledged the apparent, Boas calls into question the universalizing theoretical framework of monolinear evolutionism. "A grand structure has been reared," he explains (mimicking the tone of the evolutionist enthusiasts), "in which we see our present civilization as the necessary outcome of the activities of all the races of man that have risen in one grand procession, from the simplest beginnings of culture, through periods of barbarism, to the stage of civilization that they now occupy." That grand structure depends on a specific interpretation of a great number of apparent cultural parallels and, he admonishes, "it seems desirable to understand more clearly what this theory of parallelism of cultural development implies" (181). One thing it implies is an integrated, sequential, parallel evolution in all cultures that is simply not supported by archaeological evidence.

The theory of parallel development, if it is to have any significance, would require that among all branches of mankind the steps of invention should have followed, at least approximately, in the same order, and that no important gaps should be found. The facts, so far as known at the present time, are entirely contrary to this view. We find, for instance, large areas of the world inhabited by people well advanced in the arts of life, but who have never made the discovery of pottery, one of the essential steps in the advance of civilization. Pottery is not found in the extreme southern parts of Africa, in Australia, in northeastern Siberia, in the whole northwestern part of North America, and in the extreme south of South America. (182–83)

Another implication of the theory is "the assumption that the same cultural features must always have developed from the same causes, and that all variations are only minor details of the grand uniform type of evolution" (184). This Boas refutes by insisting as he had earlier that logically, like results could certainly be produced by unlike causes, and by marshalling empirically based evidence of such exceptions. His attack on totemism, for example, (which Freud perhaps should have known about) explains that

I am convinced that . . . the phenomenon is not a single psychological problem, but embraces the most diverse psychological elements. In some cases the people believe themselves to be descendants of the animal whose protection they enjoy. In other cases an animal or some other object may have appeared to an ancestor of the social group, and may have promised to become his protector, and the friendship between the animal and the ancestor was then transmitted to his descendants. In still other cases a certain social group in a tribe may have the power of securing by magical means and with great ease a certain kind of animal or of increasing its numbers, and the supernatural relation may be established in this way. It will be recognized that here again the anthropological phenomena which are in outward appearances alike are, psychologically speaking, entirely distinct, and that consequently psychological laws covering all of them cannot be deduced from them. (190–91)

Boas urges a very specific counter to the tendency to generalize facilely from perceptions of cultural similarity: "In order to interpret correctly these similarities in form, it is necessary to investigate their historical development" (193).

On the Spencerian theory (and widely popular conception) that evolution necessarily involves a progress from simple to complex, Boas grants that industrial progress and other activities involving reasoning do indeed show such a developmental pattern, but that other endeavors often do not. For instance, drawing on his extensive knowledge of primitive languages he claims that they are,

> on the whole, complex. Minute differences in point of view are given expression by means of grammatical forms; and the grammatical categories of Latin, and still more so those of modern English, seem crude when compared to the complexity of psychological or logical forms which primitive languages recognize, but which in our speech are disregarded entirely. On the whole, the development of languages seems to be such, that the nicer distinctions are eliminated, and that it begins with complex and ends with simpler forms, although it must be acknowledged that opposite tendencies are not by any means absent. (194)

Thus Boas invalidates the "grand structure" of the evolutionists primarily by methodological, epistemological means, countering their essentially metaphysical interpretation of universal process with a particularist, empiricist, historicist approach.

Having disposed of the monolinear evolutionist view and its powerful preconceptions and prejudgments, Boas attempts to establish what really are "Some Traits of Primitive Culture." He puts race aside for this discussion, having determined "there is no close relation between race and culture" (196), and he begins with a painstaking demonstration that for all people, civilized as well as primitive, habits and beliefs proceed from emotional, subrational, culturally inherited sources, and that their rationales and explanations are essentially only secondary elaborations. The difference, then, between primitive and civilized inheres in the fact that the civilized have a highly developed tradition of rational interpretation and a powerful trust in it; they hold to their beliefs and habits less fervently and are more amenable to change. Psychologically, Boas is not far from the Freudian and Jungian views of the operation of the rational and the irrational in all human mentality, although without their concept of deep unconscious motivation. His concern is more with the force of tradition within each culture and the means of overcoming it, which he sees as the dialectic of human progress.

The difference in the mental activity of the primitive man, Boas claims, "is not founded on any fundamental peculiarity of the mind of primitive man, but lies, rather, in the character of the traditional ideas by means of which each new perception is interpreted." That is, since "[t]he instruction given to the child of primitive man is not based on centuries of experimentation, but consists of the crude experience of generations," and since "neither among civilized men nor among primitive men the average individual carries to completion the attempt at causal explanation of phenomena, but carries it only so far as to amalgamate it with other previously known facts, we recognize that the result of the whole process depends entirely upon the character of the traditional material" (202, 203, 204). On that cultural basis the primitive mind is generally more subjective and more susceptible to emotion in its reading of experience, more holistic and less discriminative in interpreting causality, more conservatively traditional.

In terms of Boas's model the phenomenon of taboo is a frozen vestigial tradition or ritual, totemism a tribalist fusion of traditional social and religious beliefs. Their basis in *culture* is Boas's point (Freud's later model would be quite different). Ritual is for Boas one of the principal markers of the primitive: "In our day the domain of ritual is restricted, but in primitive culture it pervades the whole life" (229). Consistent with his idea of the power of emotion and cultural inheritability he sees evidence of specific rituals being independently, subrationally persistent: "It has been proved in many cases that rites are more stable than their explanations; that they symbolize different ideas among different people and at different times" (229–30).

Myth and its symbolism he explains similarly:

The same kind of tales are current over enormous areas, but the mythological use to which they are put is locally quite different. Thus an ordinary adventure relating to the exploits of some animal may sometimes be made use of to explain some of its peculiar characteristics. At other times it may be made use of to explain certain customs, or even the origin of certain constellations in the sky. There is not the slightest doubt in my mind that the tale as such is older than its mythological significance. The characteristic feature of the development of the nature myth is, first, that the tale has associated itself with attempts to explain cosmic conditions . . . ; and, secondly, that when primitive man became concious [*sic*] of the cosmic problem, he ransacked the entire field of his knowledge until he happened to find something that could be fitted to the problem in question, giving an explanation satisfactory to his mind. While the classification of concepts, the types of association, and the resistance to change of automatic acts, developed unconsciously, many of the secondary explanations are due to conscious reasoning. (234–35)

Thus for Boas the significances of myths are not generic or essential but only culturally and temporally specific. And furthermore, he sees primitive myths as ultimately societally based. In contrast to civilized societies' attempts to explain natural phenomena scientifically in terms of "the principle of causality," Boas asserts, is primitive societies' regular association of observations relating to cosmic phenomena with purely human happenings. . . . It seems to my mind that the characteristic trait of nature myths is the association between the observed cosmic events and what might be called a novelistic plot based on the form of social life with which people are familiar. (230–31)

The widespread similarity of certain ideas and myths among various far-flung peoples he suggests might be explained by Adolf Bastian's notion of "elementary ideas," which to Boas seems very like "[Wilhelm] Dilthey's conception of the limitation of possible types of philosophy." The notion of "the fundamental sameness of forms of human thought in all forms of culture, no matter whether they were advanced or primitive" involves, Boas admits, "a certain kind of mysticism," but it nevertheless serves to explain the apparent uniformity underlying so much diversity of cultural expressions (171–72). Such is Boas's rather mundane hypothetical equivalent of Jung's archetypes.

Seemingly one of the most important "elementary ideas" of primitive thought is "the idea of the solidarity of the horde," and in its modification over time Boas sees a very significant difference between civilized and primitive societies. (His demonstration is also an implicit lesson in social morality to a country rife with racism, and a Western world fulminating with rival nationalisms and standing on the doorsill of World War I.) The cumulative result of humankind's effort "to eliminate traditional elements, and to gain a clearer and clearer insight into the hypothetical basis of our reasoning" is that "reasoning becomes more and more logical" and what is handed down "has been thought out and worked out more thoroughly and more carefully." The deep suspicion of the Other, "founded largely on the idea of the solidarity of the horde, and of the feeling that it is the duty of every member of the horde to destroy all possible enemies," is gradually outgrown, Boas says, in the advance of reasoning and of the understanding of the reasoning processes, and "[w]e can trace the gradual broadening of the feeling of fellowship during the advance of civilization" (206–7).

Just as Boas sees societies tending to become (evolutionarily?) more moral by becoming more skeptical about their inherited traditions, more impartial in their thinking, and more epistemologically self-aware, he also can envision them becoming more relativistic, more able at least to sense (since they can never really know) the rightness of another culture's ways and views as seen from their own perspective. And this is what gives moral importance to the discipline of anthropology: "The general theory of valuation of human activities, as developed by anthropological research, teaches us a higher tolerance than the one which we now profess" (208–9).

The tenth and final chapter, "Race Problems in the United States," stands as a kind of coda to the rest of the book. Boas here acknowledges shifting to a sociopolitical focus and intent: "We will now turn to the question what these results of our inquiry teach us in regard to the problems that confront our modern civilization, particularly our nation." But of course the assault on racism and the insinuation of more liberal and humane alternatives has been a subtext of the entire study, just as it has been an abiding theme of all of Boas's anthropological work. His strategy here continues—intensifies, actually—the attack on "the hypothetical character of many of the generally accepted assumptions," although he regrets the need for this, since "the political question of dealing with all these groups of people is of great and immediate importance" (251–52), and the fate of millions is in danger of being determined according to the terms of unscientific, emotionally based, atavistic notions. (This turn-of-the-century period was a time, we need to keep in mind, of the widespread influence of such racist theorists as De Gobineau, Paul Topinard, Josiah Nott, and others, whose heritage would continue to fulminate in Madison Grant's 1916 *The Passing of the Great Race*.)

The first racist idol Boas attacks is the notion of "mongrelization": the presumed deleterious effect on the racial purity of the American population of indiscriminate immigration and intermixing. There can be no mongrelization without a prior state of purity, and Boas demonstrates through an extensive survey of the history of European populations—their migrations, conquests, and intermixings—that "we may dismiss the assumption of the existence of a pure type in any part of Europe, and of a process of mongrelization in America different from anything that has taken place for thousands of years in Europe" (260). Thus Boas, aiming his critique directly at his predominantly European-descended audience, has undercut the basis of that particular brand of ethnocentric superiority.

Further, he shows that the fear that immigration will cause "a degradation of type by the influx of so-called 'lower' types" is allayed by his earlier finding that "the types which come to our shores do not remain stable, but show such important modifications, that many of the differences of the human types of Europe seem rather ephemeral than permanent, determined more by environment than heredity" (261, 262). He admits that the full effects of intermixture cannot be foreseen, but "[w]ould it not be a safer course to investigate the truth or fallacy of each theory rather than excite the public mind by indulgence in the fancies of our speculation?" (264). Hypothetically calculating the mathematics of population intermixture, he points out that "if the choice of mates is left entirely to accident" and the two populations are equal in number, . . . "there will be in the fourth generation less than one person in ten thousand of pure descent." But whatever the population proportions, "it is obvious that intermixture, as soon as the social barriers have been removed, must be exceedingly rapid" (267). But of course those barriers, especially the legalized and quasi-legalized enforcements of atavistic perceptions of difference, are precisely the problem.

Focusing his final discussion on "the negro problem in the United States," Boas reinvokes his conclusions that "no proof of an inferiority of the negro type could be given, except that it seemed possible that perhaps the race would not produce quite so many men of highest genius as other races" (268). (Is it his dismay or distrust concerning that latter conclusion that prompts him to embed it in a triad of weakening qualifiers: *it seemed possible, perhaps*, and *quite so many?*) And again he discounts difference, recalling his earlier point that differences between the races are much less significant than those within them.

That context having been established, he launches into a survey of a great variety of accomplishments—social, material, artistic, and other—of Negro cultures in Africa. Using anthropological information, some of which had informed his 1906 address at Atlanta University that had greatly inspired then-history-professor W. E. B. Du Bois, he demonstrates that "the traits of African culture as observed in the aboriginal home of the negro are those of a healthy primitive people, with a considerable degree of personal initiative, with a talent for organization, and with imaginative power, with technical skill and thrift." And for purposes of this particular argument he adds, "There is nothing to prove that licentiousness, shiftless laziness, lack of initiative, are fundamental characteristics of the race. Everything points out that these qualities are the result of social conditions rather than of hereditary traits" (271). Making that more specific, Boas goes on,

> The traits of the American negro are adequately explained on the basis of his history and social status. The tearing-away from the African soil and the consequent complete loss of the old standards of life, which were replaced by the dependency of slavery and by all it entailed, followed by a period of disorganization and by a severe economic struggle against heavy odds, are sufficient to explain the inferiority of the status of the race, without falling back upon the theory of hereditary inferiority. (272)

Thus, Boas teaches, "there is every reason to believe that the negro, when given facility and opportunity, will be perfectly able to fulfill the duties of citizenship as well as his white neighbor" (273). That

word *neighbor* was probably chosen very strategically for its sublimi-
nal ethical effect.

Boas then attacks racist attitudes directly, trying to deny them any
shred of legitimacy. There is no real "race instinct" of the whites, he
claims, putting the term in quotation marks like some kind of vestigial
exhibit. It's just the old fear of the lower, less privileged social classes
by those of higher status, "an expression of social conditions that are
so deeply ingrained in us that they assume a strong emotional value."
We need more scientific study, he repeatedly urges, as an antidote to
vestigial superstitions and as guidance toward policy in such vastly
important matters, and "I think we have reason to be ashamed to con-
fess that the scientific study of these questions has never received the
support either of our government or of any of our great scientific institutions" (274).

Research is needed especially with regard to our understanding of
the mulatto: "we hardly know anything on this subject" (274). The
prevalent notion that the mulatto's "vitality is lower" is neither supported by research nor adequately accounted for in terms of heredity,
Boas claims, again interested in turning the causation toward social
factors. But his discussion of mulattoes, because of the lack of hard
scientific information, is spottily organized and highly conjectural.
"It seems reasonably certain," he says, that in the distant future the
number of full-blooded negroes will decrease and there will be "a
continued increase of the amount of white blood in the negro community" (275), but the effects of this do not seem apparent. Intermixture is quite natural and will increase wherever it is not rigorously
prohibited: "that there is no racial sexual antipathy is made sufficiently clear by the size of our mulatto population" (275–76). The
policy of Southern states to prevent racial intermixture Boas characterizes as "erroneous," and this and the plea for more scientific study
is all the persuasion he can marshal for a troubling subject on which
reliable scientific information is scant.

Finally, as an *envoi* to the whole of *The Mind of Primitive Man*,
Boas appeals to his audience directly, urging on them again and quite
specifically his ethic of applied relativity:

> I hope the discussions contained in these pages have shown that the data
> of anthropology teach us a greater tolerance of forms of civilization dif-
> ferent from our own, and that we should learn to look upon foreign races
> with greater sympathy, and with the conviction, that, as all races have con-
> tributed in the past to cultural progress in one way or another, so they will
> be capable of advancing the interests of mankind, if we are only willing to
> give them a fair opportunity. (278)

Boas's program was of enormous consequence in reconfiguring twentieth-century anthropology, and this despite its incomplete and somewhat ambiguous theoretical basis and the many variations introduced by his students/followers. Subsequently and consequently, cultural anthropology would be more scientifically sophisticated in its approaches and methods; more relativistic in its language and interpretations; more particularistic, more historicist, more emic in its research; and newly focused on culture as determining human belief and endeavor, both collectively and individually.

And of course it utterly reconfigured the notion of the primitive. The old polygenist and evolutionist usages, supported by biological or progressivist frameworks, would not survive in ethnographic interpretation for much longer, and depth psychology would draw the term ever closer to its own set of significations. In the larger nonscientific community the term still had considerable currency and potency, but the questions and qualifications introduced by Boasian anthropology were substantial increments of understanding.

Modernist literary writers tended to deconstruct notions such as the primitive too, although very much in their own terms and by their own means, not at all traceable to direct anthropological influence. Likewise their abandoning (implicitly repudiating) narrative omniscience and experimenting with points-of-view that were local, fallible, eccentric; in particularizing the details of cultural mores and the struggles of individuals within the predetermining webs of society they were envisioning the human world in terms very like the relativized standpoint and relativized culture of Boas and his followers. Granted that fallible point-of-view and social determinism had long been staples of Western literature, still, in the twentieth-century exploration into mind-realm beyond culture-bound absolutes, the new movement in anthropology put the availability and justification for such forays just a bit closer at hand.

7

Relativizing Interpretation: William Faulkner and *Light in August*

LITERARY SCHOLARS HAVE LONG SINCE DISPELLED THE MYTH—probably derived from the subject matter of his books and his own propensity for self-image making—of Faulkner's being some kind of provincial, folksy prodigy. As more has been brought to light about his life and letters, his acquaintanceships and his known reading, a clearer picture has emerged of an author very well read and very much into the culture of his times. But he seems to have accessed that culture (and the human nature he saw as comprising its basis) through experience and literature—rarely through science or other predominantly intellectual disciplines. He was steeped in the Western literary tradition—the Bible, Shakespeare, *Moby-Dick*, *Don Quixote*, Balzac, Dostoevski, Keats, and so forth; in contemporaries Joyce and Conrad as well as his American cohort—Hemingway, Dos Passos, Sherwood Anderson, Hergesheimer, Aiken, O'Neill, and on and on, and in the talk about them and their concerns; and of course steeped, too, in the talk and the foibles and legends of his region and his own little postage stamp of soil. But other than his knowledge of the one-volume abridgement of *The Golden Bough* (and isn't it for most purposes a literary performance too?) there is scant evidence of engagement with extraliterary writings.

Take, for example, his relationship to Freudianism. Faulkner himself brushed off the allegations of Freudian influence so many critics wanted to see as the basis for the morbid psychology they found in his books: "What little of psychology I know the characters I have invented and playing poker have taught me. Freud I'm not familiar with," he remarked late in his career; and as his close friend, mentor and promoter Phil Stone recalled, "He wouldn't read Freud. I tried to get him to. I taught *at* him, but he wouldn't listen. He wasn't interested in psychology." But still, in his fiction he seems to have been able to reflect, perhaps intentionally to intimate, concepts and figures

191

from contemporary psychological discourse.* The ethnographic insight in his works, let me state at the outset, seems to have been his
own, relatable only very hypothetically and distantly to popular and
historical sources. We won't presume to find influence of anthropological theory here, but rather some ingenious analogues to its definitions of difference and its methods of describing cultures.

Coming of age in the South, Faulkner lived in the presence of a very
conspicuous, often primitivised Other, and he seems to have inherited
and to have carried with him for a considerable time some very fixed
ideas about racial difference and the nature of that Other. But at the
same time, as his biographers show, he had much less surety about
himself—which life to lead, which career to follow, which literary
styles to adopt, which image to project to the outside world in his
dress, his stories about himself, his attitudes. He seems to have been
on a multiple quest to discover who he really was and how to conceal
himself from discovery: essentially, how to take on guises that would
give him self-definition, autonomy, and at the same time character in
the eyes of the world. His amazing successes came by way of his
imagination: in the work of his imagination he could intensely, virtually emically inhabit the minds and worlds of characters often only
very marginally like himself. And as his career developed his vision
widened, as did the empathy which that sort of first-person compre-
hension of other characters entailed, giving him greater insight even
across the boundaries of difference.

His modernist experiments with polyvocality in *The Sound and the
Fury* and *As I Lay Dying* had taken him across lines of class and age
and gender—even past the boundaries of mental competence and san-
ity. Underneath the characters' turmoil Faulkner the maker held
back, feeling and articulating all that sound and fury vicariously, judging or interpreting only implicitly, and never directly revealing anything about himself. With *Light in August*, then, he would employ a
narrator who could considerably broaden and sharpen the social vision projected in the earlier novels (*Flags in the Dust* and *Sanctuary*
included), inhabit again a highly differentiated set of individual characters, and at the same time, in vividly construing the mentality and
ambiguous social position of a presumed mulatto, test the South's ultimate boundary of difference.

Light in August presented difference from the inside of the other

---

*The quotes are from Gwynn and Blotner 1995, 268 and Richardson 1969, 210.
Faulkner scholars offer a great variety of interpretations of his connection to Freud,
none definitive, and each of them (including mine) conforming to a particular view
of his creativity and intellectuality.

side with its depiction of Joe Christmas (as Arii Taimai, Brutus Jones, and Jim Harris had also been depicted), while the anthropologists of the day were still working on techniques for attaining emic, Boasian understanding purely from their own side of the transaction. More recent ethnographers try to cross that line, to concoct texts with what James Clifford describes as "polyphonic authority," that decenter the participant-observer and employ a dialogic or multivocal technique (Clifford and Marcus 1986, 53–54). Faulkner's *Light* is interesting in this context: *fictionally* polyphonic, with a narrator/arranger trying to achieve the effect of polyphony and operating on the assumption that events in human experience are *events-as-perceived*, framed and mediated and interpreted in individual and often peculiar ways. Of course imitating the speech and the mental categories of fictional characters and the interpretations they make of each other, in their world and their terms, is a tradition of novelistic presentation that reaches back in English language literature to the time of *Humphrey Clinker*, but Faulkner's relativization of the polyphony has some original and distinctly modernist aspects.

Not only does it nonjudgmentally present the disparate characters in their own and each others' and the larger community's terms, but it further diversifies the presentation by developing each of the numerous story-matrices in its own specific fashion. Each individual story emerges in its own narrative type and tone, and draws significance from its own system of symbols and analogical and mythological referents, but is still part of a diverse ensemble including all the others. The novel's overall pattern thus has strong elements of discontinuity and of internal intertextuality, its viewpoints conglomerated, incompletely coordinated. To read it is to experience tragedy and fabliau, saga and bucolic tall tale, *bildungsroman*, detective story, romantic comedy, Balzacian social drama, Gothic tale of the unwilling slide into primitivism, and genre dramas of the tragic mulatto, sexual obsession, emotional paralysis, and so forth. At the same time, and quite situationally, the novel evokes various elements of classic, religious, historical, and regional myth and history, psychoanalytic theory, and so forth.

The entropy of the novel is essential; its elements remain in some ways disparate; its characters' travails are self-contained often not only as personal concerns but as literary performance. But the powerful suggestiveness of this assemblage will keep readers and critics fascinated for a good while to come. Critics with a poststructuralist bent have recently been making the best sense out of the novel, stressing what Martin Kreiswirth, for example, calls "the wholly dialogical and thus indeterminate nature of the text's ordering of materials." He concludes his analysis of the novel with this observation:

> The different narratives cannot come together but can only keep each other, as it were, in line; through a carefully orchestrated process of mutual subversion and deconstruction, the reader repeatedly experiences new and unstable horizons of expectation and, more importantly, the vanishing points of those horizons. *Light in August* thus keeps both the individual narrative voices and the silences between those voices inexhaustibly present. It is this kind of truly polyphonic structure that Bakhtin sees as the special province and ultimate goal of the novel as a genre. (1987, 77–78)

In the late stages of the writing process Faulkner did very careful carpentry (see especially Regina Fadiman's 1975 study of the formation of the text—*Faulkner's "Light in August": A Description and Interpretation of the Revisions*), but the prior matters of what to include and how extensively, how to develop it, where to place it and how to focus it seem to have been products of intuitive insight—his going off into whatever felt like it had promise—rather than of any more rationalistic or preplanned program. This is Michael Millgate's interpretation too:

> Faulkner exercised a wholly new degree of structural freedom in . . . allowing each narrative sequence to expand according to its own inherent logic, introducing each new sequence and each new character at precisely the point required in order to throw the maximum illumination upon some nodal point in the action—usually one of those moments of arrested time that he sought so persistently to explore and understand in terms of the full multiplicity and complexity of all their implications in the present and all of their antecedents from the past. (1987, 34)

As Faulkner would explain in an interview long after its composition (Gwynn and Blotner 1995, 199), the "light" of *Light in August* was a personally evocative aura; very likely the story matrices themselves came from that same deep, preconscious, intuitive zone. Although the product of submitting to such a subconscious/conscious area of imagination might have been simple incoherence or the mindless repetition of cultural bias, another potential product (and the one Faulkner seems to be striving to attain) is a de-intellectualized vision, in which feeling and empathy and the subtlest sense of human happenstance refocus perception at a level beneath the abstractions and sureties of what one thinks one knows. Thus, in the art of fiction there can be this potential—nonscientific and entirely within the imagination of the author—to attain the ambition of the ethnographer of evading at least partially the ego- and ethnocentric determinants of perception, determinants Boas and Jung saw as "tainted" secondary elaborations. Faulkner's *Light* is another of his exercises—more freely imagined, more broadly ambitious than its predecessors—in nontheoretical knowing.

To bring it off he needed a very particular type of narrator. The narrator of *Light* is protean, able (in either direct or indirect discourse) to position himself variously as character, as witness to characters' words and doings, or as master-compiler and juxtaposer—using at any particular point whatever perspective maximizes that fictional moment's significance and intensity. Critic Francois Pitavy in a careful survey of the gradations of this narrator's involvement points up its fluidity: "the distinction is often blurred between the dramatization of a character's inner consciousness and the narration or description by an omniscient author" (1982, 67). This narrator has a subtle and very comprehensive sense of the context and implications of human actions—"what's on it" in any human situation—and he is highly literate, with an ability to relate the characters' travails to literary and mythic analogues. He has a deep sense of the way history can determine the lives of some of his characters—even beneath the level of their awareness. He recognizes the powerful interaction of society and the individual, and has an ability to identify situations that reveal important characteristics of the culture and of human makeup in their working-out. As Arthur Kinney observes, "The final focus . . . is never on fact, but is rather on the perception of fact or the alternative ways of seeing facts" (1978, 8); thus the novel relativizes explanatory interpretation. It is as if a human community is too diverse, too multiply and obscurely motivated to be represented in absolute terms. The truth is in the ensemble, and to some extent in the very discontinuity of that ensemble.

The novel is a paradoxical performance: a decidedly fictive, highly manipulative piece of storytelling; yet, insofar as it is given over to intuition and to what-would-likely-happen, it constitutes a subtle reading of the object society, and one that deconstructs society's standard categories and judgments along the way. What it does by way of resignifying human difference and difference's markers, such as race and primitiveness, is especially important. What are ordinarily taken to be essential differences are revealed as social constructions in this context. When even the narrative approaches vary from folk fabliau to high tragedy to detective story, and the metaphorical interpretive frames vary from Dionysian to Marian to Freudian, all bets are off on the novel's having a central vision that presents itself as unified and absolute. Each of the narrative and interpretive frames has its own subset value-system, and none can finally singly prevail. Reading the novel is an experience in the relativity of interpretation; as André Bleikasten puts this Faulknerian message, "To begin to know the world, then, is to acknowledge that the meanings we bring to it are little more than the precarious fictions of our desires and the erratic impositions of our wills" (1990, 356).

   Lena Grove is the starting and ending point of the novel, and part of the novel's relativity accrues from her radical distance from the travails of its male protagonists. Whatever happens to Joe Christmas is beyond her interest or her ken and affects her only indirectly. Gail Hightower is no real person to her, despite his having delivered her baby and having experienced the exhilaration of a rare (though temporary) triumph because of it. His final ethical realizations (in which she does not figure), seemingly philosophically ultimate in the narrative, are actually penultimate, in a way counterpoised by a casual observer's story of Lena's subsequent wandering. Byron's baffled relocation of his life and interests on her behalf seem to leave her virtually unaffected, simply going her own way, following her own deepest whim, with him increasingly present, perhaps inevitable in her future, but clearly ancillary to it. As critic Olga Vickery has pointed out, Lena's presence and perspective "dispel . . . the obsessions of society" (1964, 80).
   Take one of Lena's typically low-intensity passages—of an anonymous driver taking her into Jefferson—and note the narrator's fluidity in moving from external observer to summarizer of Lena's thoughts to transcriber of them, whichever location enables him to maximize (for this bit of the storytelling) both humor and dramatic crosscurrent. Note, too, how this fluid positioning enables him to represent Lena's inattentiveness, her naive, self-absorbed disengagement, as if to demonstrate that there are other preoccupations, other perspectives than are the concerns of this particular time and place:

   The driver does not look at her. "How far have you come, looking for him?"
   "From Alabama. It's a right fur piece."
   He does not look at her. His voice is quite casual. "How did your folks come to let you start out, in your shape?"
   "My folks are dead. I live with my brother. I just decided to come on."
   "I see. He sent you word to come to Jefferson."

She does not answer. He can see beneath the sunbonnet her calm pro-
file. The wagon goes on, slow, timeless. The red and unhurried miles un-
roll beneath the steady feet of the mules, beneath the creaking and
clanking wheels. The sun stands now high overhead; the shadow of the
sunbonnet now falls across her lap. She looks up at the sun. "I reckon it's
time to eat," she says. He watches from the corner of his eye as she opens
the cheese and crackers and the sardines, and offers them.
"I wouldn't care for none," he says.
"I'd take it kind for you to share."
"I wouldn't care to. You go ahead and eat."
She begins to eat. She eats slowly, steadily, sucking the rich sardine oil
from her fingers with slow and complete relish. Then she stops, not
abruptly, yet with utter completeness, her jaw stilled in midchewing, a
bitten cracker in her hand and her face lowered a little and her eyes blank,
as if she were listening to something very far away or so near as to be
inside her. Her face has drained of color, of its full, hearty blood, and she
sits quite still, hearing and feeling the implacable and immemorial earth,
but without fear or alarm. "It's twins at least," she says to herself, without
lip movement, without sound. Then the spasm passes. She eats again. The
wagon has not stopped; time has not stopped. The wagon crests the final
hill and they see smoke.
"Jefferson," the driver says.
"Well, I'll declare," she says. "We are almost there, aint we?"
It is the man now who does not hear. He is looking ahead, across the
valley toward the town on the opposite ridge. Following his pointing
whip, she sees two columns of smoke: the one the heavy density of burning coal above a tall stack, the other a tall yellow column standing apparently from among a clump of trees some distance beyond the town.
"That's a house burning," the driver says. "See?"
But she in turn again does not seem to be listening, to hear. "My, my,"
she says; "here I aint been on the road but four weeks, and now I am
in Jefferson already. My, my. A body does get around." (Faulkner 1990,
28–30)

It seems at first like a simple country anecdote, but it has a complex
charge of meanings about the variousness of humanity and of human
situations. The narrator sits back, amused, phlegmatic, seemingly letting the scene develop in a way in which it reveals its own humor, its
own sagacity, to a curious reader. And what it shows is Lena profoundly attuned inwardly to her own developing biological and ma-
ternal destiny and amazed at the result of her perambulating, radically
disengaged from the curiosities and concerns of the others around
her. Later we learn of the simultaneity of this scene: Joanna is dead;
the house is burning; folks are gathering to search out the "nigger
murderer"; Christmas is hurtling himself into a circular, self-

contending, self-destroying getaway; Hightower is about to have his depressive self-exile violated by what he most fears; and yes, "A body does get around."

While the fable of Lena is like a backcountry tall tale (counter to all rational expectation she actually finds Lucas and has him presented to her and their baby!), the narrator's representation of her evokes resonances of *The Golden Bough* and the Christian narrative of the Nativity. This technique, much commented on by Faulkner critics, gives his characters generally a great deal more depth, more potential for diverse significance, than would be the case if they were depicted purely naturalistically. It is also a technique that suggests Faulkner's familiarity with contemporary notions such as Frazer's about pre-Christian ritual, Jung's about imagery derived from the archetypes of the collective unconscious, and T.S. Eliot's about the "mythic method" that could be "a way of controlling, of ordering, of giving a shape and a significance to the immense panorama of futility and anarchy which is contemporary history" (1923, 483). But Faulkner has not bought into any of those models of myth-use. His use of traditional myth is situational, and as we shall see he is not at all averse to the practice (regarded by Boas, by the way, as typical of the cross-cultural adoption of mythic elements) of revising or even countering the significances of the borrowed motifs.

The mythic aura the narrator attaches to Lena is primeval, but variously so. Echoes of the natural world, of fertility, maternity, nurture, and so forth are the associations critics have explored. Hugh Ruppersburg's detailed and useful study *Reading Faulkner: "Light in August"* demonstrates the syncretism in Faulkner's evocations of the Virgin Mary, Mary Magdalene, Helen of Troy, and *The Golden Bough*'s Diana of the Grove (1994, 18), and he and other recent critics have hedged the myth-based interpretations with acknowledgments of the situational nature of the allusions. Francois Pitavy, for example, warns that "It must be remembered then that the use of mythological allusion is only one of the many tools, as Faulkner himself might have said, used to extend a character beyond the limitations of his actual context" (1982, 80); and André Bleikasten tempers the myth-enthusiasm (his own included) by observing that "Lena is both more and less than a replica of her mythic models" (1990, 277). Yes, indeed, both more and less: a Virgin Mary who is by her own admission (and Byron's tardy but vivid recognition) not a virgin at all; a fertile earth-mother of a Magdalene; a bumpkin Helen licking sardine oil off her fingers; a Diana whose power is in her passiveness and dependency.

Can we imagine mythic allusion as reciprocal, as both signifying and countersignifying? Then not only is Lena greatly enhanced by the mythic company in which the narrator places her, but those cultural myths of purity and beauty and power are to some extent brought to earth by association with their alleged earthy avatar. The possibilities expand and wander for us, but Faulkner was probably not in any conscious sense deconstructing those venerable myths, was he? His own recollection of his striving toward a Lena-aura has been much quoted as an explanation of the book's title, but it demonstrates the way his intuition played around the regions of myth, imagery, and cultural antiquity, cultivating possibility rather than definition:

> [I]n August in Mississippi there's a few days somewhere about the middle of the month when suddenly there's a foretaste of fall, it's cool, there's a lambence, a luminous quality to the light, as though it came not from just today but from back in the old classic times. It might have fauns and satyrs and the gods and—from Greece, from Olympus in it somewhere. It lasts just for a day or two, then it's gone, but every year in August that occurs in my country, and that's all that title meant, it was just to me a pleasant evocative title because it reminded me of that time, of a luminosity older than our Christian civilization. Maybe the connection was with Lena Grove, who had something of that pagan quality of being able to assume everything, that's—the desire for that child, she was never ashamed of that child whether it had any father or not, she was simply going to follow the conventional laws of the time in which she was and find its father. But as far as she was concerned, she didn't especially need any father for it, any more than the women that—on whom Jupiter begot children were anxious for a home and a father. It was enough to have had the child. And that was all that meant, just that luminous lambent quality of an older light than ours. (Gwynn and Blotner 1995, 199)

Byron Bunch seems quite differently conceived, and is certainly quite differently used in the novel. No avatar of deities and luminous lambencies, Byron is purely local, purely contemporary. Not only an actor in his own (comic) drama of the confounding of rationality and personal consistency, he is also a valuable informant through whom the narrator can maintain both distance from the events and relativity of interpretation. The narrator's reliance on Byron is one of the things that Faulkner substantially augmented in his process of revising and assembling; according to Regina Fadiman, "On numerous occasions he situated his narrator in Byron Bunch's consciousness, employing Bunch as observer, auditor, and judge" (1975, 65). Early in the novel Byron informs Lena of Joanna Burden's background, in the process conveying to her and to us his (and his culture's) very unreflective sense of the significance of racial difference as well as his own extremely innocent sense—his innocence here matching hers—of what might have been going on at the Burden place:

"It's a right big old house. It's been there a long time. Don't nobody live in it but one lady, by herself. I reckon there are folks in this town will call it a judgment on her, even now. She is a Yankee. Her folks come down here in the Reconstruction, to stir up the niggers. Two of them got killed doing it. They say she is still mixed up with niggers. Visits them when they are sick, like they was white. Wont have a cook because it would have to be a nigger cook. Folks say she claims that niggers are the same as white folks. That's why folks dont never go out there. Except one.... Or maybe two, from what I hear. I hope they was out there in time to help her move her furniture out. Maybe they was." (53)

But it is as the innocence is dispelled and Byron performs his informant's role for the benefit of and in collaboration with Hightower that so much is accomplished for Faulkner's narrator by this indirection. Because of their eccentricities and their differences, the two characters provide a rich resource for establishing the events of the novel as events-as-perceived. Matter-of-fact Byron, immensely curious about other folks and the gossip about them despite his self-sworn vows of self-management and nonmeddling; and evasive, depressive, past-haunted ex-reverend Hightower, trying so hard and so vainly to shut out the human world and its powerful proclivity for moral outrage: together they help the narrator to some intricate countercurrents of interpretation. Byron is no *tabula rasa*—he has a very clear and deeply imprinted sense of what's right and how to be helpful—but the accounts he brings to Hightower are basically plain and nonjudgmental reports, even in several cases purportedly direct transcriptions of conversations of others or of the stories others had been told. (The narrator sometimes takes Byron's nonmanipulative reportage four or even five narrative levels deep, showing how the community's thought and action develop by showing how information and stories disseminate, all within Byron's ken. See a fine demonstration of this in Ruppersburg 1983, 45.)

But Byron's stories are virtually all traumas for Hightower. He brings him news of Lena's arrival and his own increasingly compromising involvement with her welfare, of the fire at the Burden place, of Christmas and Lucas Burch/Joe Brown as bootleggers and living at Joanna's, of Brown's allegations of Christmas's and Joanna's relationship, of the discovery of the murder, of the beginning of the investigation, and of Brown's allegation that Christmas is a nigger. Byron relates this litany of horrors matter-of-factly, although regretting the need "To tell on two days to two folks something they ain't going to want to hear and that they hadn't ought to have to hear at all" (79). (Of course his mission is probably at least partly to prepare

Hightower, against all the ex-minister's inclinations and resolutions, to agree to marry Lena and Lucas.)

Hightower, gradually comprehending the vast range of moral transgressions, their potential consequences, and his own potential entanglement, reacts increasingly negatively, from an initial point at which "Byron can see in the other's face something latent, about to wake, of which Hightower himself is unaware, as if something inside the man were trying to warn or prepare him" (81), to a final point at which "the man . . . sits there with his eyes closed and the sweat running down his face like tears. Hightower speaks: 'Is it certain, proved, that he has negro blood? Think, Byron; what it will mean when the people—if they catch. . . . . . . Poor man. Poor mankind'" (100). This narrative situation functions to relativize interpretation, surely, to deepen and complicate our sense of what people can make out of what happens, at the same time that it dramatizes the telling itself, even introducing a measure of oblique and dark humor into the whole diverse concoction.

Part of the relativization involves the semantics of racial difference. "Christmas is part nigger," Byron says; "'Part negro,' Hightower says" (89). The narrator indicates to us via this socially marginal pair of friends that there are within this culture markedly differing relationships to the dominant ideology, just as there are markedly different perceptive sets and personal agendas.

That established, the narrator puts aside Byron-as-informant for an eight-chapter exploration of the mind and history of Joe Christmas. When Byron is brought back again he has saddled himself with two women—both Lena who needs sequestered and safe birthing, and Mrs. Hines who wants (inconceivably) to save her lost grandson, Joe Christmas—and again Byron's self-assumed commitments require the involvement of Hightower. The information Byron brings him is still manifestly matter-of-fact but laden with the subtexts both of his Samaritan commitments and (as Hightower realizes with dismay) of his attraction to Lena. In this complex framework we learn through Byron of Lena's lying-in at the Burden place, of Christmas's capture, of some of the local reaction to him and his crime, of Mrs. Hines's story of his parentage and birth, and of Lucas Burch's pursuit of the reward money. Again Faulkner's fictional quasi-ethnography situationally, dramatically delivered develops the idea of the intricacy of human interpretation of human experience.

In a certain sense Byron is a kind of stand-in for the reader: curious, seeking the truth, groping his way through an unfamiliar experience, willing goodness and wanting things to turn out all right. But his inner struggles and self-reproofs are comic, his most determined efforts often come to naught, and he seems to be of little consequence in the eyes of the world. The townsfolk who know him judge him as utterly reliable, utterly upright (at least before his adventuring on Lena's behalf), and utterly marginal to the concerns of moment; to the practiced eye of an outsider (the furniture dealer who witnesses the midstages of Byron's sporadically frustrated courtship), "he was the kind of fellow you wouldn't see the first glance if he was alone by himself in the bottom of an empty concrete swimming pool" (495). Insofar as Byron carries along our hopes about Lena, Hightower, the Hineses, the town, and so forth, he seems to serve as the narrator's means of caricaturing even our own well-meaning curiosity.

But it is that same quality of humane curiosity that leads Byron to ever-deeper participation in matters he originally felt should be none of his business. The same thing happens to Hightower. Determined to protect the obsessive vision of ironic Confederate gallantry that has become the matrix of his ego, he fights any and all vestiges of connection and commitment, except Byron's friendship. But that friendship becomes both Hightower's source of information about the unrenounceable world and his route to voluntary participation in a birth and in a futile attempt to avert a murder. From "I am not in life anymore" (301), he graduates, however unwillingly, to becoming an active protector of the welfare of others and a philosopher of human affairs who is able to see, at least in a hiatus before the imaginary cavalry again makes its mythic run, both his own culpability in driving his wife to her death and the deep-down identity of Joe Christmas and Percy Grimm, of victim and executioner. In the characterizations of both Byron and Hightower, Faulkner demonstrates curiosity breeding empathy and involvement. That same background assumption guides his own compositional strategy, his narrators' positioning inside even radically disaffiliated characters, developing them as understandable and even justifiable in their own terms. It's a phenomenon very like emic understanding generating compassion.

Joe Christmas is its crux in *Light*, and the crux of the question of human difference. In Faulkner's first conception of the novel he occupied no more attention than Byron or Lena or Hightower, and he definitely had Negro blood. But Faulkner seems to have felt that there was great potential in him as a character—in his background, his internal conflict, his position in society, his challenge to racial definition, his fate, whatever—and that particular intuition transformed the novel.*

---

*Regina Fadiman has traced and explained the numerous changes Faulkner made in expanding Christmas's role and problematizing his racial origin at every point (1975, 42–43, 56–58, 64, 111–13, 132–34, 150, 169).

Faulkner seems to have wanted the presentation of Christmas to be both deep and inconclusive. Difference—quasi-difference in this embodiment—becomes a complex of many aspects and significances, all of them attributive. First, there are all the various perceptions of Joe Christmas by the people who encountered him. In his first appearance in the novel Byron sees "something definitely rootless about him . . . ruthless, lonely, and almost proud" (31–32), and the other millworkers, taking him more personally, see a challenging insolence in his demeanor. Back in his orphanage childhood, the dietitian, imagining herself discovered by him in a tawdry sexual adventure, characterizes him according to her own need as "You little rat! . . . You little nigger bastard!" (122). The orphanage matron sees him as a complex problem for her institution, one needing a quiet (however compromising) solution. The Negro yardworker tells him "You dont know what you are. And more than that, you wont never know" (384). And all the while Joe has been coldly watched and brooded over by the anonymous figure of his own grandfather, convinced of his Negro blood and his damnation, and waiting for God to make His move.

To his adoptive father McEachern he is a rebellious son, stubbornly unwilling to follow God's austere path of piety and labor, while to his adoptive mother he is a poor boy needing indulgence and nurturing. To his first love Bobbie he is a young naif with a charmingly romantic appeal whose confession of negritude at first made no difference; when his public battle with McEachern spoils her easy game of prostitution, she sees it as justification for coldly, even brutally, denying him. To Southern whores, his alleged negritude evokes shock and repulsion, but in the north, boredom.

To Joanna Burden he is Negro and radically dual: both the forbidden sexual object with whom she can passionately defy her gender's and her race's strongest moral strictures (debasing her family's heritage in the bargain), and the underprivileged Other, the poorer brother who needs to be helped to self-respect and a place in society. To his "partner" Brown he is first a means of averting suspicion from himself for Joanna's murder, and then, with the announcement of the reward, a chance to get a lot of money for not much effort. For the sheriff then he is quarry, for the onlookers eager to become posse he is generic Negro-murderer-of-a-white-woman, and for Percy Grimm he is both of those things and the means of a personal consummation/vindication as well.

For Mrs. Hines he is Milly's wayward son and family, for Gavin Stevens an intricate motivational jigsaw puzzle in black and white, and for Hightower another victim of a horrible, typically human self-righteousness. The sum total of these perceptions is inconsistent, unstable, and ineluctably relativistic: each construction of Christmas essentially a product of the personal needs and perceptions of a particular person at a particular moment, each notion of racial difference a somewhat pliable norm potentially useful in the service of those needs, those perceptions.

Second, in establishing the inconclusive, attributive nature of difference in this novel, there are the more characteristically modernist means of relativizing interpretation: the variations in narrative type for different stages of Christmas's story, and their varied interpretive frameworks—the systems of symbolism, of mythic reference, of sociological and sociocultural background, of psychotheoretic structuring. Christmas is first presented to us from the outside (from Byron's point of view, although not limited by his perception) in chapters 2 and 4 as a dangerous drifter; we are given the visible menace, the rumors, the fact of the killing. He is peripheral then, though: a subplot to narratives about Lena, Byron and Hightower and their places in the society. When we shift focus to Christmas in chapter 5, the story becomes a psychological study of terrible compulsion versus human need—the interior of a fated murderer presumably on his way to do the killing. Black and white, dark and light, need and drive characterize the story then; the society is essentially passive, a field of lures and repulsions relative to his drives. Flashing back to his childhood in chapter 6—an articulation of what could only impinge upon him as something that "memory believes before knowing remembers" (119)—we have a different kind of story, though one incipiently the forerunner of what we've already read. Now it's a beleaguered orphan with a quasi-Freudian eating-nausea-sex trauma, a friendless little kid without a clue being pushed around and characterized as "nigger" by callous grownups for their own purposes. Except for the sex and the nearly gratuitous racial attribution, this story could be Dickensian, its inherent interpretive framework a matter of social criticism rather than dark psychological drives or mythic resonances.

Chapter 7 is a coming-of-age story, recounting his unrationalized, self-defining opposition to the fundamentalist strictures of his adoptive father. Here the imagery evokes Christian martyrdom—"When the strap fell he did not flinch, no quiver passed over his face. He was looking straight ahead, with a rapt, calm expression like a monk in a picture." (149)—but the religious imagery is ironically inverted, as the youth, determinedly willful and dedicated to discovering the snares of world, flesh, and devil, is being martyred by the pious father. Chapter 7 further develops the sex-and-repulsion motif in Joe's violent reaction against his own sexual initiation by the Negro girl, at this point thematically linking sex and race and blending symbolism of darkness, negritude, primitiveness, and womanness into the mix.

Chapters 8 and 9 put aside the Christian, race, and darkness symbolism and develop the romance with Bobbie in terms of a naive country courtship and the coming-of-age of a sensitive youth, again ironically however, since Joe is for so long innocent of Bobbie's profession. At this point it's a story, too, of an education in waywardness, of a youth's falling into, or rather consciously imitating, dissolute habits and violently breaking away from his home and parents. The sex-and-repulsion motif continues in the menstruation/sheep's blood episode, but for this segment of the narrative the black/darkness/negritude motif is minimal until Joe's nigger status is again invoked as justification for the beating he gets with Bobbie's repudiation of him.

Chapter 10 is a lost-loner-on-the-road story, mostly narrated as summary, with sex and negritude its main elements and a society that responds violently to Christmas's assaults on its racial norms, and yet teaching him the geographic relativity of those norms. With chapters 11 and 12 we get a kind of "descent to the underworld" in the affair with Joanna, with a good deal of quasi-Freudian imagery—passion and putrefaction, compulsion and repulsion—mixed with darkness, race, and ironic Adam-and-Eve resonance. The depth-psychological motives in *Light in August* are certainly like those propounded by Freud and Jung, but peculiarly Faulkner's own, analogous to rather than indebted to theirs, I would claim, and at that only used for particular effects in particular narrative situations.

Chapter 14 is a story of flight, and the last time the narrator puts us inside Christmas's mind, where we can feel the turmoil, and the irrational hatred of Negroes, of God and religion, and of the need to continue life at such a cost. This segment is not particularly sexual, Freudian, or Christian-sacrificial; it constitutes a defiant but ambivalent dance with death, as Christmas's ingenuity and resilience contend in his mind and his actions with his despair and sense of personal doom and damnation. If there are resonances of the character of Satan implied in Christmas's representation at this point, they are explicitly so designated by a nameless woman frightened by his gratuitous invasion of the Negro church: "already in a semihysterical state" she screamed "'It's the devil! It's Satan himself!'" (322). His actions there—as third-person reported in the narrator's summary of what the frightened messenger told—seem like unmotivated evil, as he overwhelmed and brutalized the members of the congregation with no regard for age or gender, smashed property, and "cursed God louder than the women screeching" (323).

But then in the final Joe Christmas scene, in chapter 19, the perspective, the narrative mode, and especially the inbuilt interpretive framework are quite different, as the narrator shows us Percy Grimm's pursuit from a position over his shoulder, with access to Grimm's perceptions and reactions, but with repeated allusions to the way that "he seemed to be served by certitude, the blind and untroubled faith in the rightness and infallibility of his actions" (459) and (somewhat more than metaphorically?) to "the Player who moved him for pawn" (462). Here the story moves ritualistically, like a primeval inevitability, fated from the very beginning but in its mechanisms inaccessible to human understanding. Then Christmas, nearly cornered, makes one more appearance, here to Hightower, as more-than-human ("his raised and armed and manacled hands full of glare and glitter like lightning bolts, so that he resembled a vengeful and furious god pronouncing a doom" [463]), before he suffers the execution/mutilation and thus becomes the everlasting memory of the witnesses which, as Hugh Ruppersburg correctly observes, "is the culmination of the Christ parallelism in the novel" (1994, 265).

From crime story to scripture, case study to vegetation myth, a good deal of the power of the Joe Christmas story comes from its mixture of myths and genres, and a good deal, too, of its essential indefinability. To the characters in the narrative's realm who had to deal with him (and to us, in one way of reading his character) he was nothing of a Christ or an Attis, an Oliver or a Young Werther. He was a treacherous cheap hood: razor-packing and unapproachable, he'd picked up his habits and mannerisms from Bobbie's pimps and other criminals and antisocials. He'd nurtured himself in the culture of crime, prostitution, and lowlife, and his desires and yearnings, though confused in his inner conflict, were pitilessly egocentric. His understanding of human psychology and his mode of dealing with others was through an appeal to their base motives: greed, lust, vengeance, inebriation, punishment. But the interpretive overlayers in which Faulkner clothes him problematizes all judgment. Joe Christmas's difference is multivalent, protean.

Third, there are the various ways in which Christmas attributes difference to himself, prompted or steered by situational factors and incomprehensible inner urges. His notion of his difference is originally attached to him at the orphanage by the unremitting unsympathetic surveillance by the old janitor, his fanatical grandfather, and it is associated with negritude by the other children's taunts and the Dietician's defensive accusation. Joe absorbs the notion and enacts it, variously using it, confessing it, concealing it, variously feeling within himself resigned acceptance, secretive pride, deep denial. In the throes of his adolescent turmoil he imagines telling Mrs. McEachern her tyrannical husband "has nursed a nigger beneath his own roof" (168), and the thought gives him a sense of power over her, a potential to destroy both her womanish attempt to control him with kindness and her husband's domineering spiritual pride. He actually does confront the white prostitutes with negritude in an attempt to control them, to take reviling or even beating to avoid paying. On the street he will act out his difference in overt antagonism, as either black or white, and draw the racial hostility that for him is a kind of self-confirming response.

For Christmas every relationship is adversarial, and when the relationship is relatively close he needs to feel the other's reaction to his putative negritude before he's satisfied with its terms. Thus he confesses to Bobbie, to Lucas Burch, and to Joanna, drawing the reaction, observing the result, and learning to use it. But even in that he maintains his autonomy oppositionally, however inconsistently: To Joanna's offer of a securely Negro education and profession, he responds "Tell niggers that I am a nigger too? . . . Shut up. Shut up that drivel. Let me talk." And he goes on to humiliate her personally, shifting the subject entirely to her menopausal state rather than some racially entailed future for him (277). Difference is itself an identity for him, more important than racial definition.

Difference is within too—"the human heart in conflict with itself," in one of Faulkner's favorite slogans of his later life. Christmas at various times experiences inner denial of one or the other of his racial identities, although it is notable that his denials of blackness are far more potent, deep, and detailed than those of his whiteness. He denies his whiteness through his actions, unconsciously, unreflectively. Physically and socially (and especially in flight) he gravitates toward Negroes' locales. It seems an inadvertent process, as if he were taken there by his legs or his random intuition, by some unconscious sense of where he should be or (after the murder of Joanna) by his acceptance of a fixed role in the life-and-death racist ritual he has initiated.

But his rejections of blackness are matters of an almost primal loathing. Inadvertently walking into the "shadowbrooded street" of Freedman Town surrounded by "the summer voices of invisible negroes" he suddenly feels as if in the midst of a powerful primitive vortex. "[A]s from the bottom of a thick black pit," as if threatened by the enveloping presence of "the lightless hot wet primogenitive Female" he runs for his life "up the sharp ascent" to "the cold hard air of white people" (114–15).

Earlier in his career having made a determined effort to be black, he had been unsuccessful in a very particularized, very essential way:

> He now lived as man and wife with a woman who resembled an ebony carving. At night he would lie in bed beside her, sleepless, beginning to breathe deep and hard. He would do it deliberately, feeling, even watching, his white chest arch deeper and deeper within his ribcage, trying to breathe into himself the dark odor, the dark and inscrutable thinking and being of negroes, with each suspiration trying to expel from himself the white blood and the white thinking and being. And all the while his nostrils at the odor which he was trying to make his own would whiten and tauten, his whole being writhe and strain with physical outrage and spiritual denial. (225–26)

And in the latter stage of his final flight, having duped the posse and its bloodhounds by exchanging shoes with a Negro woman,

> he paused there only long enough to lace up the brogans: the black shoes, the black shoes smelling of negro. They looked like they had been chopped out of iron ore with a dull axe. Looking down at the harsh, crude, clumsy shapelessness of them, he said "Hah" through his teeth. It seemed to him that he could see himself being hunted by white men at last into the black abyss which had been waiting, trying, for thirty years to drown him and into which now and at last he had actually entered, bearing now upon his ankles the definite and ineradicable gauge of its upward moving. (331)

In Christmas's mind, then, the blackness that is part of his own very personal essence partakes of the primitive and impends death. It incites fear and revulsion in him. Whether Faulkner's narrator wishes us to regard this reaction as generically instinctual or acculturated is undeterminable. What is evident is that Joe Christmas's sense of his own difference is a construction—one specific to his psyche, experiences and social context.

In relativizing interpretation in all the aforementioned ways, Faulkner tacitly disestablishes the conventional assumption that a culture can be accounted for in general terms. The concrete, polyvocal, nonintellectualized narrative depicts a society that certainly has its own distinct, historic characteristics, rooted in race discrimination, but is still irreducibly diverse in its population and its interconnections of individuals, society and circumstance. In this way the novel is something of an exploration of the parameters of human potential: on questions of sexuality, or religious belief, of justice or race or personal integrity, it shows us fanatical extremes, moderate middles, and the totally unconcerned. Percy Grimm and Doc Hines are, like Sheriff Kennedy, Mrs. Beard, Gavin Stevens, and the furniture dealer and his wife, possible in this society but not typical of it. Nobody is or could be.

And the myths of the society are shown to be diverse and fallible, variously believed and rooted not in history but in legends about history. We even see two of them born: the legend of the ironically slain Confederate hero, Hightower's grandfather, and the legend of Joe Christmas and his slaying-mutilation, a troubling enigma for the townspeople generally, and far more than that for the eyewitnesses, for whom "the man seemed to rise soaring into their memories forever and ever" (465). Since "reality" is really "perceived reality" in Faulkner's framework, story is part of it and story will come to define and encompass it; the "storied past" is indeed storied, and essentially so. Thus present reality, too, becomes shaped by story, since myths and notions are part of everyone's system of perception. Witness the heavy freight of storied past that Joanna Burden has shouldered throughout her life; and witness, too, her sudden transformation in the public mind from abolitionist outcast to pure-white-woman-victim-of-Negro-murderer. There are societal myths, broadly normative, that reinforce the social status quo though they are variously believed in and acted upon by individuals; and there are also more personal myths like Percy's myth of his own thwarted heroism and Joanna's of her duty to the Negro race.

But whether beliefs and myths are societal or personal, their variousness and their situational and personal adaptability mark them as fictions, having as much or more to do with subjective accommodation, adaptation, and aspiration than with the actualities to which they presumably refer. Furthermore, the situational heterogeneousness of the array of primitive, classical, pre-Christian, Christian, psychoanalytical, and Southern-historical referents suggests, similarly, that from time immemorial humankind has lived by fictions. Relativizing interpretation as Faulkner does in this novel has the effect of deconstructing the verities of both the subject and object cultures. In such a framework primitive difference and even race, its customary correlative, lose all claim to absoluteness and become situational matters of relativistic interpretation.

There is high moral tragedy here, in a society modeled as this one is on Faulkner's South, in which the boundaries are rigidly, brutally enforced and beliefs and interpretations are so diverse and fallible. For race to be such an overridingly crucial category for ranking and dealing with people, and for it to be at the same time somewhat ambiguous in its nature and significations is a discontinuity that ranks as an institutionalized moral outrage. Faulkner struggles with the problem in this novel, I think even revising his own view of the significance of "race"—and that even despite his narrator's sporadic lapses into racist characterizations.

Faulkner's work compares interestingly with that of Boas. Both men have strong senses of the moral import of their work, but Faulkner is actually less explicitly moral, perhaps counter to our expectations in a comparison of science and literature. Both men understand language to be artifactual and perspective to be inescapably relative, and thus have similar ideas of the fallibility of such abstract notions as race and the primitive. But whereas Boas is especially concerned to explain and argue the invalidity of the application of such notions in science and in sociopolitical life, Faulkner uses representations of them, in all their particularity of variousness and inconsistency, to characterize, to produce or heighten dramatic conflict, to explore society's or humanity's nature, and so forth—all by implicit means.

Both he and Boas see the greatest insight about cultures coming from studying them from the inside, understanding the viewpoint of the Other as a viable human perspective. Boas treads the line between objectivity and reflexiveness, in an attitude of emic empathy; Faulkner, building on established literary tradition, explores the Other's viewpoint subjectively, and in that Other's own language—in so doing anticipating the extra dimension of emic presentation of the ethnography of a much later day. Both were dedicated to particularity: Boas of course to the particularity of the actual people he lived among and studied, Faulkner to the particularity—at one remove from the empirical—of the imagined representations of people such as those he lived among or could imagine.

Boas was cautious, distrustful about employing the generalized, intellectualized language that previously had been the utilitarian currency in the study of other peoples, although several of his followers—Benedict, Mead, and Sapir, for instance—would go a long way in generalizing what they felt they could regard as cultural essences. Faulkner, as part of a modernist movement in writing that distrusted and even repudiated abstractions and intellectualizations, was highly sensitive to the society's heterogeneity, its interpretive entropy. Like Hemingway repudiating abstract language, and like Dos Passos, in *Manhattan Transfer* and *USA*, depicting the modernist's experience of discontinuity, personal isolation, and interrelationship by chance and coincidence, Faulkner configured a fictional society that qualified or countered or evaded many of the thematic conclusions it generated.

Thus *Light in August* issues a kind of ethnographic challenge, fictionally presenting both an analytical representation of a Southern community and a sense of the complexity of the notion of a culture as well. Boas, never finally defining "culture," and despite his necessary reliance on the idea of ethnographic authority and the languages of scientific discourse, public information and persuasion, certainly knew intracultural complexity and the many ways a culture could resist conceptualization. His encouragement of the study of the individual in society, like that same deep concern of Faulkner, is but another aspect of that knowing.

8

Relativism and the Reflexiveness of Interpretation: Margaret Mead and *Coming of Age in Samoa*

A complete elimination of the subjective use of the investigator is of course quite impossible in a matter of this kind but undoubtedly you will try to overcome this so far as that is at all possible.

—Franz Boas to Margaret Mead,
15 February 1926

Franz boas knew well the impossibility of absolute objectivity in studying human difference, but he could offer his followers little guidance in the "elimination of the subjective use of the investigator" beyond encouraging an awareness of the problem, suggesting some perspective-shifting ideas for thinking beyond the gravitational pull of one's own cultural background, and providing the tacit example of his own painstaking and often uninterpreted collections of specifics—linguistic, physical, material, storied and societal. Margaret Mead, carrying out the Boasian program of participant-observer fieldwork and cultural deterministic interpretation, was able to become the most widely known and respected anthropologist in the United States in the years before and just after World War II. Today, however, although she still is a figure of very great cultural importance, her work does not have much lasting importance for anthropology. And its fallibility is relatable to that problem of "the subjective use of the investigator" versus the implied objectivity of her conclusions.

Mead's career was launched stratospherically with the publication of her very first book, *Coming of Age in Samoa,* in 1928. The text itself is a fascinating one, deconstructing and reconstructing a number of standard notions about primitive and civilized peoples, and doing it with sufficient particularity, force, and literary flair for a wide public audience to be wholly taken with it. As a contribution to the discourse on human difference, based in Boas's idea of the enormous effect of culture in determining the particulars of difference, it fosters these interpretations: (1) racial difference is of so little, so indeterminate a consequence that it can be virtually left out of a comparison of peoples of different cultures; (2) primitiveness can be viewed in the modernist way as in some of its aspects possibly worthy of emulation by Western cultures; (3) ethnography can function as cultural critique: a study of a radically other culture can serve as a critique of the anthropologist's own culture; (4) gender characteristics and expectations are culture-specific and open to reconceptualization and revision; and (5) personality and individuality, and their conflicts with society, are culture-specific and potentially valuable as ethnographic indicators.

Historically, her importance to the discourse on human difference is principally in the realm of theory, challenging its conventional concepts and expanding the range of its purposes and possibilities. Her ethnographic methods were too casual for later anthropologists (and not up to the high empirical standards of some of her contemporaries), and her very preoccupation with theory, impelling her study of each particular culture toward some ultimate thematic interpretation—some reification, actually—that would define that culture's essential character, led her into shaping and steering her findings and assuming an attitude toward her subject culture that finally was both reflexive and condescending.

She was young and inexperienced when she set out for Samoa for her first adventures in the field, but she was bright, quick to catch on, and so self-confident that, in her write-ups at least, she would never falter in her assumption of authority. Fifty years later, looking back on the experience, she emphasized the methodological uncertainty she had felt: "The truth was that I had no idea whether I was using the right methods. What were the right methods?" She saw her Boasian training as weak in method but strong in interpretation: "I really did not know much about field work. The course on methods that Professor Boas taught was not about field work. It was about theory—how material could be organized to support or to call into question some theoretical point" (Mead 1972, 151, 137). Significantly, that orientation seems to have shaped not only *Coming of Age* but nearly all her later work: the real payoff is rarely in the details but characteristically in the theoretical point that she set forth as the issue.

It was Boas who set the terms of her Samoan project. Attitudinally he had trained his students carefully, in the process setting them at odds with many of the polygenist and evolutionist doctrines and preconceptions:

Our training equipped us with a sense of respect for the people we would study. They were full human beings with a way of life that could be compared with our own and with the culture of any other people. No one spoke of the Kwakiutl or the Zuni—or any other people—as savages or barbarians. They were, it is true, primitive; that is, their culture had developed without script and was maintained without the use of script. That was all the term "primitive" meant to us. (Mead 1972, 140–41)

(Yes indeed—Mead and the other Boasians had learned to try to limit that term "primitive" to meaning nothing more than "lacking a written language.")

The individual direction Boas gave Mead was quite specific. As she later explained, "Boas, always tailoring a particular piece of research to the exigencies of theoretical priorities, time, place, and personal ability, wanted me to study adolescence. In the end we compromised. I took his problem and he consented to my choice of Polynesia" (1959b, 42). The problem as he conceived of it at the outset was aimed at challenging regnant theories of adolescent development, and it clearly implied cultural comparison. As he explained in a letter to Mead near the time of her departure,

> I am sure you have thought over the question very carefully, but there are one or two points which I have in mind and to which I would like to call your attention, even if you have thought of them before.
>
> One question that interests me very much is how the young girls react to the restraints of custom. We find very often among ourselves during the period of adolescence a strong rebellious spirit that may be expressed in sullenness or in sudden outbursts. In other individuals there is a weak submission which is accompanied, however, by a suppressed rebellion that may make itself felt in peculiar ways, perhaps in a desire for solitude which is really an expression of desire for freedom, or otherwise in forced participation in social affairs in order to drown the mental troubles. I am not at all clear in my mind in how far similar conditions may occur in primitive society and in how far the desire for independence may be simply due to our modern conditions and to a more strongly developed individualism. (Mead 1959b, 42–43)

Boas's principal interest was that theoretical issue of the cultural determination of the psychological manifestations of adolescence—in one sense an attack on what he saw as the naive and culture-bound assumption that psychosocial development had certain inevitable, universal stages. At the same time, though, he was introducing in the very terms of his project protocol the idea that the individual and her relation to her particular society were important factors in the whole anthropological enterprise. Although in literary practice the crises of individuality had of course all along been a vital revelatory element, anthropologists had focused at a more general level, bypassing individual differences (or unaware of them) and characterizing their subject cultures in terms of generalized societal beliefs and behaviors. The question of how or why an adolescent girl might express anguish or rebellion toward her tribal customs was far beneath the notice of Morgan or Brinton or Frazer.

The psychoanalysts (who as we have seen also dabbled in ethnology) had an interest in the conflict of individual and society, but Freud's interest in the situation of the individual in primitive cultures was focused on his vision of universal biological determinants like the Oedipus Complex, and Jung simply elevated the limitation of viewpoint of the earlier anthropology into a characteristic of human reality: "if we go right back to primitive psychology, we find absolutely no trace of the concept of an individual. Instead of individuality we find only collective relationship or what Lévy-Bruhl calls *participation mystique*" (Jung 1971b, 10). The quasi-psychological approach that Boas and Mead were developing would thus focus on individuality and its conflicts recognized as part of primitive life and particularized within specific cultures.

And it also moved anthropology in the directions of relativism and sociopolitical liberalism. The home culture of the anthropological observer was not necessarily in the position of superiority; the conditions of social discontent were not unreformable, immutable functions of generic or evolutionary processes. These theoretical aspects of the program were entirely suited to Mead, and the chance it gave her to reengage adolescence and to open the lives of women to anthropological investigation made it much more attractive. Her biographer, Jane Howard, makes a particular point of this latter, quoting Mead's statement that

> [w]hat she would learn in Samoa, she hoped, would "add appreciably to our ethnological information on the subject of the culture of primitive women. Owing to the paucity of women ethnologists, practically no ethnological [work] has been done among women as such, and this investigation offers a particularly rich field for the study of feminine reactions and participation in the culture of the group." (Howard 1984, 76)

Boas's "tailoring a particular piece of research to the exigencies of . . . personal ability" certainly fit Mead ideally.

Mead brought a great deal to the Samoan project, but still it was not enough. Intellectually, she was loaded. Not only was there the Boasian program, but there were also several years of engagement with the important discourse of the day on psychology, epistemology, educational philosophy, and so forth; her correspondence and her memoirs bristle with references to Freud and Jung and Einstein, and especially to developmental psychologists Stanley Hall, Jean Piaget, and Kurt Koffka, who piqued her curiosity regarding nature-nurture issues. She also admitted to knowing Bernard Malinowski's *The Father in Primitive Psychology* (published in 1927, as she was writing her monograph), which implicitly challenged Freud's view of the universality of the Oedipal father-son relationship with revelations about local Trobriand Island social organization. Discussions with her early academic mentor and later close personal friend Ruth Benedict shaped and focused many general issues for both of them. Mead had surveyed the published studies of various Polynesian cultures—studies of mythologies, of social organization, of art and material cultures and migrations. The complex similarities and differences of the various Polynesian cultures led to a great deal of variousness and speculation in South Seas ethnology, but it left a relatively clear field for an interpreter of the Manu'an sector of American Samoa.

In retrospect, however, Mead can be seen as underprepared in some respects. She landed among her Manu'an subjects "after six weeks of concentrated work on the language, and a small amount of work with a few selected informants" (Mead 1969, 4), and the brevity of this preparation seems to have introduced an element of inaccuracy into her interpretations.* Also, she drew her conclusions after just six months' residence among the Manu'ans, and although her contact with them was daily and extensive, she found the need to "remain aloof from native feuds and lines of demarcation" by residing with a U.S. Navy Chief Pharmacist's Mate and his wife for four of those months. Still, she felt that, given her immersion in the lives and accounts of virtually all of the adolescent girls of the society, she was able to attain a unique and nuanced view of the Manu'an culture.

There was no great difference in ethnographic standards between *Coming of Age* and the general run of anthropological writings of the period, but fifty-one years later it became the center of the broadest and possibly the most troubling controversy in anthropology to that point and well beyond. In 1983 Australian anthropologist Derek Freeman published *Margaret Mead's Samoa: the Making and Unmaking of a Myth*. His book was an attack on Franz Boas and the whole program of his followers to emphasize cultural rather than biological determinants in human populations, but it was also an attack

---

*Martin Orans offers a detailed critique of Mead's linguistic shortcomings in 1996, 20–23.

on the American who had the reputation as the world's leading anthropologist. Thus it was sure to draw a crowd, both inside and outside the profession, and aggressive prepublication marketing made sure that it would.

As Freeman saw the situation of the latter 1920s, Boas had been in search of a negative instance that would destroy the premise that the stages in human development were biologically determined, and he sent Mead into the field to find that instance, which she, inexperienced as she was, dutifully did by misunderstanding and misrepresenting the Samoans. Thus "In this book I adduce detailed empirical evidence to demonstrate that Mead's account of Samoan culture and character is fundamentally in error" (1983, xii), Freeman claims, meaning to put the whole cultural determinist paradigm off the tracks.

Mead's conception of the Samoan culture as easygoing, very mild in its passions and prohibitions, and her interpretation of Samoan adolescence as a relatively easy, sexually uninhibited passage into well-defined social and gender roles was predisposed, Freeman alleges, by Boas's theoretical program and Mead's own personal predilections. Her adolescent girl informants were either too eager to tell their interviewer what they knew she wanted to hear or they deliberately misled her for their own amusement. Freeman supported his attack with his own findings (although they were not from the same time period, informant class or island locale as Mead's) and his own interpretation of the general tenor of Samoan culture as morally strict, often harsh toward adolescents, with a very high regard for virginity.

The anthropological profession took the controversy very seriously; throughout the 1980s and 1990s dozens of articles and books and reviews on the subject appeared, the list of authors comprising something of a roll call of contemporary cultural anthropologists. There is no need to recapitulate the controversy here: the relative accuracy of Mead's or Freeman's accounts is not as significant to the present inquiry as is the nature of the language, categories, and rhetoric of Mead's historic account. But in general it should be noted that anthropology's reevaluators tended to side with Mead, although often with serious reservations about some of her methods and/or her reliance on generalized interpretation. There is no doubt that she was the sentimental favorite in this contest. Much of her work and her thinking about cultures and their relationships had been stimulating if not methodologically formative for the anthropologists who grew up on her writings, whatever her later role as questionable guru on world issues.

Freeman got somewhat less positive treatment, often credited with calling attention to the standards of ethnographic method, but often being seen as misrepresenting the Boasian views he meant to refute, selectively exaggerating counterposing details in his version of Samoan society, or (like Mead) being too much enthralled by the drive to define a fundamental ethos of Samoan culture. His whole theoretical program of recentering cultural anthropology on a sociobiological basis could not stand as very defensible, influential, or productive. And there were also personal responses possibly affecting commentators: Why had Freeman apparently held back his attack for so many years until Mead was dead and could no longer answer him? Why was he being so totally and seemingly grudgingly negative? Were nature versus nurture, biological versus cultural determinism really such absolutely bipolar, such impassioning alternatives?*

By and large what recent anthropologist readers generally have wanted from *Coming of Age* is something methodologically and rhetorically much more like the ethnographies of their own much later time. But the peculiar character of this text and its positioning among the texts Mead produced are worth considering in an attempt to understand how to take it. Although the fact is seldom noticed, *Coming of Age* is only one of several writings Mead derived from her original Samoan research, each of them having a different focus, purpose, and audience. *Coming of Age* (1928) of course focuses on adolescent sexuality, and was published and marketed by a commercial press and aimed at a broad and not particularly professional audience. The book-length *Social Organization of Manu'a* (1930) focuses ethnographically on a wide range of characteristics of Manu'an society (with no mention of adolescent girls), offering what Mead claimed as its "central theoretical contribution . . . the discussion of the dynamics of the kinship systems and the way in which political forms and kinship forms reflect and provide models for each other" (1969, xiii). *Social Organization* was published as bulletin 76 by the Bernice P.

---

*Of the great number of valuable pieces on the Freeman-Mead controversy I'll recommend the following as ones that I relied on most substantially. First, there is the symposium edited by Ivan Brady in *American Anthropologist* 85 (Dec. 1983, 908–47) and these book-length studies: Lowell D. Holmes, *Quest for the Real Samoa* (1987); James E. Cote, *Adolescent Storm and Stress* (1994); and Martin Orans, *Not Even Wrong* (1996), which offers evaluation of Mead's field notes and comparison of them to her final text. Of individual articles, there are: Marvin Harris, "Margaret and the Giant Killer" (*The Sciences* 23 [1983] 18–21); Robert I. Levy, "Mead, Freeman and Samoa" (*Ethos* 12 [Spring 1984] 85–92); Richard Feinberg, "Margaret Mead and Samoa" (*American Anthropologist* 90 [Sept. 1988] 656–63); Nancy Scheper-Hughes, "The Margaret Mead Controversy" (*Human Organization* 43:1 [Spring 1984] 85–93); and the judicious summary account in George W. Stocking, Jr., *The Ethnographer's Magic* (1992) 324–38.

Bishop Museum and written specifically for the anthropological profession.

In the journal *Psyche* (1928b), Mead attacked a prominent notion about primitive psychology with "A Lapse of Animism among a Primitive People." In *Journal of the Royal Anthropological Institute* (1928c), she displayed a typically American theme with a typically cultural determinist framework in "The Role of the Individual in Samoan Culture." And for a more popular audience and with a more political (postcolonial *and* pro-American) message, she published "Americanization in Samoa" in *American Mercury* (1929).

Mead seems to have had a strong sense of shaping her texts for particular purposes, venues and audiences. Theodore Schwartz has put it somewhat more caustically: "Her fieldwork had to serve many purposes, including providing the license for prescription and prophesy" (1983, 928). But at any rate it is worthwhile to try to particularize her sense of exactly what she meant *Coming of Age* to be.*

She subtitled the book "A Psychological Study of Primitive Youth for Western Civilization," thereby defining difference as her subject—difference in a polar sense, opposed to the civilized phenomena familiar to her readers, and difference with a pedagogical intent, possibly even an implied agenda of liberal social reform. Her introduction explains her ethnographic effort wholly within the Boasian theoretical problematic. Of the textual result of her deep engagement with the adolescent girl population of Manu'a she says, "In the following chapters I have described the lives of these girls . . . [a]nd through this description I have tried to answer the question which sent me to Samoa: Are the disturbances which vex our adolescents due to the nature of adolescence itself or to the civilisation?" (1928a, 11). Her original appendices (which she later characterized as "impersonal, cast in the mold of a technical book" [1973, vi]) stressed the facts that her research had covered a broad range of Samoan culture, but that her text would not: "Although a knowledge of the entire culture was essential for the accurate evaluation of any particular individual's behaviour, a detailed description will be given only of those aspects of the culture which are immediately relevant to the problem of the adolescent girl" (1928a "Appendix II," 262–63).

---

*George Stocking argues (1992, 316n) for the consistency of Mead's basic interpretations in *Coming of Age* and *The Social Organization*, pointing out that "it is doubtful that all the issues that have been raised regarding her Samoan ethnography can be resolved by compartmentalizing the 'popularized' and the 'professional.'" Agreed: ethnography is ethnography in whatever costume, and the ethnographic shortcomings of *Coming of Age* certainly aren't excusable by reference to discursive genre. Still, I feel it is important to understand what she meant that book to deliver and not expect it to deliver something else.

When she looked back on the text from a distance of thirty-plus years (in a period of greater methodological sophistication), it was its pedagogical mission to her home culture that she emphasized as the key to its character. "During the . . . winter . . . 1927–1928, I was writing *Social Organization of Manu'a*, happy in the freedom to write more technically, after my attempt to make the material on Samoan adolescence intelligible to educators in *Coming of Age in Samoa*," she wrote in 1959 (1959a, 206). In the preface she added to the 1973 reprinting of the text, she insisted on its being viewed as historical ethnographic text, with its pedagogical intent being a primary and pioneering feature:

> I can emphasize that this was the first piece of anthropological fieldwork which was written without the new paraphernalia of scholarship designed to mystify the lay reader and confound one's colleagues. It seemed to me then—and it still does—that if our studies of the way of life of other peoples are to be meaningful to the peoples of the industrialized world, they must be written for them and not wrapped up in technical jargon for specialists. As this book was about adolescents, I tried to couch it in language that would be communicative to those who had most to do with adolescents—teachers, parents, and soon-to-be parents. I did not write it as a popular book, but only with the hope that it would be intelligible to those who might make the best use of its theme, that adolescence need not be the time of stress and strain which Western society made it. (1973, ii–iii)

In a 1965 statement she even claims that she wrote the book's final two chapters—the ones directly addressing the situation of adolescents in the United States—in response to a request of William Morrow, the publisher who was considering the manuscript after it had been rejected by Harper and Brothers (1965, 123–25). In private she admitted that in the effort "she pushed speculation 'to the limit of permissibility'" (Stocking 1992, 316).

Thus, however ethnologically pure her intentions in going to Samoa in the first place, Mead certainly responded to a mixture of agendas and influences in producing this particular text. That there should be conflict between some of these agendas—for instance, between the implied professional mandate to represent the Manu'ans according to the highest ethnographic standards, and the impulse to send a reformist message to the folks back home—should be no surprise. Boas offered her, as far as we know, no methodological help or supervision in producing the text, although his *The Mind of Primitive Man*—as an ethnological book aimed at revising beliefs and preconceptions of the audience back home—might have served as a model.

Actually Mead takes this genre to a new level, as George Marcus and Michael Fischer point out in *Anthropology as Cultural Critique*:

> This is the source of difference between Franz Boas and his student, Margaret Mead, who became *the* model of the anthropologist as cultural critic. Boas used ethnography to debate residual issues derived from the framework of nineteenth-century evolutionary thought and to challenge racist views of human behavior, then ascendant. Mead, and others like Edward Sapir, Elsie Clews Parsons, and Ruth Benedict, were much more focused in their cultural criticism. They began to use anthropology's subjects as specific probes into American conditions of the 1920s and 1930s. While Boas himself had been a critic of intellectual doctrines that had great social implications, his students were primarily critics of society under the banner of relativism. (1986, 119)

Martin Orans in his recent study of Mead's notes, methods, and conclusions, suggests the category of "creditable humanistic inquiry" as a designation of the genre of her two major Samoan texts, which (like Derek Freeman's counter-study), in having insufficient methodological precision, are scientifically "not even wrong" (1996, 131). In whatever generic framework we place it, though, *Coming of Age* is an original and culturally valuable work that "under the banner of relativism" indeed attacks the ethnocentricity of the civilized world's view of the "primitive," but at the same time has a complex problem with its own reflexiveness.

The voice through which Mead presents *Coming of Age* establishes a self-characterization having two major attributes: She represents herself both as being fully authoritative on issues dealing with primitive and civilized cultures, adolescent development, and systems of educating and maturing the young, and as having experienced deep immersion in the culture of a specific part of American Samoa. From the outset there is no hesitancy or uncertainty, however broad or complex the issue. And there is no citation of other observers and little attempt to offer empirical evidence in support of general interpretations—routines that necessarily support the different approach she takes in *Social Organization of Manu'a*.

The introduction begins by challenging the conventional view of the stormy adolescence as we know it in our civilization—is it actually an essential component of human psychological development as authorities like Stanley Hall and the general run of public opinion would have it, or is it instead culturally produced and thus amenable to mitigation through educational reform? Launching the book as an inquiry on this issue, *Coming of Age*'s speaker doesn't come around to mentioning Samoa until page nine. And then it is not Samoa-as-ethnographic-subject, but Samoa-as-case-in-point. Since there is no controlled-conditions laboratory for testing hypotheses about human development, she observes,

> [t]he only method is that of the anthropologist, to go to a different civilis-ation and make a study of human beings under different cultural condi-tions in some other part of the world. For such studies the anthropologist chooses quite simple peoples, primitive peoples, whose society has never attained the complexity of our own. . . . A primitive people without a written language present a much less elaborate problem and a trained stu-dent can master the fundamental structure of a primitive society in a few months. . . . [Especially] in an uncomplex, uniform culture like Samoa. (1928a, 7, 8, 11)

The audience assumed by this presumptuously authoritative speaker is an educated U.S. group interested in issues of education, perhaps amenable to suggestions for reform ("from this contrast we may be able to turn, made newly and vividly self-conscious and self-critical, to judge anew and perhaps fashion differently the education we give our children" [13]), and naive about anthropology. The Samoan sub-ject society is characterized as instructive in its difference, and as sim-pler. Especially simpler. Mead uses that term insistently; in this book cultural simplicity is a prime category of difference, although there is no expectation that a simple society need stay simple. So this for-the-time-being simple society becomes a kind of elaborate control group in this experiment, interpretable in terms of the intellectual perspec-tive of Western anthropology.

Faulkner's invention of a particular voice to maximize the revela-tions in *Light in August* had avoided the kind of distancing produced by this speaker-self fashioned by Mead, had gotten closer to the sub-ject in its own terms, even granting its fictionality. And Henry Adams, taking on the voice and the causes of Arii Taimai as a persona, put himself, albeit with some markedly civilized baggage, relatively uncondescendingly into the realm of Tahiti. As a playwright, O'Neill had to imagine his characters presenting themselves without an over-layer of explicit ethnocentric interpretation. Mead, intending to real-ize the lives of the Samoans from the inside, to see what Manu'an mores and conventions meant to adolescent Manu'ans, still had much of the burden of the conventions of anthropological presentation—its presumption of authority, its presumably higher level of civilized-world interpretive language.

Within its historical context Mead's approach is logical and insightful, certainly, although anthropologically such an assumption of the easy interpretation of simple cultures wouldn't wash today, given the far deeper sense of cultural particularity that has evolved—largely out of the Boasian approach—and its condescension is quite apparent to our distinctly postcolonial mindset. More recent ethnography has taken many different, often experimental or quasi-literary approaches to the production of text, as James Clifford observes. As he says of the "participant observation" mode of establishing ethnographic authority, "it is worth taking seriously its principal assumption: that the experience of the researcher can serve as a unifying source of authority in the field" (Clifford and Marcus 1986, 35).

Mead does very much mean her firsthand experience of Samoa to establish her authority. Once Samoa is introduced into the inquiry, her firsthand perceptions and how to convey them become a principal concern, especially insofar as they establish for the reader a sense of difference: of the typical "primitive adolescent girl" of her experience, she states

> She spoke a language the very sounds of which were strange, a language in which nouns became verbs and verbs nouns in the most sleight-of-hand fashion. All of her habits of life were different. She sat cross-legged on the ground, and to sit upon a chair made her stiff and miserable. She ate with her fingers from a woven plate; she slept upon the floor. Her house was a mere circle of pillars, roofed by a cone of thatch, carpeted with water-worn coral fragments. Her whole material environment was different. Coconut palm, breadfruit, and mango trees swayed above her village. (9–10)

"I was there," her introduction as much as asserts, "and such particulars of difference as these are what I needed to work through to arrive at the generalizations I will present to you."

But she goes farther in this direction. In her chapter II: "A Day in Samoa," she takes a quite literary approach, emphasizing atmosphere and mood, picturesque detail and erotic framing: "As the dawn begins to fall among the soft brown roofs and the slender palm trees stand out against a colourless, gleaming sea, lovers slip home from trysts beneath the palm trees or in the shadow of beached canoes, that the light may find each sleeper in his appointed place" (14). An anthropological embarrassment, this descriptive piece is reminiscent (although probably not consciously so) of Melville's description of a typical day in the Typee valley and any number of South Seas accounts and fantasies whose principal objective was exoticism. We can imagine Mead meaning to engage her audience, to validate her participant-observer status, to contextualize her analysis of adolescent behavior in this culture.

But its ethnographic distortion has been condemned in terms from the carefully measured ("Although the compression of typical activities into a typical day is an accepted literary device, it tends to distort perspective on the tempo of village life"—according to Lowell Holmes [1987, 109]) to the snidely dismissive ("This is a discursive, or perhaps I should say chatty and feminine, book with a leaning toward the picturesque, what I call the rustling-of-the-wind-in-the-palm-trees kind of anthropological writing, for which Malinowski set the fashion"—in the opinion of E. E. Evans-Pritchard [1964:96]).* Whatever authority Mead gained from her foray into atmospheric description was gained only with her lay audience.

It is important but seldom noticed that there is little atmospheric description in the book after that controversial chapter. Having established the vision of "A Day in Samoa," Mead continues the book basically as an exposition of the Manu'ans' social habits and mores.

Although apparently never meaning *Coming of Age* to be taken as a scientific text for scientists, Mead nevertheless strives to establish it as an inquiry based on science, bearing that particular claim to authority. The introduction sets up the project in terms of a scientific experiment, explains what anthropologists do and how that involves a careful consideration of the effects of social environment, gives a personal example of participant observation at work, and indicates how this sort of science can be of social benefit. The exposition that makes up the body of the text—the summary-description of Samoan ways and institutions especially in relation to the maturation process of girls—presents only very occasional indicators that this is a scientific study based on data. There is, for instance, the one sample response she quotes and the others in the appendix she cites to illustrate what she presents as the simple set of traits by which Samoans interpret character (125–30), and the transitional reminder that "[a]s far as our material permitted, an experiment has been conducted to discover what the process of development was like in a society very different from our own" (195).

It is in the five appendices that Mead gives the text its most prominent scientific markers: describing and justifying her methods; graphically enumerating some of her data; explaining her use of informants, of testing, of cross-referencing. She justified bypassing quantitative methods (with Boas's encouragement, by the way), saying "the type

---

*It should be noted that both of these commentators value Mead's study in other respects, however.

of data which we needed is not of the sort which lends itself readily to quantitative treatment. . . . [T]he student of the more intangible and psychological aspects of human behaviour is forced to illuminate rather than demonstrate a thesis" (260). And she articulately defended her use of a cross-sectional study of the adolescent population rather than a linear study over time. The language of science was in these several ways central to her claim to authority and authenticity. With introduction and appendices the text is plausibly framed in science, although in between, in the descriptions and general characterizations of Samoan culture, we simply have to trust her authority.

In her representation of the lives Samoan adolescent girls Mead stresses their casual bringing up by the whole community, their household and baby-tending duties, their freedom to explore their sexuality, and the narrow but socially supported adult roles open to them. Children are nothing special in Manu'a: they are expected to stay out of the way and to look after the younger family members and run errands, but they are otherwise free to wander and to interact and to witness whatever happens in the community—births, burials, sexual intercourse, or whatever. Their position in the family keeps them subordinate to anyone older, but should they feel oppressed or unfairly treated, they are free to leave that household and live, temporarily or permanently, with more congenial relatives. Girls have little or no contact with boys until adolescence, but then they overcome their shyness (however gradually) and freely experiment with sexuality, usually with a number of partners. Marriage is a matter of formal interfamilial arrangement, often involving little romance, and it is very simply dissolved at the wish of either partner. The mature woman has household, food-providing, and procreative duties, but little involvement in the society's management or traditions.

Mead's representations of Samoans are consistently racially neutral. I have found only a single reference to race or color in the text, a statement in the introduction that Samoa is "a South Sea island about thirteen degrees from the Equator, inhabited by a brown Polynesian people"; and this in a discussion that has just previously emphasized that in choosing their most valuable sources of insight, anthropologists "choose primitive groups who have had thousands of years of historical development along completely different lines from our own, whose language does not possess our Indo-European categories" (8–9). Her causal explanations never refer back to racial characteristics, even in situations in which those of another 1920s theorist might well have: For two examples, "The Samoan background which makes growing up so easy, so simple a matter, is the general casualness of the whole society" (198); and "for the explanation of the lack of conflict we must look principally to the difference between a simple, homogeneous primitive civilisation, a civilisation which changes so slowly that to each generation it appears static, and a motley, diverse, heterogeneous modern civilisation" (206). Difference for Mead is a cultural thing, having nothing to do with racial stock.

Nor is the Samoans' moral behavior any indicator of essential difference. Mead presupposes cultural relativism: their "civilisation" is as much a "civilisation" as ours, and with none of the customary suggestions of barbarism or atavism. In treating their familial and sexual mores her language goes well beyond the neutral, tending to be approving, admiring. No wonder. These areas Mead feels most strongly about; they are at the root of her case against American society as she has known it. Of the Manu'an child's home life she says, in an obvious tone of approval,

> Few children live continuously in one household, but are always testing out other possible residences. And this can be done under the guise of visits and with no suggestion of truancy. But the minute that the mildest annoyance grows up at home, the possibility of flight moderates the discipline and alleviates the child's sense of dependency. No Samoan child, except the *taupo* [the community virgin-princess], or the thoroughly delinquent, ever has to deal with the feeling of being trapped. There are always relatives to whom one can flee. (42–43)

Of a girl's normal course of social maturation, she says,

> adolescence represented no period of crisis or stress, but was instead an orderly developing of a set of slowly maturing interests and activities.... To live as a girl with many lovers as long as possible and then to marry in one's own village, near one's own relatives and to have many children, these were uniform and satisfying ambitions. (157)

In no way can moral inferiority be attributed to these people, thus presented. Mead's liberal moral sense and her reformist zeal reinforce her strong intercultural belief in basic human worthiness. The intellectual ground bass is a Boasian litany: "Each primitive people has selected one set of human gifts, one set of human values, and fashioned for themselves an art, a social organization, a religion, which is their unique contribution to the history of the human spirit" (13). And the descant is the emotion in her veneration for the Samoans' cultural difference: "it is conceivable that the Samoan child is not only handled more gently by its culture but that it is also better equipped for those difficulties which it does meet" (208). The moral mission of *Coming of Age* is not only to teach respect for difference, but also to reverse American culture's interpretation of the primitive. And (implicitly throughout and explicitly in conclusion) to problematize America's social and sexual norms.

The principal criteria by which Mead evaluates cultures are complexity, as we noted before, and naturalness. Since the eighteenth century Western writers have associated simple and friendly native people with closeness to nature, usually Edenic nature. Mead's version of the Edenic myth, however, specifies that it is the social accommodation of the facts of human biology rather than some mystical associative simplicity that makes the people of this culture effectively and enviably natural. "All of these children had seen birth and death," she explains, and it is "inevitable that children should see intercourse, often and between many different people" (133, 135). To the elders of the society, who have themselves been brought up this way, the situation is entirely appropriate, because "[t]o them, birth and sex and death are the natural, inevitable structure of existence, of an existence in which they expect their youngest children to share" (220).

Note especially that primitive sexuality—that preoccupation of so many "civilized" visions (explicit or suggested, scandalous or frightening or enticing) of the presumed naïve lasciviousness of dark-skinned natives—Mead presents as a matter of the Samoans' superior knowledge: "from the Samoans' complete knowledge of sex, its possibilities and its rewards, they are able to count it at its true value" (222). There is no obsessive guilt, no tangle of id and ego: Mead's slant is psychological but distinctly un-Freudian here. Implicitly counterpoising American society's intellectual turmoil about sexual liberation and psychosexuality, she depicts these natives in their simpler culture manifesting an enviable level of understanding of and accommodation to the facts of life.

Coming of Age's Samoans' culturally based psychological qualities also make their lives more comfortable, more enviable, and certainly less menacing (they, the dark-skinned Others) than the general run of 1920s textually presented primitives. Mead refers again and again to "the Samoan civilisation which discounts strong feeling," to "the lack of deep feeling which the Samoans have conventionalised until it is the very framework of all their attitudes toward life" (206, 200). Especially this quality comes out in Mead's consideration of the erotic lives of maturing girls. "[T]he lesson is learned of not caring for one person greatly, not setting high hopes on any one relationship" (199), of not conflating erotic adventure and passionate attachment, of not even feeling passionate attachment. (Mead parenthetically notes that her Samoans "greeted the story of Romeo and Juliet with incredulous contempt" [155–56].) There is a strongly favorable and quite possibly personal value judgment implied in the diction Mead uses in discussing this characteristic insofar as the topics of romantic love and family ties are concerned.

Yet there is a price to be paid, Mead implies, for the advantages of "the general casualness of the whole society" (198): "no prominence is given to the subtler facts of intelligence and temperament" (130), and "we may . . . feel that important personalities and great art are not born in so shallow a society" (200). But she sees adequate recompense in such social advantages as "the painless development from childhood to womanhood" (200). Mead explicitly does not mean to be taken to be describing every primitive culture, but her Samoa is one example that effectively disposes of the universality of any assumption equating primitiveness and uncontrolled instinctual behavior.

Beneath the very significant cultural shaping of psychological responses, however, are some basic human responses that Mead assumes are operative in the same way whatever the culture. Her chapter XI depiction of "The Girl in Conflict," for example, treats individual cases in which her readers can feel the emotional logic. They are such as Ana, illegitimate daughter of a chief, abandoned by her promiscuous mother and finding refuge in the household of an aunt who, partly motivated by disapproval of the mother, forced on the girl a self-image as frail and inept, "too delicate for a normal existence." In Ana's recoil, "she became a church member, gave up dancing, clung closer to the group of younger girls in the pastor's school and to her foster home, the neurasthenic product of a physical defect, a small, isolated family group and the pastor's school" (169).

Mala, whose parents were dead, "was a scrawny, ill-favoured little girl, always untidily dressed," who "lived with her uncle, a sour, disgruntled man of small position" and his divorced niece, both of whom "worked her unmercifully." Characterized by Mead as having become "treacherous" and "insinuating," Mala had transgressed two of the most important strictures of the society: she stole and she played with boys, acting and dressing boyishly, even though her position among the boys was the very lowest (178–79).

As Mead admits in one of the long autobiographical chapter introductions in *An Anthropologist at Work: Writings of Ruth Benedict*, "The chapter on 'The Girl in Conflict' . . . began with a question which Ruth Benedict had taught me to ask: 'Were there no conflicts, no temperaments which deviated so markedly from the normal that clash was inevitable?'" (208). Humanly, generically inevitable, we might add, and recognize that the specific descriptions of the situations within individual families, both normal and deviant, set against the rules and mores of Manu'an culture, put us imaginatively into the characters' lives and lead us to feel the characters' tensions. Regardless of the exoticism of environment or customs the text presents, we become for the moment like them and they like us: they are humanized by their particularization. Essential difference is abolished in the individuation of the Benedict/Mead culture-and-personality approach.

Fundamentally, it is the Samoan culture Mead is defining rather than the Samoans as a people. Definitions of the people inhere in things not said, in things implied or assumed, such as the absence of reference to race or of criticism of their morality, and the assumption that in their situation we would feel and act in quite similar ways. Psychologically we're all of the same stuff; difference in race or culture is in no way difference in essence. Mead's cultural determinism by no means entails a thoroughgoing relativism.

What, then, does it mean for a people to be "primitive" in Mead's sense of that term? It means they have a simpler culture and no written language; that they have clearer and fewer cultural guidelines for individual development, and that this entails a somewhat reduced capacity for artistic or intellectual accomplishment; that they are quite possibly more natural in their behavioral patterns and personal relationships; that they are not necessarily driven by instinct any more than are we "civilized." "Primitive" is a quality of a culture, not of a people or a racial stock.

Thus *Coming of Age in Samoa* provided an important contribution to Americans' cultural understanding, partly by bypassing and undermining prevalent value-laden ethnocentric categories and concepts, and partly by attempting to particularize a "primitive" culture in terms that respected it as a culture. And this in addition to the fact that the book itself admits to having as its primary purpose the examination of a theory of adolescent development.

But under the surface there is this basic oppositional pull in the book between its particularization of the Samoan culture and its use of that particularization to drive home Mead's theoretical point. We learn a good deal that is quite specific about the Manu'ans, their mores and habits and even their problems, but the ways in which that information is couched (and perhaps even arrived at?) is highly dependent on intercultural comparisons and on categories from the civilized world. "The oppressive atmosphere of the small town is all about them," Mead declares, and "privacy of possessions is virtually impossible" (125). "Romantic love as it occurs in our civilisation, inextricably bound up with ideas of monogamy, exclusiveness, jealousy and undeviating fidelity does not occur in Samoa" (105), and so forth. Granted that such expressions all have the readership in mind, serving the rhetorical function of clarifying comparisons, still their sources are specific features of United States society imported into Samoa as presumably ethno-neutral interpretive categories.

Looked at in terms of recent ethnographic standards, her issues and categories are ethnocentric in themselves: the crisis of adolescent girls in society was a contemporary U.S. issue, as were the relative strictness or laxity of sexual behavior and the possibly inhibiting effect of the nuclear family arrangement. What bothers Samoans is given little notice, while Mead pursues her issues. She even employs Western aesthetic and psychological standards in viewing their behaviors: in explaining the Samoans' untypically individualistic public dancing she notes that "this emphasis on individuality is carried to limits which seriously mar the dance as an aesthetic performance" (117–18). And, although she (and Franz Boas too, in his Foreword) expressly reject psychoanalysis as a generically explanatory scheme, her interpretation of the dance, for example, invokes as a conclusion "the function of informal dancing in the development of individuality and the compensation for repression of personality in other spheres of life" (121). (Yes, although Freud's theories were propounded with an evolutionist ethnology in mind, traces of their influence certainly are observable in the hypotheses of even the most dedicated of cultural relativists.)

For anthropologists of the last two decades, *Coming of Age* was simply too obsessed with proving its point, with establishing an interpretive configuration of Samoan culture that would stand in vivid contrast to U.S. culture. This characteristic made the book vulnerable to Derek Freeman's attack, "the leitmotif of her depiction being the notion of *ease*" (1983, 84) being contradicted by his own idea of Samoa's strict and more sinister configuration. Martin Orans in reviewing Mead's field materials exposes her tendency to force a configuration:

> Because Mead requires a halcyon Samoa for her argument of a less stressful adolescence, we are therefore entirely prepared for her failure to report cases of rape, violence, revolution, and competition that the field materials indicate she was aware of. But what of the surprising number of cases she was aware of? (1996, 120–21)

James Clifford concludes that "Mead's 'experiment' in controlled cultural variation now looks less like science than allegory—a too sharply focused story of Samoa suggesting a possible America" (1988, 102). Nancy Scheper-Hughes identifies as a limiting factor of Mead's early work and Freeman's "the old culturalist idea that everything in a society must adhere to a single configuration or a pattern," she pointing out, too, that "[t]he error is to think of 'culture' as a single integrated reality somewhere 'out there' waiting to be accurately described" (1984, 90, 91). Bradd Shore declares that "the problem is not ethnographic, but epistemological," that "neither a personality nor a culture can be sufficiently characterized by unidimensional themes purged of the conflicts and contradictions that lie at the heart of the human condition" (1983, 936, 937). (The culture Faulkner envisions in *Light in August*—as very particularly determinant, but still vastly diverse and entropic—embodies much of the epistemological and sociological sophistication that these latter-day cultural anthropologists have come to require. Such literary performances indeed have had the potential to give them a good deal of purchase on their very complex discipline.)

But if Mead's representation of Samoa is adversely affected by her allegiance to a configurationist approach, what shall we say of her representation of American society? Here her categories and issues all come from the culture under observation, but there is no attempt to offer evidence, and the language is unrestrainedly biased. Science lapses here in the final chapters, as Mead with a strong admixture of emotion presents intuitive conclusions as self-evident truths. "What are the rewards of the tiny, ingrown, biological family opposing its closed circle of affection to a forbidding world," she asks, later concluding that "[i]n our ideal picture of the freedom of the individual and the dignity of human relations it is not pleasant to realise that we have developed a form of family organisation which often cripples the emotional life, and warps and confuses the growth of many individuals' power to consciously live their own lives" (212, 214). The line taken here is congruent with much of the liberal reformist social criticism that was familiar to her, but the empirical base of her judgments seems to be simply her own experience, rooted provincially in white upper-middle and middle class urban and suburban society. And strangely enough, we can imagine a kind of reciprocity of perspective-warping: just as her representation of the Samoan culture seems to have been much affected by her comparative reading of the American, so too the faults she stresses in American society often seem negative reflections of the counterpoised culture of Samoa.

There is no doubt that *Coming of Age in Samoa* remains a very problematic text. But neither is there any doubt about the importance of its contribution to the growing literature on issues of difference, race, and primitiveness, or to the growing understanding that the so-called primitive cultures were made up of individual persons rather than generic populations. And much of the book's importance involves its introduction of the "other gender" into anthropological study—as the first in a series of South Seas studies that she was to produce in which, as Louise Newman points out, "Mead brilliantly redeployed these constructions of primitive sexuality to prompt Americans to reconceptualize their understanding of sexual differences and gender relations" (1996, 244). The reconceptualizing prompted by *Coming of Age* was to involve sexual activity, romance, marriage, and divorce.

Societally, however, as Mead saw, Samoan gender roles were rigid, and the careers of mature women involved adjusting to the social roles dictated by their husband's rank, carrying out domestic and childbearing duties, working hard in the fields, and (for a few) becoming an expert and a teacher in some craft limited to women. As she characterizes them, "old women are usually more of a power within the household than the old men." They "rule by force of personality and knowledge of human nature" rather than by any official authority (194). But the limitation of the range of *Coming of Age*'s gender reconceptualizations cannot diminish the force of its inherent feminist message—witness Bonnie Nardi's 1984 attack on Freeman in *Feminist Studies*: "I argue here that Freeman attacks feminism by attacking Mead, a powerful symbol of female liberation" (327).

Mead saw her Samoa of 1926 as temporarily hovering in a hiatus of colonialism. "The new influences have drawn the teeth of the old culture. Cannibalism, war, blood revenge, the life and death power of the *matai*, . . . the discomfort due to widespread disease—all these have vanished," (276) she proclaims, and Samoan civilization is characterized by its "flexibility, . . . the result of the blending of the various European ideas, beliefs, mechanical devices, with the old primitive culture" (272). Impure and impermanent, Samoan culture seems to her to have flourished in the way it has because of a chance economic factor: it is virtually "an island without resources worth exploiting" (277). The atypicality of American Samoa was vividly present to Mead, although it was only in other writings that she treated that particular contrast.

From New Guinea she wrote in one of her letters from the field, "Such flimsy structures of a hundred or so white men govern and exploit this vast country—find gold, plant great plantations, trade for shell, hide their failures in other lands, drink inordinately, run into debt, steal each other's wives, go broke and commit suicide or get rich—if they know how" (1977, 63–64). And in her *American Mercury* essay praising the administration by the American navy in Samoa she enumerates the casually malicious effects on the natives of the usual colonialist occupation, concluding that "[t]his is cultural death and has proved to be only a deferring of racial death in Hawaii" (1929,

264). The complex issue of Mead's opinions about and relationship to South Pacific cultures is one that develops largely in later phases of her career and is beyond the scope of my topic here, but it is important to note her sense that in Manu'a she was studying a rare historical exception to the ordinary course of colonialism.

Coming of Age in Samoa is certainly a book of its time and place—radical much in the style of 1920s liberalism and still struggling to free itself from the ethnocentric categories and overconceptualization of the older patterns of ethnographic understanding. But it was in some ways forward-looking and innovative, and it gave American notions of difference in race, civilization, and culture distinctly new trajectories.

9

Improvising Ethnography: Zora Neale Hurston and *Tell My Horse*

Man, like all the other animals fears and is repelled by that which he does not understand, and mere difference is apt to connote something malign.
                              —Zora Hurston, "What White Publishers Won't Print"

To accept as "moral" only those values held moral by the whites, to regard as "culture" only those practices that have the sanctions of a European past is a contributory factor in the process of devaluation.
                              —Melville Herskovits, *The Myth of the Negro Past*

HURSTON'S SENSE OF THE SIGNIFICANCE OF HUMAN DIFFERENCE was very like that of her white anthropologist contemporary Herskovits. She similarly rejected the conventional attributions of the term "primitive," and her program for addressing the root issue of racism was similar to his: fight it with understanding. Like Boas, who had personally served as her anthropological mentor, and Mead and Herskovits, she located difference principally in culture, but her approach was personal and intuitive—fundamentally and explicitly—so that in her ethnographic writings she factored in the inescapable reflexiveness of personal and cultural viewpoint far differently than did they. Aiming at a general audience in *Mules and Men* and *Tell My Horse,* Hurston interwove a complex and seemingly spontaneous characterization of herself-the-investigator, experiencing and reacting to and even instigating the investigative situation. The result was a pair of texts without the standard self-stipulated aura of objective scientific authority but with interesting connections to the narrative fallibility of contemporary fiction, to the personalizing conventions of contemporary travel accounts, and to the epistemological sophistication of the ethnography of a much later period.

Personally, Hurston is an anomaly. An individualistic, multiply talented woman, she was fiction writer, folklorist, ethnographer, raconteur and cultural critic by turns and sometimes all at once. To her contemporaries she could seem any or all of these, and yet basically none of them fully and officially. She never (until quite recently) achieved a niche in American culture. She stood out as a kind of amateur, an original, an improviser whose works were often only partially successful and difficult to classify, sporadically appreciated, and set against the grain of much contemporary African American literature.

The combination of her race and her gender put her on a marginal track on which recognition and even economic survival were tenuous at best, and this despite the help she got from several influential white friends (Boas, writer-critic-promoter Carl VanVechten, patrons Fanny Hurst, and Mrs. Osgood Mason). Her status was the key determinant of her career. As ethnographer or as any kind of professional intellectual her credentials were mixed and, in respect to their ability to get authority for her voice, clearly inferior (unlike Mead, whose academic degrees and social placement guaranteed a certain amount of authority, and whose lingo simply arrogated it).

Cross currents of influences on her abounded: Alain Locke and his *The New Negro*; Nancy Cunard and her odd compilation *Negro*; Langston Hughes and his works and his ways as a Hurston collaborator; W.E.B. Du Bois; the rebellious intellectuals and journals and the whole intricate give-and-take of the Harlem Renaissance (a source of much stimulation, much comradery, much contention for her); VanVechten and the white liberal supporters of Negro art; her paternalistic Professor Boas and the cultural determinists; the complex and conflicting aims of commercial publishers, of funding agencies, of possessive patrons, and so forth. Never, however, as far as I have been able to discover, any influence of Freudianism—as we shall see, Hurston employed quite different systems of interpretation. But through it all (and, yes, in spite of much of it) Hurston's irrepressible personal self comes through: witty, ironic, self-possessed, sassy, Zora is a "rush" even when dealing with her most serious concerns.

In his biography of Hurston, Robert Hemenway makes this point as part of his explanation of Hurston's lack of a clear professional role: "Zora never became a professional academic folklorist because such a vocation was alien to her exuberant sense of self, to her admittedly artistic, sometimes erratic temperament, and to her awareness of the esthetic content of black folklore." He cogently goes on to point out that in her writing, "eventually immediate experience takes precedence over analysis, emotion over reason, the personal over the theoretical" (1977, 213). In his introduction to her autobiography, *Dust Tracks on a Road*, he proposes viewing her as bicultural:

Born in an all-black town, she collected folklore in all-black communities, spent the last years of her life writing for a black newspaper while substitute teaching in a segregated school, and was buried in a segregated cemetery. No matter how far she traveled, Eatonville was home. The public Hurston was a graduate of Barnard, a Guggenheim Fellow, a writer for the *Saturday Review*, the *American Mercury*, and the *Saturday Evening Post*, a book reviewer for the *New York Times* and the *New York Herald Tribune*, a woman who moved easily in an integrated world.

A writer whose career has assumed this pattern exhibits a certain biculturalism. (Hurston 1984, xviii)

The use of bipolar terms has become standard in Hurston criticism, focusing her anomalousness in contrasts between black home-girl and Barnard-grad anthropologist, between folk and intellectual cultures, African and European mythos, literary and scientific expression, subjectivity and objectivity, and so forth. Bipolarity has played a very useful part in structuring our understanding of Hurston's works, although several recent cautionary notes have been expressed: one by Barbara Johnson who, looking at "her strategies and structures of problematic address" is led to consider "Hurston's way of dealing with multiple agendas and heterogeneous implied readers" (1985, 317); another by Karen Jacobs, who notes an "overall instability in her thought," "an inconsistent relationship to her methods and materials . . . which arguably testify as much to Hurston's internal conflicts and divisions as to her elusive, editorially shaped and culturally constrained position as a speaking subject" (1997, 339).

Boas saw Hurston as talented and resourceful, a potentially valuable researcher of folklore, folkways and linguistics. The fieldwork he put her onto was similar to what he had been getting from George Hunt, his informant for much of his research on the Kwakiutl Indians (although Hurston's independence and sophistication were to determine that the end products would come out quite differently). He directed her research and helped her obtain funding (at least initially, before Mrs. Mason took control), and he endorsed her books, even when they took a more freestyle approach than was then current in ethnography. She cited him as mentor and a paramount role model in science, characterizing him as "the greatest anthropologist alive, for two reasons. The first is his insatiable hunger for knowledge and then more knowledge; and the second is his genius for pure objectivity. He has no pet wishes to prove. His instructions are to go out and find what is there" (Hurston 1984, 174). She could accept the whole cultural relativist program—and that not as if it were learned but as if it were her natural way of seeing things.

The formative moment in her career came when Boas commissioned her to revisit her girlhood home in Eatonville and several other Southern locales to gather folklore. As recounted by Hemenway, "She was sponsored by Columbia University's anthropology department. The Association for the Study of Negro Life and History was paying expenses. . . . . [And t]he task was to record the songs, customs, tales, superstitions, lies, jokes, dances, and games of Afro-American folklore" (1977, 84). On that 1927 adventure she not only got a whole rush of appreciative nostalgia about her childhood locale and its people, but the experience of lore-gathering too, by techniques some of which were canonical and some personally improvised. It gave her a sense of identity as ethnographer, and a sense of mission too: to give the lower-class rural Negro culture the recognition and respect she felt its people—her people—deserved. Years later Alice Walker would recognize this motive and give it her full appreciation: what African American readers could feel was

the *joy* over who she was showing them to be: descendants of an inventive, joyous, courageous, and outrageous people: loving drama, appreciating wit, and, most of all, relishing the pleasure of each other's loquacious and *bodacious* company.

This was my first indication of the quality I feel is most characteristic of Zora's work: racial health—a sense of black people as complete, complex, *undiminished* human beings, a sense that is lacking in so much black writing and literature. (1986, 64)

A different but related part of Hurston's mission also seemed to be to establish a similar legitimacy for Hoodoo, to free it from outrageous popular misconceptions and show it as an alternative religion with a logic and a power of its own.

She took the role of participant-observer to the limit and beyond, revealing not only her own "insatiable hunger for knowledge and then more knowledge," but a limitless relish in participation, be that in store-porch storytelling, dancing and hanging out in backcountry joints and jukes, or undergoing initiatory rites of Hoodoo practitioners. She was not at all shy about precipitating adventures that might show the people at their most fervently typical.

She wanted to serve up the folklore and -ways pure and straight and from the bottom of the culture (LET THE PEOPLE SING was the title she chose for the program of amateur-performed spirituals she wanted to show as superior to the "highly arranged spirituals" white audiences in America had been getting [Hurston 1984, 207]). Nevertheless there is a question about the accuracy and purity of her collecting. She herself would have been the first to point out that there is no possibility of establishing a definitive word-for-word text of an oral folktale or -song: too many people have their own ways of telling and singing, their own elaborations and memory lapses. But at the same time in her lore-collecting and her ethnographic (and semi-ethnographic) texts she seems to have moved rather freely among the roles of collector, mediator, interpreter, and even creator. "Her re-writing grew out of her desire to emphasize the esthetic significance of the folklore performance," Hemenway claims by way of defense, although he acknowledges that "Hurston's rewriting and tampering with material, even done solely for the purposes of clarity, would be anathema to most modern folklorists" (1977, 126). And, we might add, to many folklorists of her own day.

Somewhat like Mead she had a sense of accommodating the style and presentation of her writing to the interests of a particular audience and publishing situation. The first fruits of her fieldwork in the American South were published as a scholarly article, "Hoodoo in America" in *The Journal of American Folklore* (Hurston 1931). The persona of the investigator is virtually invisible in that piece, which is principally the uninterpreted presentation of accumulated materials. The investigator makes some minimal acknowledgment of how she got the information but basically the article presents descriptions of Hoodoo practitioners, principles, practices, substances and parapher-nalia, stories of cures and curses, and so forth—and that just strung out, not even very systematically. Four years later she used the same material in the Hoodoo segment of *Mules and Men*, but edited and slightly altered and more personalized, positioned after her extended account of the many various stories and songs she had gathered, and of the adventure of her gathering them.

Mules and Men, the first of her two ethnographic works aimed at a general audience, was issued in 1935, completed eight years after her gathering of the materials and then only after advice from publishers and some substantial reconsideration of the material's possibilities. She had published stories even before her Florida folklore-collecting expeditions, and in the time between the collecting and the composi-tion and publication of *Mules* she had followed diverse impulses: writ-ing stories, a novel, plays, and theatrical revues; staging revues and a concert program, attempting to establish a college program in Negro dramatic arts; beginning and quickly abandoning a PhD program in anthropology at Columbia. In her prime she tended to go in many directions at once, although the urge to be a literary writer seems to have predominated. No wonder then that personal narrative would be

what both framed and flavored the folklore and ethnography of
Mules.

Boas gave the book a dedicatory preface, lauding Hurston in white-
fatherly terms for her ability as a kind of native participant-observer
to provide new information about cultural phenomena previously
difficult for anthropologists to access:

> It is the great merit of Miss Hurston's work that she entered into the
> homely life of the southern Negro as one of them and was fully accepted
> as such by the companions of her childhood. Thus she has been able to
> penetrate through that affected demeanor by which the Negro excludes
> the White observer effectively from participating in his true inner life.
> Miss Hurston has been equally successful in gaining the confidence of the
> voodoo doctors and she gives us much that throws a new light upon the
> much discussed voodoo beliefs and practices. Added to all this is the
> charm of a loveable personality and of a revealing style which makes Miss
> Hurston's work an unusual contribution to our knowledge of the true
> inner life of the Negro. (Hurston 1935, xiii)

But Hurston, after giving an appreciative nod in the direction of "the
spy-glass of Anthropology" (1) for the perspective it gave her on the
down-home stories she now could certify as indigenous folklore,
goes on to describe the ethnographic adventure in lingo that projects
a country-wise vernacular Zora:

> I didn't go back there so that the home folks could make admiration over
> me because I had been up North to college and come back with a diploma
> and a Chevrolet. I knew they were not going to pay either one of these
> items too much mind. I was just Lucy Hurston's daughter, Zora, and even
> if I had—to use one of our down-home expressions—had a Kaiser baby,
> and that's something that hasn't been done in this Country yet, I'd still
> be just Zora to the neighbors. If I had exalted myself to impress the town,
> somebody would have sent me word in a match-box that I had been up
> North there and had rubbed the hair off of my head against some college
> wall, and then come back there with a lot of form and fashion and outside
> show to the world. But they'd stand flat-footed and tell me that they
> didn't have me, neither my sham-polish, to study 'bout. And that would
> have been that. (1935, 2)

The linguistic approach could hardly be more different from that of
her entry in *The Journal of American Folklore*, and in addition to its
making far livelier reading, more attractive to readers (and to prospective publishers), ethnographically it establishes a different order of authority for its presenter. Hurston presents herself as, yes indeed, an
academically trained folklorist embarking on a scientific enquiry, but

also as one who can talk the talk of the subject peoples, speak virtually from the inside of the culture in presenting information (and, of course, recording the individual tales and telling styles) for the ostensible purpose of satisfying the scientific curiosity outside. Not that much of her explanation isn't delivered in standard, educated American English, but ultimately the ethnographic authority established in the language of *Mules* derives not from a generic professional erudition, but from an implied linguistic oneness with the subject people and their stories. And the fact that Hurston seems so obviously enjoying the language—and the culture and the stories and songs that are inherent in it and expressed through it—gives the book that sense of "joy" that Alice Walker so appreciated, at the same time that as discourse it managed (in Hemenway's more intellectualized terms) "to assert black humanity by emphasizing its anthropological warrant" (1977, 214). Henry Louis Gates Jr. coined the term "speakerly text" to apply to Hurston's monological evocation of "a profoundly lyrical, densely metaphorical, quasi-musical, privileged black oral tradition" (1988, 174).

This is a radical departure from the objectivity urged by Boas (as in his admonition to Mead, above [p. 212]), but it is something more—something that takes Hurston in the direction of later twentieth-century anthropological writing. As has been pointed out (albeit somewhat exaggeratedly) by Karen Jacobs, Boas's "almost positivist insistence on the untainted, unmediated scientific gaze as a tool for producing reliable knowledge" is what is compromised by Hurston, and compromised in the direction of a more sophisticated (and more suitably relativistic) epistemology (1997, 333–34). And I would have it that Hurston's self-representation in *Mules* constitutes not merely a switch from objective to subjective, absolutist to relativist viewpoints, but the creation, fictionwise, of a presenting persona, a protagonist-narrator who, speaking in different dialects for different situations, is herself a bit of a fabrication, a means to reveal—and to embody—the insights that author Hurston thought most important. Thus the Zora-narrator is a postulated subjectivity through which the whole array of characters and relationships, of myths, stories, "lies" and Hoodoo practices and beliefs can be presented without assuming a no less artificial pose of ethnographic objectivity that would risk misrepresenting and possibly undervaluing their inner logic. The bonus in the bargain is the entertainment-and-insight package that is that Zora character, both subject and voice.

Thus human difference in *Mules* was presented from a complex, of-it-but-not-of-it perspective, its linguistic positioning in effect somewhat like that which fixed our identification in the Other as we followed Joe Christmas. Hurston's fiction—although I am putting it outside the bounds of this inquiry—has this same characteristic of language and perspective, carrying us through quasi-emically on the dreams, resilience, and resourcefulness of the protagonists (like Janie Crawford Killicks Starks Woods questing for a self-fulfillment free from domination and abasement), and also on the richness, wit, and legitimacy of the rural black culture (like the ingenious challenging of individual and social mores by the store-porch banterers, and the communal cohesion of the workers "on the muck"). In communicating her first folklore-gathering and -assimilating efforts to a general audience Hurston manifested what Michael North has identified as "a conception of performative language in which even the most playful utterances accomplish serious social work" (1994, 185).

Interestingly, despite the unconventional-for-its-time presentation, *Mules* was (and is) recognized as having ethnographic value. Melville Herskovits drew on it in his 1941 work *The Myth of the Negro Past*, a major study intended to dispel the racial devaluation embodied in incomplete and fallacious versions of Negro history. Herskovits portrays the African heritage as complex, various, and highly developed, and he attempts to trace its survivals in Negro cultures of the Western Hemisphere. At one point he recommends "Hurston, who discusses the Negro point of view with the intimacy of inside knowledge" (252), and, in recognition of the value of *Mules* for the kind of anthropological inquiry he is carrying on, in which reliable information is scarce, he states that

> Some indication of the acculturative accommodation can, however, be illustrated by an example taken from the recent, informally reported collection of Florida tales published by Hurston, that have never been subjected to comparative analysis and are from an area where no previous collections of any appreciable size have been made. (274)

(Apparently "informally reported" material is of ethnographic value in 1941 even in the absence of fully sanctioned scientific prose.) The anthropologist could especially draw on her reporting of her first-hand Hoodoo experiences for information valuable in drawing his conclusions: "There is much in Hurston's descriptions of the initiations she experienced into various cult groups that can be referred to recurrent practices in West Africa, and in the Catholic New World countries where pagan beliefs of Africa have persisted" (248). Herskovits' *The Myth of the Negro Past* and Hurston's earlier *Mules and Men* had the similar aims of demythologizing the African American population and of legitimizing their culture and the study of it, although their strategies and their languages were as different as their own stations in life and their own creative styles.

Tell My Horse (1938) continued and in a way culminated Hurston's quest for language that could make difference unthreatening, respect-inducing, and separable from conventional (racist) primitive/civilized, superiority/inferiority axes. Her anthropological spy-glass again helped somewhat, although her personal sense of what was real and what was right gave her most of her insights, most of her expressiveness. Her rationales—esthetical, semiscientific, semi-intellectual—were sometimes confused, but her impulses were humane, her confidence unimpedable, her genius a matter of feelings and figurativeness.

In the mid-1930s Hurston used her reputation for insider expertise in Hoodoo to win a Guggenheim Fellowship to study Obeah practices in Jamaica and Haiti. That sponsorship, along with that of Mrs. Osgood Mason (who fancied herself as knowing a thing or two about the folklore of primitives and how it should be treated and appreciated), and the moral support of Boas provided the practical rationale that sped Hurston very enthusiastically off for lore-gathering in the Caribbean.

The interests of her stateside supporters probably complicated her investigative agenda, though, as well as the focus of the text she would subsequently produce. Along with considerations of publishers' and readers' anticipated tastes and Hurston's whole sense of the demands of "[her] position as an African-American female writer" they provided, as Deborah Gordon has pointed out, a set of determinants "placing her work both tenuously within the field of anthropology and also outside of it because of its style. . . . *Tell My Horse* was only one example of her 'style' that did not readily fit into the literary genres available for producing African-American intellectual life, art, or folklore" (1990, 161). That text was indeed far from being freely concocted, but the diversity of Hurston's own curiosities and enthusiasms must also be figured as a factor in accounting for its looseness and variousness.

Voodoo and Life in Haiti and Jamaica is the subtitle of *Tell My Horse*, which suggests the variousness of its contents at the very outset. But the variousness—the miscellaneousness, really—of the narration's routines and approaches and of the relationships of the researcher to her subjects is not evident until the book is under way. The text is by turns ethnographical and personal, historical and con-

temporary, empirical and opinionated, earnest and ironic. What unifies it is the persona of Zora and what structures it is the sequence of
her adventures, both factors allowing or even encouraging dispersion
and digression. No wonder *Horse* has been overlooked and underval-
ued—it is of mixed genre and complex (and somewhat contradictory)
intent, and it is problematically open to any of a number of different
criteria for its evaluation.

As Hurston was researching and writing *Horse* in 1936–38 there
were two recent books about Haiti that she seems to have known
quite well: Melville Herskovits's *Life in a Haitian Valley* (1927) and
W. B. Seabrook's *The Magic Island* (1929). And they couldn't have
been more different from each other. "William Seabrook in his *Magic
Island* had fired my imagination with his account of The White King
of La Gonave" (1938, 134), Hurston admits, in explaining her own
motivation in visiting that island. Seabrook's book, following on his
previous *Adventures in Arabia*, was an adventurer's travelogue, making some attempt to describe the Haitian people and environment and
history, but driven basically by his search for the bizarre, the dangerous and the impressive, and his need to portray himself as daring and
courageous and talented at gaining the confidence of mysterious and
important personages. Photos document his presence among Voodoo
practitioners, and, with what today appears striking anomalousness,
the book includes melodramatic drawings by Alexander King: exaggeratedly Negroid caricatures, most of them sinister in tone, presented in a kind of illustrator's high modernist style. Seabrook
himself expresses a good deal of respect for the Haitian people, repudiating racist judgments and regarding Voodoo as a legitimate (even
on occasions compelling) religion. But class bias intervenes more than
just occasionally, and it reinforces both the sense of drama and the
pose of superiority the text insists on: At a soiree of the Haitian president and his social set, Seabrook decides that this society, if measured
by other than "material-mechanical-industrial standards" was "perhaps a great deal more civilized in some ways than we are. At any rate,
it often seemed to me that they lived more agreeably" (1929, 159). But
his language describing the lower classes is far different, involving
only negatives of "civilized": "[t]he Haitian peasants are thus double-
natured in reality—sometimes moved by savage, atavistic forces
whose dark depths no white psychology can ever plumb—but often,
even in their weirdest customs, naive, simple, harmless children" (91).

Herskovits's book, by contrast, is studiously ethnographic, systematic rather than dramatically selective, and (at least by contrast)
self-effacing. As he explains in an appendix-description of his methods, he and his wife spent some three months with a particular Hai-

tian people in the Valley of Mirebalais studying their social and familial organization, economy, daily routines, religion, celebrations, and ceremonies, and so forth. Herskovits tries to be thorough in his information gathering and apologizes when he is unable to be. One of his avowed primary aims is to trace elements of the African and the slavery heritages in the culture of these people. Another, developed in an appendix, is to encourage "*acculturation* studies" (1971, 327) such as this, and a third, in his conclusions (with the incipient intent of his *The Myth of the Negro Past* already in focus), was to affect the racial discourse (and the racial situation) in the U.S. by countering conventional white racist preconceptions and judgments.

Consistent with his stance (and his authority) as a scientist of his time, Herskovits maintains a focus on the Haitians as Others. He purposively stays outside their culture, observing but neither participating nor judging. His account uses a great deal of passive voice, as he seems to be trying not to put himself into it in any way. He avoids essentialist othering of the Haitians with designating or characterizing terms, although he occasionally refers to generic characteristics of "the Negro people." He obviously means to de-sensationalize, de-exoticize Haitians, and in a set of notes added in a later edition he explicitly criticizes Seabrook for his frequent excesses in representing them and their ceremonies. Ethnologically, finally (and very much in line with his Boasian matrix), Herskovits urges students of cultures not "to neglect the inner relationships that give to a culture the significance it has for those who live under it," nor to neglect "the basic principle that every culture is a unique historical continuum" (1971, 328).

Part ethnography and part travel narrative, *Tell My Horse* takes on many characteristics of Herskovits' kind of work, and many, too, of Seabrook's, but as in *Mules and Men*, Hurston's personal, original perception and expression most crucially shape the text. There are scientific standards and there are literary and intellectual genres and traditions, but Hurston will have it her own way, and this enriches, complicates, and confuses her presentation of her subject and her claim to authority.

A good many aspects of *Tell My Horse* confirm Hurston's role as ethnographer. In attempting to study the Caribbean people and their ceremonies from the inside she had two special advantages: she was black, and she had already been inducted (several times, actually) into African-based conjure religion and could demonstrate her familiarity with its myths and rituals to prospective Voodoo informants. Her text doesn't make a great deal of these qualifications to her readers, but they are clearly implied. In those extremely sexist Caribbean communities her gender often hampered her work as anthropologist, however; this she makes very clear in the text and shows how she needed persistence and ingenuity to overcome the bias. She is usually careful to account for the experiential sources of her information, citing particular occasions and persons, even giving rather full references for some of her informants. She demonstrates professional skepticism (when an informant offers to hold a ceremony for her she declines, thinking but not telling him, "I was too old a hand at collecting to fall for staged-dance affairs" [1938, 35]), and she feels it her responsibility to show disagreement among informants or to refute individual or commonly-held interpretations. In keeping with standard methodology she gets some of her information and interpretation from previous anthropological or historical writers (including Herskovits). She makes her text clearly indicate when she is quoting or paraphrasing a particular informant or source, when reporting a general opinion or legend, and when she is fabricating a particular perspective to present a more vivid version of a historical event.

She also functions as a folklorist-ethnographer: collecting and preserving accounts of myths and stories; carefully detailing settings, paraphernalia, and rituals of particular ceremonials; describing voodoo deities, their functions and habits; listing a repertoire of conjure poisons and antidotes; and presenting printed versions of Voodoo worship songs, both words and music. Hurston even includes photographs in the text, pictures she had taken that document the events she witnessed and, as Beth Harrison has pointed out, help establish her authority as an on-site observer.*

But her text does not show her aiming at Herskovits' ideal of thoroughness: she selects and dwells on certain ethnographic topics—most especially Voodoo, Zombies, secret societies, and institutionalized sexism—that would emphasize primitive difference for an American audience. Coincidentally and conveniently, these topics would also have for that audience potentially the greatest ethical and social import, and the most attractive exoticism. Hurston's approach and self-representation everywhere overflow with enthusiasm, freely compromising ethnographic objectivity, which is principally confined to enumerations and to the use of material from other authorities. The Zora-narrator explicitly relishes the natural surroundings,

---

*1996, 94. The use of photography and even motion pictures was increasingly a part of ethnographic reporting in the thirties; Hurston was not an originator of the practice, but her use of the camera avoided the stocks-in-trade of travelogue photography such as Seabrook's posing of costumed natives and of himself with Voodoo priests.

the Haitian and Jamaican people, their folkways and ceremonies, her own joining in with them, the whole adventure of being an anthropologist in the field, the expression of her own feelings—even disapproval, righteous indignation, satiric wit, or irony. The very representation of that adventuring, investigating, enthusing narrator establishes her as a subject of the book too—ancillary, but nevertheless thoroughly infused. In both of Hurston's ethnographic works after her piece in *The American Journal of Folklore*, the language is often stylish: openly, flamboyantly self-characterizing of this persona "Zora Hurston."

In *Tell My Horse* investigator/narrator Zora does not have the linguistic advantage that she had in *Mules and Men*; she is not a daughter of these parts, and although the Caribbeans' slavery heritage, African-origin folktales, and Voodoo are deeply part of her background and expertise, their languages—creolized French and pidgin English—are foreign to her, and she has to work to learn to translate them. She includes a good deal of quotation, translation, and imitative locution in *Tell My Horse*, but the principal language of her narration does not have that near-emic quality of that in *Mules and Men*. Concurrently, (and perhaps reciprocally?) she often takes the liberty in this book of openly expressing her opinions and judgments.

Implicitly, this book seems another of her attempts to reorient thinking about black peoples—to suggest the Haitians and Jamaicans are not "primitives" but humane, intelligent, resourceful peoples who have civilizations that entail their solving the basic human problems—especially problems of power and powerlessness—in their own characteristic ways. But explicitly the text indicates she feels she needs to sort out their mores; to attack as well as appreciate some elements of their societies and cultures; to set the record straight about their sexism and their cruelty, their nominal Christianity, their horrendous political history, and their misprizing of the heritage of their recently ended occupation by the U.S.

Hurston arranges the book in three parts, each part roughly focused on a major segment of her expedition and made up of a set of chapters each roughly focused on a particular subject, theme or event. "Part I: Jamaica" contains five chapters. The first sympathetically characterizes a Jamaican cult ritual she has observed, satirically attacks the island's hypocritical postcolonial racial bias, and admiringly quotes some indigenous proverbs. She introduces the cult casually: "It is important to a great number of people in Jamaica, so perhaps we ought to peep in on it a while" (1938, 13). But its underlying myth (a revisionist version of Christianity) and its ritual details are carefully observed and accounted for, along with some appreciative diction (the "very beautiful singing," the dancing, and "that tremendous exhalation of the breath" producing a ceremony that is "exciting at times" [14–15]).

"And then Jamaica has its social viewpoints and stratifications which influence so seriously its economic direction" (16), she claims, abruptly shifting to the topic of race bias. In describing Jamaican social stratification Hurston puts her own style into it, producing an irony-loaded polemic against racism and sexism. "Jamaica is the land where the rooster lays an egg," she begins, scathing "the aim of everybody to talk English, act English and *look* English," where a class structure premised on the superiority of the former colonial masters devalues black people and results in "a frantic stampede white-ward to escape from Jamaica's black mass," and where a person no matter what his or her heredity or coloration can be declared *legally* white (16). Such an absurd bias devalues womankind as well, as the mulatto will indeed insist on his or her part-white status "until you get the impression that he or she *had* no mother" (19). "The situation presents a curious spectacle to the eyes of an American Negro" (18), the narrator asserts, worrying the question of assimilation versus separation, seeing the situation in American terms as an attitudinal throwback, and suggesting tongue-in-cheek that "in His Majesty's colony it may work out to everybody's satisfaction in a few hundred years, if the majority of the population, which is black, can be persuaded to cease reproduction. That is the weak place in the scheme" (18). The language in this highly stylized cultural analysis is that of irony and absurdity, ethnographically unconventional and out of tone with the rest of the chapter, but effectively raising questions about differentiation by race and deconstructing prevailing notions of race and gender dominance, not only in Jamaica but in the world in general.

The chapter ends with a different sort of set piece, declaring its thesis with its introductory transition: "But a new day is in sight for Jamaica. The black people of Jamaica are beginning to respect themselves." And it goes on to praise their proverbs as "particularly rich in philosophy, irony and humor" (19–20), quoting and translating twelve of them, and then citing the work of several Jamaican artists working with Jamaican forms. The folklorist combines with the art critic here to (again) urge a revaluation of black culture.

Hurston shifts discursive mode, tone, idiom, and so forth in this manner throughout the entire book, and critics (principally literary critics) have offered a number of different explanations for this departure in her writing from the unity that is one of Western authorship's most valued compositional principles. Cases can and have been made for the shifting approach as expressive of Hurston's "biculturalism" or of her "double consciousness" as an African American; as a strategy by which she accomplishes the blending of outsider and insider perspectives to "mediate between objective and subjective viewpoints without privileging either," or achieves "strategic positionality," or "resistance to any single defining discourse" (see Hemenway 1984, xviii; Gates 1990, 296; Harrison 1996, 93; Hernandez 1995, 148; O'Connor 1992, 151). If there is a conscious compositional theory behind Hurston's practice it might conceivably be related to her notions of an essence of Negro expression such as she sets forth in "Characteristics of Negro Expression," an essay she supplied for Nancy Cunard's massive and diverse 1934 collection, *Negro*. Mightn't the category of unity be something Hurston purposefully avoided on racial esthetic grounds? Here are points she makes about two of the "Characteristics," *angularity* and *asymmetry*:

> Anyone watching Negro dancers will be struck by the same phenomenon. Every posture is another angle. Pleasing, yes. But an effect achieved by the very means which a European strives to avoid. . . .
> It is the lack of symmetry which makes Negro dancing so difficult for white dancers to learn. The abrupt and unexpected changes. (1980, 54–55)

Or, to consider a more mundane possibility, perhaps it was just the desire to include all her notes, all the various interesting pieces of information and insight that led to all the variety in mode and idiom— just a roughly chronological ordering of different windows on different aspects of Hurston's experience in the culture.

The second chapter continues in a miscellaneous, spontaneous way. The Zora-narrator gets an exceptional invitation to a "curry goat feed," a ceremonial celebration that "is something utterly masculine in every detail" (22), an invitation she uses to add to the exclusiveness of her ethnographic authority. She not only records the details of the celebration, but names and identifies particular individuals who took some specific ceremonial role or related to her in some specific way.

And then the narrative shifts to detail an extensive discussion she had with a male informant who argued vehemently that "women who went in for careers were just so much wasted material" (27). Zora "did not agree with him and so I gave him my most aggravating grunt. I succeeded in snorting a bit of scorn into it" (29), but she let him run on, presumably to hang himself for the American readers by the extremity of his sexism. But then he arranges for her to spend two weeks with a group of "specialists who prepare young girls for love" and the narrative takes a quite different turn. The narrator is obviously awed by the subtle and meticulous indoctrination and physical stimulation of the girls. They are taught that their only role in life is to provide sexual satisfaction for a man, and yet Zora, this time without a snort, celebrates the inductee going forth to her consummation "no nerve-racked female behaving as if she faced her doom," but "with the assurance of infinity" (33). At this moment in Hurston's experience, eroticism seems to have conquered both her deep-seated feminism and her trust in the intellectuality that would ordinarily rule the ethnography that she is presumably doing. Through her persona she seems at any and all times determined to say exactly what she felt, composing her ethnographic study reflexively, to be sure, but openly, candidly so—and if that were to sacrifice consistency along with unity, so be it.

Just two chapters later Hurston takes a very different tack on the issue of the place of women in Jamaica. There in a sarcastic polemical mode she exposes the triple tyranny of dominance by gender, race, and class:

> Of course all women are inferior to all men by God and law down there. But if a woman is wealthy, of good family and mulatto, she can overcome some of her drawbacks. But if she is of no particular family, poor and black, she is in a bad way indeed in that man's world. She had better pray to the Lord to turn her into a donkey and be done with the thing. It is assumed that God made poor black females for beasts of burden, and nobody is going to interfere with providence. (76)

This fifth chapter, "Women in the Caribbean," is not developed in connection to a specific experience as were each of the foregoing chapters, and it makes no reference to the various earlier strikes on the issue of gender. It stands as a kind of postscript to the Jamaican adventure, out of keeping in tone and intent with ethnographic writing, but strong in the impacts of its sarcasm, of the pathos it develops in one particularized example of a poor spinster exploited and defiled, and of the pity it evokes in picturing poor black women forced to work at breaking rocks for a bare subsistence. Here is how the narrator describes their feet: "They look so wretched with their bare black feet all gnarled and distorted from walking barefooted over rocks. The nails on their big toes thickened like a hoof from a life time of knocking against stones. All covered over with the gray dust of the road, those feet look almost saurian and repellent" (77).

"It is a curious thing to be a woman in the Caribbean after you have been a woman in these United States" (75), Hurston says, heavily understating her introduction to this topic. But the cultural comparison that develops is vivid, pervasive, and passionately personal, between the experience of the American woman, "Miss America, World's champion woman" free to speak her mind and take a place in the world, and that of her downtrodden Jamaican sisters. The chapter vents Hurston's anger and sympathy as it argues for her vision of social justice, although it also blows her cover as relativistic ethnographer and puts her at a judgmental distance from the culture and the people she is studying. But are ethnographers expected not to have feelings or principles? Or are they expected not to acknowledge them? Candid, involved in the emotion of the remembered moments, this chapter (and other passages like it) problematizes ethnographic discourse. Not disciplined emic investigation at all, this chapter represents another perspective, another irrepressible intent, and one that is not at all relativistic.

Between these unrelated discussions of the position and potential of women are two important chapters very different in what they accomplish. Chapter three recounts Hurston's visit—practically a pilgrimage—to Accompong and the Maroons. There, "I could feel the dead generations crowding me," she confesses: "Here was the oldest settlement of freedmen in the Western world, no doubt. Men who had thrown off the bands of slavery by their own courage and ingenuity. The courage and daring of the Maroons strike like a purple beam across the history of Jamaica" (35).

The narrator claims to have concealed her mission as ethnographer throughout this episode, presenting herself to head man Colonel Rowe as a naive and enthusiastic traveler staying on for some undeterminable purposes, but

> [w]hat I was actually doing was making general observations. I wanted to see what the Maroons were like, really. Since they are a self-governing body, I wanted to see how they felt about education, transportation, public health and democracy. I wanted to see their culture and art expressions and knew that if I asked for anything especially, I would get something out of context. (36)

And to us, her readers, she presents herself semicomically, at first victimized by her transportation, Colonel Rowe's "wall-eyed, pot-bellied mule. . . . Maybe it was that snappy orange-colored four-in-hand tie I was wearing that put [the mule] against me. I hate to think it was my face" (34). Then (letting us in on her observational strategy) she "just sat around and waited" (36), gathering folklore and observing a medicine man's magic. Finally—intervening rather than sitting and waiting—she "kept on talking and begging and coaxing until a hunting party was organized" (45), a hunting party that would take her through a long and arduous adventure revealing a good deal both about the Maroons' hunting culture and about Zora's own semicomic sufferings and misfortunes.

Her language throughout this chapter variously and complexly reflects the reverence she felt for the Maroons, her projection of her own seriocomic role, and her purpose of observing and recording for posterity and the outside world the realm of these relatively secluded people. Her claim to authority as a methodologically sophisticated anthropologist quickly evaporates. But we can imagine that white American readers' residual racist fear or distrust of those notorious and independent Maroon rebels (however fearsome their popular reputation) might be somewhat alleviated by Hurston's account of going like an informal and naive traveler into the presence of a hospitable and fascinating people.

In her fourth chapter the Hurston-narrator follows out her interest in ceremonies, especially those dealing with death and after-death, especially as practiced and believed in by the people on the lowest level of the society. "The most universal ceremony in Jamaica is an African survival called 'The Nine Night.' . . . In reality it is the old African ancestor worship in fragmentary form," she declares (taking on at this point a basically scholarly stance and language), "[t]he West African tradition of appeasing the spirit of the dead lest they do the living a mischief" (54). With an anthropologist's attraction toward the presumably pure and primal reinforcing her own sympathy for the lowest classes, Hurston reports on her attendance at a "Nine Night" among "the barefoot people, the dwellers in wattled huts, the donkey riders, [who] are at great pains to observe every part of the ancient ceremony as it has been handed down to them" (54). She gathers a number of tales about the dangerous tendencies of the unquiet spirits of the recently departed, the "duppies," from a gathering of informants, and in her retelling she attempts to represent something of their own lingo: "But some duppy is rude, man. Some duppy will come even if nobody don't send call him." And showing again that she knows that there are no definitive folktales, the Hurston-narrator includes her informants' disagreements about duppies' powers and susceptibilities (61–63).

Here (as elsewhere) Hurston's most interesting innovation with language is basically literary—her use of impressionistic imagery and figurativeness.

At last a way-off whisper began to put on flesh. In the space of a dozen breaths the keening harmony was lapping at our ears. Somebody among us struck matches and our naked lights flared. The shapeless crowd-mass became individuals. A hum seemed to rise from the ground around us and became singing in answer to the coming singers and in welcome to the dead. (55–56)

Such language merges the observer with the participants and carries the reader along too, in a single interpretive perception. In her "Characteristics of Negro Expression" Hurston had set out as a primary postulate that "the metaphor is of course very primitive," and in this ethnographic work the metaphor is used to carry us back, pictorially and emotionally, into accord with the celebrants' state and her own: "There is the thunder of drums subtley [*sic*] rubbed with bare heels, and the ferocious attack of the rackling men. The thing has begun. They are 'making house for duppy.' The hands of the drummers weave their magic and the drums speak of old times and old things" (71). It is as if she were accepting the inner significance of the ceremony, not acting as an outside observer. And we can feel her figurative response uniting her (and us) with the celebrants.

The dance, too, produces a similar figurative emotional response: "Now the scores of dancers circled the tombs. . . . There was a big movement and a little movement. The big movement was like a sunset in its scope and color. The little movement had the almost imperceptible ripple of a serpent's back. It was a cameo in dancing" (71–72). Then in describing the end of the ceremony, Hurston even attempts to reconstruct the feel of the experience rhythmically, intermixing quotation and metaphor: "Hand a' bowl. . . . Cocks crowing raucously. . . . Day a' light. . . . Night took on a deathly look. . . . Want ingwalla. . . . The spirit went out of the drums. . . . Fum dee ah. . . . The sun came up walking sideways" (74; her ellipses).

Changing the venue to Haiti with Part II, Hurston begins by devoting its four chapters principally to "Politics and Personalities of Haiti"; human difference here—in keeping with the Boasian paradigm (and in some ways like the assumption base of Henry Adams's anticolonialist text)—is firstly a difference of particular history. The history of Haiti had been particularly dire and bloody, a story of brutal occupation, genocide, failed colonialism, corruption-riddled attempts at self-rule, frequent insurrection, U.S. intervention and occupation, and afterwards a somewhat tenuous independent stability. In her account Hurston seems to be variously improvising, trying to bring out the drama and irony she sees in the Haitian background. Along with some straight-out historical summary, she offers an imaginary eyewitness account, a vision of events as the fulfillment of an imagined prophesy, an extended imaginary conversation, a number of satiric or laudatory judgments, a number of figurative associations with Western myth and legend—with Joan of Arc, Moses, Damon and Pythias, David and Jonathan—and so forth. In keeping with her approach in the rest of the book, the story of the Zora-narrator gathering the history and relating it to the Haiti around her is also part of the whole story. The expository method is informal, seemingly situational, and unmistakably literary.

Its interpretations and judgments clearly indict the earlier colonial influence: the most undesirable characteristics of the Haitian people—they are beset by habits of lying, cruelty, self-deception and blame shifting—are linked by the narrator to the decades of European oppression. These characteristics are not racial or primitive or essential but products of specific historical processes acting on fallible, generic human nature. The recently terminated U.S. occupation is praised, both explicitly and implicitly, and in making her points the narrator fictionalizes both an argumentative opponent and a prophesy. She argues down a hypothetical Haitian who wants to place all the blame for Haitian poverty and misgovernment on the occupation; and an imagined prophesy that the "black plume against the sky . . . shall give fright to many at its coming, but . . . shall bring peace to Haiti" she identifies as "[t]he smoke from the funnels of the U.S.S. *Washington*[,] . . . a black plume with a white hope" (86, 93). Although she doesn't regard the occupation as having been an unqualified success, Hurston, on site among the Haitian people, sees the drama of Caribbean history much the way the *National Geographic* writers had (above, pp. 140–41), except that she is far less condescending about the Haitians themselves.

Throughout her various representations in this section, Hurston maintains the supposition that human difference is basically historical. Generally, Haitians are competent, moral, humane, and yearning for peace and stability in a world made violent by the greed and ambition of a few. Their society being profoundly classist and their economy sparse, they survive by whatever means a poor and historically oppressed people can contrive. Their shifts (especially their adaptations and elaborations—both doctrinal and ceremonial—of African and European religions) are evidences of both their ingenuity and their determination to persist.

The book's third and final section, "Voodoo in Haiti," develops in greater detail the several aspects of Haitian culture that would probably seem most alien to a U.S. audience, but Hurston wants to reveal them not as Frazerian barbarities but as likely and—in some surprising ways—effective accommodations to the natural and sociocultural conditions of their lives. As an ethnographer with a mission, she means to de-vilify Voodoo, and up to certain limits to demystify it as

well. The difficulties of the job are formidable. The negative sensa-
tionalizing by outsiders, endemic in U.S. popular arts and press, presents one great obstacle. The classism of upper-class Haitians is
another ("since Voodoo is openly acknowledged by the humble only,
it is safe to blame all the ill of Haiti on Voodoo" [114]). Even prior to
those problems of presentation, there has been the difficulty of access
for any non-Haitian to the practices and beliefs of a secret and under-
ground cult. But Hurston combats the misconstruals with rhetoric,
first-hand information, and insider testimony; and the difficulty of
access with her own expertise in U.S. Hoodoo and with her indomitable ingenuity, openness, daring, and charm. Boas might well have been
proud of her on both counts.

The chapters in Part III are, like the others in the book, digressive
and various in their approaches, reflecting Hurston's multiple agendas
and serendipitous prose, but she has a consistent, anthropologically
relativistic sense of Voodoo's fundamental nature, deeply colored by
her own fascination with it. "It is the old, old mysticism of the world
in African terms," the narrator claims, "[i]t is the worship of the sun,
the water and other natural forces. . . . There is no mystery beyond
the mysterious source of life," the mystery of sex and regeneration
(137). She takes the position that there is a primal religious intuition
linked directly to the human condition in the natural world; that this
intuition is observable in all societies, primitive or civilized; and that
particular ceremonies and representations of the spirit realm are historical outgrowths of particular cultural circumstances. Thus Haitian
Voodoo offers a set of spiritual figurations relative to and equivalent
to others such as the Christian.

The narrator shows a strong diffusionist bent in explaining basic
intercultural religious similarities at the same time she carefully picks
her way through the tangle of African, Christian, and indigenous Haitian elements that embody the primal in Voodoo. For example, in explaining the "supreme Mystere" Damballah Ouedo, she states that
"All over Haiti it is well established that Damballah is identified as
Moses, whose symbol was the serpent"; but dismissing the influence
of Christianity in the new world as too localized and too recent to
produce this identification, she goes on to say that

> It is more probable that there is a tradition of Moses as the great father of
> magic scattered over Africa and Asia. Perhaps some of his feats recorded
> in the Pentateuch are the folk beliefs of such a character grouped about a
> man for it is well established that if a memory is great enough, other mem-
> ories will cluster about it, and those in turn will bring their suites of mem-
> ories to gather about this focal point, because perhaps they are all

scattered parts of the one thing like Plato's concept of the perfect thing. (139–40)

Since "as yet no Haitian artist has given an interpretation or concept of the loa [the deities]," the Haitians tend to use borrowed images and iconography. Yet "Damballah is the highest and most powerful of all the gods, but never is he referred to as the father of the gods as was Jupiter, Odin and the great Zeus" (141). And Erzulie Freida "has been identified as the Blessed Virgin, but this is far from true. Here again the use of the pictures of the Catholic saints has confused observers who do not listen long enough. Erzulie is not the passive queen of heaven and mother of anybody. She is the ideal of the love bed" (144).

Similarly the narrator notes in the Voodoo rituals how the primal is expressed eclectically: as part of the ceremony initiating a candidate, in the midst of sacrificial foods and soon-to-be-sacrificed live chickens, "the houngan places him upon the leafy couch and recites three Ave Maria's, three Credos and the Confiteor three times. Then he sprinkles the couch with flour and a little syrup . . ."; (147), and so forth. From this basic perspective Hurston's narrator acts as descriptive ethnographer, cataloging Voodoo's principal loa, describing several ceremonies specific to them, transcribing several chants, and including photos of several ceremonies-in-progress. She admits that "this work does not pretend to give a full account of either Voodoo or Voodoo gods," and she laments the fact that "an intelligent man like Dr. Dorsainville has not seen fit to do something with Haitian mysticism comparable to Frazier's [sic] The Golden Bough" (153). Her coverage is selective and clearly shaped and seasoned by the Hurston touch, but nevertheless pioneering and quite specifically informational.

The people characterized and reflected through their participation and their reactions to Voodoo are for the most part earnest, pious folk, although in the course of the narrative Hurston shows that there are skeptics, fanatics, secularists, opportunists, splinter cultists, bureaucratic reassurers, and so forth—a whole melange such as constitutes a complex society in any human community. The Zora-narrator expresses great admiration for those individual houngans who seemingly quite freely requite her earnest and submissive curiosity with detailed information and instruction. She characterizes them as wise and even worldly men fully convinced of the efficacy of their faith (at times her praise being so direct that we might suspect that she intends it to get back to them). Dieu Donnez, for example, "lives in a compound like an African chief" (161), but "[t]here is nothing primitive about the man away from his profession. He is gentle but intelligent and business-like. All of his lectures had to be written. He took ashes and drew the signatures of the loa on the ground and I had to copy them until he was satisfied" (166).

The people are generally presented as believers, and as devout rather than credulous. They brim with tales and legends of the powers of the invisible, and they faithfully follow through the intricate ceremonies that placate, cajole or ward off those powers. Voodoo's deity is multiple, the gods' domains and influences are often ambiguous or conflicting, stories of their doings and their effects in the everyday world abound, and Hurston's narrator attempts to record and discriminate among these as faithfully as possible.

A subtext of her treatment is the ways the Haitians rely on Voodoo in trying to understand and control their world. Their gods are in many ways as diverse and unpredictable—and unreliable—as is their world, and Voodoo is shown to be a complex of explanations that offers at least some reassurance of understandability and some hope of one's being able to intervene in the working out of one's own fate. The ceremonies are one form of such intervention, and the use of specific spells and substances are another, and the Zora narrator is very specific in describing the former and cataloging the latter. Along with the fulfillment of its other agendas, personal and ethnographic, the text thus presents the Haitians as trying through their belief in the causal agency of invisible forces to attain some modicum of power over the vagaries and misfortunes of human existence in the face of widespread poverty and a history of oppression and political turmoil.

The information Hurston presents about Voodoo is interspersed among accounts of her adventures and discoveries. A short chapter on her stay on Isle de la Gonave tells of the sacred stones of Voodoo and how she came to hear of them, but it makes some personal points as well: she visited there because Seabrook's book had "fired my imagination," and while there "I found on this remote island a peace I have never known anywhere else on earth" (156, 158). (The narrator is a personal Zora only up to certain limits, though, principally regarding Hurston's gathering of ethnographic information: Hemenway's biography points out that Hurston's being on that island "released a flood of language and emotion"—a consequence of her inability to smother a love affair she had left behind—and resulted in her writing *Their Eyes Were Watching God* in seven weeks during her stay there [1977, 230–31]. This important personal fact isn't mentioned in *Tell My Horse*.)

A longer chapter on a stay in Archahaie features Hurston's witnessing the rites for a deceased houngan—carefully described in all its ceremonial details and colored with her impressions and responses along the way. She witnesses several paranormal events: When suddenly "[t]he body of the dead man sat up with its staring eyes . . . it was so unexpected that I could not discover how it was done" (163); and when a man in a state of possession bursts into the ceremony bringing "a feeling of unspeakable evil," a "menace that could not be recognized by ordinary human fears . . . everybody seemed to feel it simultaneously and recoiled from the bearer of it like a wheat field before a wind" (164). When later a sacrificial chicken "leaped in its death agony and crashed into me, [m]y heart flinched and my flesh drew up like tripe" (173).

The narrator's impressionistic and metaphoric accounts personalize and authenticate her experiences, and they tend as well to involve her more deeply, more emically, within the belief system of the Voodoo practitioners: as she interprets that dead houngan's action, "no one knows what was said to the dead man to get him to relinquish the mystere [the supernatural spirit] but he had sat up, bowed his head with its unchanging eyes and laid back down . . ." (163). As her observations, so charged with empathy and presence, shade into Voodooistic interpretations, the text acts to carry the audience virtually over into the Haitian frame of beliefs too. For example, as she tells of the Haitians' belief in the likelihood of misfortune that is the result of incurring an obligation to the sinister Petro gods, she affirms, "If you make a promise to the Petros *it is going to be kept*" (179; her emphasis). Frequently it is thus the case that the narrator's language functions to connect her subjects and her readers, even across what seem to be the most daunting of chasms of background and belief.

Not surprisingly, given the multiple roles the narrator is playing, ambiguities and discontinuities abound in her chapter on Zombies, as her written account in this (thematically focused) chapter riffles through firsthand experiences, hearsay evidence, gathered folklore, social and economic explanation, scientific hypothesis, and so forth. She disclaims absolute knowledge at the outset: "What is the whole truth and nothing else but the truth about Zombies? I do not know, but I saw the broken remenant [*sic*], relic, or refuse of Felicia Felix-Mentor in a hospital yard" (189). The experience of confronting—and photographing—that supposed Zombie stands as the emotional baseline of her account, and around it flourish varying tales and analyses.

As the narrator continues, her viewpoint, her authority, her sense of context seem to vary situationally. She sifts Zombie lore like a folklorist for its consensuses, its discrepancies, and its origins; like a religious scholar for its consensual informational content; and like a novelist for its effect. In other frames she contextualizes Zombies in terms of issues of social class or economics. For one thing, the issues separate the Haitian social classes: "I was told by numerous upper class Haitians that the whole thing was a myth. They pointed out that the common people were superstitious, and that the talk of Zombies had no more basis than the European belief in the Werewolf" (190–91). For another, so the conventional opinion runs, Zombies are often the recently deceased who have been exhumed and revivified for economic purposes, supplying for unscrupulous plantation owners an easily exploitable, abusable labor supply, since they are physically capable but mentally dead. Hurston doesn't explore the symbolic psychological function of the Zombie in this fundamentally exploitive economic system, but she examines the fear the bereaved relatives of any class feel about the possible fate of their dead. In still another frame she constructs vivid fictional scenarios (shades of Frazer?) based on what she has heard about how Zombies are created.

Her encounter with the supposed Zombie typifies her several roles. "I had the rare opportunity to see and touch an authentic case," she explains, claiming anthropological authority in a typical way. "I listened to the broken noises in its throat, and then, I did what no one else had ever done, I photographed it" (191). "[T]he sight was dreadful. That blank face with the dead eyes" (206). Recounting the experience personally leads her to affirm at one point that "I know that there are Zombies in Haiti. People have been called back from the dead" (191). At another point, however, discussing that individual with a doctor, "It was concluded that it is not a case of awakening the dead, but a matter of the semblance of death induced by some drug known to a few. Some secret probably brought from Africa and handed down from generation to generation" (206). In not inquiring deeply into her experiences or her sources, the narrator sustains the irresolvability of the issue of Zombies.

The phenomenon of possession is essential to Voodoo, and the Zora-narrator, apparently fascinated, returns to it repeatedly in her text. Of course: given the society she comes from and is writing to, negation of rationality and individual selfhood is bound to inspire fear and awe. In some of the ceremonies she describes, inducing the loa to inhabit oneself and becoming trancelike or ecstatic seem to be the purpose of the whole ritual. Her language at times can even empathetically take on the character of possession, enthusiastically shedding any vestige of its scientific objectivity, as in this episode telling of the time that she heard a much-admired informant telling of his out-of-self experiences:

> Dr. Reser began to tell of his experiences while in the psychological state known as possession. Incident piled on incident. A new personality

burned up the one that had eaten supper with us. His blue-gray eyes glowed, but at the same time they drew far back into his head as if they went inside to gaze on things kept in a secret place. . . . As he spoke, he moved farther and farther from known land and into the territory of myths and mists. . . . Whatever the stuff of which the soul of Haiti is made, he was that. You could see the snake god of Dahomey hovering about him. Africa was in his tones. He throbbed and glowed. He used English words but he talked to me from another continent. He was dancing before his gods and the fire of Shango played about him. Then I knew how Moses felt when he beheld the burning bush. Moses had seen fires and he had seen bushes, but he had never seen a bush with a fiery ego and I had never seen a man who dwelt in flame, who was coldly afire in the pores. (272)

In other circumstances the loa seems to take possession of individuals willy-nilly, forcing behavior that is neither personally typical nor humanly rational. Zombihood is one special kind of godless possession in which individual will and personal consciousness are permanently extinguished, and there are other kinds as well, induced by spells cast by one's enemies or by certain potent substances introduced into one's food or environment.

Possession by the god Guedé is of a special type that the Zora-narrator especially admires, (and the author adopts as a metaphor for the kind of speaking out her narrator is doing throughout much of the book), because "he belongs to the blacks and the uneducated blacks at that," and "he does and says the things that the peasants would like to do and say" (232). Supposedly, when a person is "mounted" by Guedé, he or she is entirely under the god's control, and "'Parlay Cheval Ou' (Tell My Horse), the loa begins to dictate through the lips of his mount and goes on and on. Sometimes Guedé dictates the most caustic and belittling statements concerning some pompous person who is present" (234). "This manifestation comes as near a social criticism of the classes by the masses as anything in all Haiti," the narrator claims, as "[t]he people who created Guedé needed a god of derision. They needed a spirit which could burlesque the society that crushed him," and supposedly poorly fed and shabbily dressed, "he bites with sarcasm and slashes with ridicule the class that despises him" (233). Hurston's narrator's bias in favor of the lowest, blackest classes (although alternatively mixed with admiration for headmen and houngans and doctors—she's not a doctrinaire classist) here again suggests the ingenuity and the culture-specific efficaciousness of peasant folkways, as "[t]hat phrase 'Parlay cheval ou' is in daily, hourly use in Haiti and no doubt it is used as a blind for self-expression" (234).

While members of the upper classes and their officials generally dismissed the talk of Zombies, possession by loa, secret societies, and even Voodoo itself as the superstitious misinformation of the uneducated, narrator Zora soon began to get advice from a few of her personal sources that her delving deeper would put her at risk. Should she inquire more deeply into the possibility that some people know of a specific drug that produced Zombies? She reports her informant, Dr. Legros, despite his own apparent scientific orientation, advising against it, telling her "perhaps I would find myself involved in something so terrible, something from which I could not extricate myself alive, and that I would curse the day that I had entered upon my search" (206).

A young woman who had become friends with Hurston advised her against her whole project of investigating Voodoo: "You know, you should not go around alone picking acquaintances with these houngans. You are liable to get involved in something that is not good" (199). And another warns her against following the sound of a drum in the night to what is supposedly a ceremonial of a secret sect: "Some things are very dangerous to see, Mlle. There are many good things for you to learn. I am well content if you do not run to every drum that you hear" (212).

Although she represents herself as undaunted by those friendly but quite urgent warnings, subsequent events (as we must learn from other textual sources) affected the depth and nature of her inquiry. As reported by biographer Hemenway,

> While deep in her studies in a remote part of the bush, she was taken violently ill; as she wrote privately, "It seems that some of my destinations and some of my accessions have been whispered into ears that heard. In consequence, just as mysteriously as the information traveled, I HAVE HAD A VIOLENT GASTRIC DISTURBANCE." She was in bed for two weeks, so shaken that she asked to be carried to the home of the American counsel. She withdrew enough money from the bank to pay for the trip to the States. . . . "For a whole day and a whole night, I'd thought I'd never make it."

"Zora Hurston was convinced that her illness and her Voodoo studies were related," Hemenway concludes; "She backed off from continuing the intense research and began to make plans to finish *Tell My Horse* on American soil" (1977, 247–48).

Hemenway sees a deleterious effect on the book from her backing off: "*Tell My Horse* was written by an author pulling her punches," he complains (1977, 248). Wendy Dutton has characterized Hurston's role in the research and writing as "problematic," in that having become "much more of a participant than an observer," and "having been initiated, she was bound by secrecy. Having seen the long arm of Voodoo in action, she knew full well what the punishment was for talking" (1993, 140). There is no doubt that Hurston backed off on her research, never penetrating the most secret, most sinister and dangerous observances. But as an improvising ethnographer with more than a little literary flair, she found ways to extend the range of her eyewitnessing. *Tell My Horse* does indeed represent the ceremonial creation of Zombies, the sinister "give man" oaths made with the Petio gods, and even the ceremony of human sacrifice by the outlawed fanatical Secte Rouge. Hurston gathered what information she could about these practices from outsiders who had lived in their presence and knew the rumors and the lore, and on that basis she fictionalized accounts, vividly, like an eyewitness, of how these practices might occur. It's impure, imagination-illuminated ethnography, but still it embodies what information was available from such secondhand sources and presents it coherently and dramatically (see esp. 195–98 and 224–31)—and while we are within those narratives, we hardly feel that the punches are being pulled.

Subsequently in the text neither does she pull away from explaining and listing—much more like a bona fide ethnographer—the special poisons and antidotes characteristic of the Voodoo culture. *Tell My Horse* had reached a broad sort of climax—both emotional and positional—with the chapters on the Voodoo ceremonies, Zombies, secret societies, and "tell my horse," but in the closing-out of the book Hurston still plays all her investigator-narrator roles, still gathers in all the various forms of information and judgment in characterizing the Haitians. "Graveyard Dirt and Other Poisons" collects information and historical and anecdotal testimony about Voodoo poisons in an ethnological framework:

> What is most interesting is that the use of poisons follows the African pattern rather than the European. It is rare that the poison is bought at a drug store. In most cases it is a vegetable poison, which makes them harder to detect than the mineral poisons so often used by the Europeans. . . . It is a clear case of an African survival distorted by circumstances. (253)

And somewhat similarly, folklorist-conservationist Zora later appends to her text a collection of Voodoo songs and chants, both words and music. But first the chapter "Dr. Reser" praises one of her favorite informants (a white houngan!) to the skies, recounts several paranormal events she witnessed while under his tutelage, and presents his evaluation of the Haitians: "They are infinitely kind and gentle and all that I have ever done to earn their love is to return their unfailing courtesy" (261). Again in this chapter she prides herself on her skill as an ethnographer and her subtlety as a strategist: "the most important reason why I never tried to get my information second-handed [*sic*] out of Dr. Reser was because I consider myself amply equipped to go out in the field and get it myself" (266).

Field researcher, ethnographer, Voodoo believer and admirer, very personal friend of informants, tourist vividly reporting her adventures and responses, the Zora-narrator concludes the book quite unanalytically with "God and the Pintards," a mythic story she got from Dr. Reser, and which she means to apply to the Haitian character to explain why "[w]ith all their ineptitude for certain concepts that the Anglo-Saxon holds sacred, the Haitian people have a tremendous talent for getting themselves loved" (273). Pintards were guinea fowl of God who ate up so much of the rice He had planted in His heavenly fields that He determined to get rid of them. Sending angels, one after another, armed with shotguns failed because each was distracted and charmed into dance when "the great mass of pintards crowded into the tree singing and making rhythm" (274). Then when God himself went to do the job, they redoubled their festiveness and soon had Him dancing too. He then thought of the perfect solution: if He sent the pintards to earth, He would not only save His rice but He would give joy and laughter to a place where "it is sad . . . and nothing goes right." The pintards landed in Guinea, and "that is why music and dancing came from Guinea" (275). And with that celebration of human difference, the literary Zora has gotten the last word.

As a whole, then, *Tell My Horse* does many things, offers many insights, experiments with many perspectives, but it does indeed defuse difference and deconstruct primitiveness, and to a considerable extent it does that by conveying information from the inside of the Jamaican and Haitian cultures. Emic, culturally relativistic in her approach yet without muting her own judgments, Hurston represents the Caribbean peoples as different from white (and to a lesser extent other black) Westerners in their particular, situationally-modified relation to their African cultural origins, in the residues of their colonial domination, in their particular envisioning of a spirit world and plausibly natural ritualistic approach to it. Race and ethnicity inevitably signal difference, as she sees it, but culture and history determine their significance. Primitiveness is a matter of intercultural judgment, and relative to the one doing the judging. It is not in any way essentially linked to race. As she would write in 1942, "After all, the word 'race' is a loose classification of physical characteristics. It tells nothing about the insides of people" (1984, Appendix).

That Hurston would express her theory of race in a homely every-day locution is typical of her treatment of human difference. Her writing implies no absolute language of difference, no absolute positioning of an observer from which such language could be generated.* One might as well be personal, since what one could be sure about were her own perceptions, impressions, and opinions. And, especially if one were confident and self-possessed (and a good writer too), she could forego the lingo and the artificial frameworks of contemporary social science and say the thing as plainly and as entertainingly as she could. Attending to—and enjoying!—the lingo of the people she was studying (never condescending) then became another dimension of this linguistic relativism. Ethnographer Hurston—participant-observer-advocate—got herself almost fully into the Caribbean cultures, took out what most interested her, and wrote it up with a great deal of relish and a great deal of Zora, constructing and angling and innovating each portion of her text so as to maximize the effect along with the information. The result is an ethnoliterary mongrel, but a valuable and interesting one that never thinks down on its subjects as "primitive."

---

*D. A. Boxwell (1992, 610), invoking Clifford Geertz's theory of anthropological nonobjectivity, credits Hurston with recognizing "the illusory nature" of the ethnographic language of her day. See also Beth Harrison (1996, 96–97), linking Hurston's nonobjective ethnography to first-person travelogue, diary, and other such traditions.

A Brief Afterword

THE PERIOD 1878–1940 WAS ONE OF RADICAL REORIENTATION BOTH OF Western intellectuality and of the relationships of peoples, away from the simple ethnocentric rationality that had so authoritatively dominated understanding and judgment. Anthropology and literature in the United States were deeply involved—as both cause and effect—in that reorientation. Both anthropology and literature were undergoing rapid modification through the efforts of their most venturesome practitioners. Anthropologists were of course exploring new zones—accessing peoples never before systematically studied, and developing new methods of understanding and representing those peoples' lives and societies and minds. Literary writers, too, were exploring new internal and external zones—of consciousness, of social experience, of human variability—and experimenting with the techniques of their craft, traditional and newly innovated.

For both Boasian historical particularism/cultural determinism and literary modernism, the developing of new insight involved the deconstruction of some traditional verities and an increased engagement with issues of epistemology and methodology. Experimenting with standpoint and point of view, with language and the voice and authority of the narrator/expositor, with psychological interpretation and interiority, with the concept of culture and its internal configurations and external significances, with new ideas about myth and symbol and their social and psychological roles, both disciplines were accumulating complex new understandings that involved the abandonment of much of what was formerly thought of as known. Polygenist racial theory, monolinear evolutionism, Western cultural standards as universals, the pose of omniscience in narrative or expository writing, absolutism in any of its forms, all were relegated to obsolescence. And the concepts of race and the primitive were among them.

I don't mean to lose sight of the unbridgeable differences between anthropology and literature. There is no possibility of obliterating the boundary between (on the one hand): a discipline that involves empirical study of real people in real places; that has widely agreed upon standards of practice and professionalism; and that develops as a sci-

264

ence develops, with criteria for evidence-gathering and verification; and (on the other) another that employs the imagination of an individual person in the creation of fictional characters and circumstances based on his or her apprehension of the world. Still, similarities and analogues of approach, insight, and method almost suggest, in this particular historical context, a common project.

We see in the authors I have specifically focused on here an enormous awareness of—and suspicion of—preconception, and a striving to develop methods of observation and representation meant to penetrate to actualities beneath or beyond standard and traditional understandings. Beginning with the notion that a particular individual point of view originating from a particular culture was the only valid and truthful standpoint for perceiving and interpreting the teeming actual world, they each attempted to reconceptualize human realities relativistically. This naturally involved an act of the imagination, an attempt to see the world and human experience, belief, society, routine, and fate as they would appear to a Tahitian or a Kwakiutl, an African American or a self-designated mulatto, a Samoan adolescent or a Haitian Voodooist. Human specifics *in situ* was what they strove for: a realization of difference in mindset, signification, and language that would leave behind any sense that difference was in itself inferiority.

I maintain that the twentieth century's growing beyond the reflexiveness and absolutisms it was heir to was to a very great extent a result of individual imagination and creativity, of personal difference: individual thinkers and artists inventing new increments of possibility. The ethical results are observable in the reconfigurations, the marginalization of the notions of race and the primitive. Never again would they be what they had been, prompting and justifying what they had prompted and justified.

References

Ackerman, Robert E. 1987. *J. G. Frazer, his life and work.* New York: Cambridge University Press.

Adams, Henry. 1891. Primitive rights of women. *Historical essays*, 1–41. New York: Charles Scribner's Sons. [Orig. pub.1876].

———. 1947. *Tahiti by Henry Adams: Memoirs of Arii Taimai.* Ed. and intro. Robert E. Spiller. New York: Scholars' Facsimiles and Reprints. [Orig. pub. 1901].

———. 1982. *The Letters of Henry Adams*, vols. 2–4. Ed. J. C. Levenson, Ernest Samuels, Charles Vandersee, and Viola Hopkins Winner. Cambridge, Mass.: Harvard University Press.

Aldrich, Charles R. 1931. *Primitive mind and modern civilization.* New York: Harcourt, Brace.

Bell, Michael. 1972. *Primitivism.* London: Methuen.

Berkhofer, Robert F. Jr. 1978. *White man's Indian: Images of the Indian from Columbus to the present.* New York: Knopf.

Bigsby, C. W. E. 1987. Four early plays. In Harold Bloom, ed., *Eugene O'Neill*, 133–44. New York: Chelsea.

Black, Stephen A. 1999. *Eugene O'Neill: Beyond mourning and tragedy.* New Haven, Conn.: Yale University Press.

Bleikasten, André. 1990. *The ink of melancholy.* Bloomington, Ind.: Indiana University Press.

Boas, Franz. 1911. *Handbook of American Indian languages.* Smithsonian Institution, Bureau of American Ethnology, Bulletin 40. Washington: Government Printing Office.

———. 1931. *The mind of primitive man.* New York: Macmillan. [Reprint of 1911 ed.].

Bogard, Travis. 1972. *Contour in time: The plays of Eugene O'Neill.* New York: Oxford University Press.

Bone, Robert. 1965. *The Negro novel in America.* New Haven, Conn.: Yale University Press.

Boon, James. 1982. *Other tribes, other scribes: Symbolic anthropology in the comparative study of cultures, histories, religions and texts.* Cambridge: Cambridge University Press.

Boxwell, D. A. 1992. "Sis Cat" as ethnographer. *African-American Review* 26 (4): 605–17.

Brady, Ivan, ed. 1983. Special section: Speaking in the name of the real: Freeman and Mead on Samoa. *American Anthropologist* 85 (4): 908–47.

Brinton, Daniel G. 1890. *Races and peoples.* Philadelphia, Pa.: David McKay.

———. 1897. *Religions of primitive peoples.* New York: G. P. Putnam's Sons.

Carroll, Charles. 1900. *The Negro a beast.* Savannah, Ga.: Thunderbolt Press.

Chabrowe, Leonard. 1976. *Ritual and pathos: The theater of O'Neill.* Lewisburg, Pa.: Bucknell University Press.

Chalfant, Edward. 1994. *Better in darkness: A biography of Henry Adams, his second life 1862–1891.* Hamdon, Conn.: Archon Books.

Chester, Rear Admiral Colby M. 1908. Haiti: A degenerating island. *National Geographic* 19: 200–217.

Clifford, James. 1988. *The predicament of culture.* Cambridge, Mass.: Harvard University Press.

Clifford, James, and George E. Marcus, eds. 1986. *Writing culture: The poetics and politics of ethnography.* Berkeley, Calif.: University of California Press.

Codere, Helen. 1959. The understanding of the Kwakiutl. In Walter Goldschmidt, ed., The anthropology of Franz Boas. *The American Anthropologist* 61 (5) pt. 2 (Memoir 89): 61–75.

Colson, Elizabeth. 1974. *Tradition and contract: The problem of order.* Chicago: Aldine.

Conn, Peter. 1983. *The divided mind: Ideology and imagination in America, 1898–1917.* New York: Cambridge University Press.

Connor, Steven. 1990. The birth of humility. In Robert Fraser, ed., *Sir James Frazer and the literary imagination,* 61–80. London: Macmillan.

Cooley, John. 1982. *Savages and naturals.* Newark, Del.: University of Delaware Press.

———. 1986. In pursuit of the primitive: Black portraits by Eugene O'Neill and other Village Bohemians. In Victor A. Kramer, ed., *The Harlem Renaissance reexamined,* 51–64. New York: AMS.

Cote, James E. 1994. *Adolescent storm and stress: An evaluation of the Mead-Freeman controversy.* Hillsdale, N.J.: L. Erlbaum.

D'Acierno, Pelligrino, and Karen Barnaby, eds. 1990. *C. G. Jung and the humanities.* Princeton: Princeton University Press.

Darnell, Regna. 1998. *And along came Boas: Continuity and revolution in Americanist anthropology.* Amsterdam: John Benjamins.

———. 2001. *Invisible genealogies: A history of Americanist anthropology.* Lincoln, Neb.: University of Nebraska Press.

Darwin, Charles. 1966. *On the origin of species.* Cambridge, Mass.: Harvard University Press. [Facsimile of 1859 ed.].

———. 1981. *The descent of man.* Princeton: Princeton University Press. [Repr. of 1871 ed.].

Deloria, Philip J. 1998. *Playing Indian.* New Haven, Conn.: Yale University Press.

Dixon, Thomas. 1903. *The leopard's spots: A romance of the white man's burden 1865–1900.* New York: Doubleday, Page.

Dutton, Wendy. 1993. The problem of invisibility: Voodoo and Zora Neale Hurston. *Frontiers* 13 (2): 131–52.

Eastman, Charles. 1931. *From the deep woods to civilization.* Boston: Little, Brown. [Orig. 1916].

Eliot, T. S. 1923. Ulysses, order, and myth. *Dial* 75: 480–83.

Encyclopaedia Britannica. 11th ed. 1910. s.v. Haiti. vol. 12: 824–27.

Engel, Edwin. 1953. *The haunted heroes of Eugene O'Neill.* Cambridge, Mass.: Harvard University Press.

Estrin, Mark W., ed. 1990. *Conversations with Eugene O'Neill.* Jackson, Miss.: University Press of Mississippi.

Evans-Pritchard, E. E. 1964. *Social anthropology and other essays.* New York: Free Press.

————. 1965. *Theories of primitive religion.* Oxford: Oxford University Press.

Fabian, Johannes. 1983. *Time and the Other: How anthropology makes its object.* New York: Columbia University Press.

Fadiman, Regina K. 1975. *Faulkner's "Light in August": A description and interpretation of the revisions.* Charlottesville, Va.: University Press of Virginia.

Falk, Doris. 1958. *Eugene O'Neill and the tragic tension: An interpretive study of the plays.* New Brunswick, N.J.: Rutgers University Press.

Faulkner, William. 1990. *Light in August: The corrected text,* ed. Noel Polk. New York: Vintage. [Orig. pub.1932].

Feinberg, Richard. 1988. Margaret Mead and Samoa: Coming of age in fact and fiction. *American Anthropologist* 90 (3): 656–63.

Fielding, Willliam J. 1922. *The caveman within us.* New York: Blue Ribbon Books.

Fletcher, Alice C. 1891. The Indian Messiah. *Journal of American Folk-Lore* 4 (12): 57–60.

Floyd, Virginia, ed. 1981. *Eugene O'Neill at work.* New York: Frederick Ungar.

Fortes, Meyer. 1969. *Kinship and the social order.* Chicago: Aldine.

Fraser, Robert, ed. 1990. *Sir James Frazer and the literary imagination.* London: Macmillan.

Frazer, Sir James. 1911. *Taboo and the perils of the soul.* Vol.2 of *The golden bough,* 3rd ed. London: Macmillan.

————. 1914. *Adonis, Attis, Osiris.* Vol. 4 of *The golden bough,* 3rd ed. London: Macmillan.

————. 1922. *The golden bough.* 1 vol. abridged. New York: Macmillan.

————. 1935. *Totemism and exogamy.* London: Macmillan. [orig. 1910].

————. 1966. *The magic art and the evolution of kings. The Golden Bough,* vol.1. New York: St. Martins. [Reprint of 1911 ed.].

Fredrickson, George M. 1971. *The Black image in the White mind.* New York: Harper and Row.

Freeman, Derek. 1983. *Margaret Mead and Samoa: The making and unmaking of an anthropological myth.* Cambridge, Mass.: Harvard University Press.

Freud, Sigmund. 1918. *Totem and taboo: Resemblances between the psychic lives of savages and neurotics,* trans. A. A. Brill. New York: Moffat, Yard.

————. 1949. Why War? In James Strachey, ed., *Collected papers of Sigmund Freud,* vol. 5: 273–87. London: Hogarth Press. [Orig. pub.1932].

————. 1950. *The interpretation of dreams,* trans. A. A. Brill. New York: Random House. [Orig. pub. 1913].

————. 1959. 'Civilized' sexual morality and modern nervous illness. In James Strachey, ed., *The complete psychological works of Sigmund Freud,* vol. 9: 181–204. London: Hogarth Press. [Orig. pub. 1908].

————. 1961a. *Civilization and its discontents.* In James Strachey, ed., *The standard edition of the complete psychological works of Sigmund Freud,* vol. 21. London: Hogarth Press. [Orig. pub. 1930].

———. 1961b. *The future of an illusion*, trans. James Strachey. New York: W. W. Norton. [Orig. pub.1928].

Gates, Henry Louis Jr. 1986. *"Race," writing and difference*. Chicago: University of Chicago Press.

———. 1988. *The signifying monkey*. New York: Oxford University Press.

———. 1990. Afterword: Zora Neale Hurston: "A Negro way of saying," in Hurston, *Tell my horse*. New York: Harper and Row.

Gelb, Arthur and Barbara. 1962. *O'Neill*. New York: Harper.

Gillett, Peter J. 1972. O'Neill and the racial myths. *Twentieth Century Literature* 18 (1): 111–120.

Goldschmidt, Walter, ed. 1959. The anthropology of Franz Boas: Essays on the centennial of his birth. *The American Anthropologist*, 61 (5) pt. 2, memoir 89.

Goldwater, Robert John. 1986. *Primitivism in modern art*. Cambridge, Mass.: Harvard University Press.

Gordon, Deborah. 1990. The politics of ethnographic authority: Race and writing in the ethnography of Margaret Mead and Zora Neale Hurston. In Marc Manganaro, ed., *Modernist anthropology*, 146–62. Princeton: Princeton University Press.

Gossett, Thomas F. 1997. *Race: The history of an idea in America*. New York: Oxford University Press.

Gould, Stephen Jay. 1981. *The mismeasure of man*. New York: W. W. Norton.

Grant, Madison. 1923. *The passing of the great race: Or, the racial basis of European history*, 4th ed. New York: Scribner's. [Orig. 1916].

Gwynn, Frederick, and Joseph L. Blotner. 1995. *Faulkner in the university*. Charlottesville, Va.: University of Virginia Press.

Harris, Marvin. 1964. *The nature of cultural things*. New York: Random House.

———. 1968. *The rise of anthropological theory*. New York: Columbia University Press.

———. 1983. Margaret and the giant killer. *The Sciences* 23 (4): 18–21.

Harrison, Beth. 1996. Zora Neale Hurston and Mary Austin. *Melus* 21 (2): 89–106.

Hegeman, Susan. 1999. *Patterns for America: Modernism and the concept of culture*. Princeton: Princeton University Press.

Hemenway, Robert E. 1977. *Zora Neale Hurston: A literary biography*. Urbana, Ill.: University of Illinois Press.

———. 1984. Introduction to Hurston, *Dust tracks on a road*. Urbana, Ill.: University of Illinois Press.

Hernandez, Graciela. 1995. Multiple subjectivities and strategic positionality: Zora Neale Hurston's ethnographies. In Ruth Behan and Deborah A. Gordon, eds., *Women writing culture*, 148–65. Berkeley, Calif.: University of California Press.

Herskovits, Melville J. 1941. *The myth of the Negro past*. New York: Harper.

———. 1953. *Franz Boas: The science of man in the making*. New York: Scribner's.

———. 1971. *Life in a Haitian valley*. New York: Doubleday. [Orig. pub.1927].

Hinsley, Curtis M. Jr. 1981. *Savages and scientists: The Smithsonian Institution and the development of American anthropology, 1846–1910*. Washington, D.C.: Smithsonian Institution Press.

Holmes, Lowell D. 1987. *Quest for the real Samoa*. South Hadley, Mass.: Bergin & Garvey.

Homans, Peter. 1979. *Jung in context*. Chicago: University of Chicago Press.

Howard, Jane. 1984. *Margaret Mead: A life*. New York: Simon and Schuster.

Hume, Robert A. 1951. *Runaway star: An appreciation of Henry Adams*. Ithaca N.Y.: Cornell University Press.

Hurston, Zora Neale. 1931. Hoodoo in America. *Journal of American Folk-Lore* 44: 317–417.

———. 1935. *Mules and men*. Philadelphia: J. B. Lippincott.

———. 1938. *Tell my horse: Voodoo and life in Haiti and Jamaica*. New York: J. B. Lippincott.

———. 1979. What white publishers won't print. In Alice Walker, ed., *I love myself when I am laughing*, 169–73. Old Westbury, N.Y.: Feminist Press. [Orig. pub. 1950].

———. 1981. Characteristics of Negro expression. *The sanctified church*, 49–68. New York: Marlowe. [Orig. 1934].

———. 1984. *Dust tracks on a road*, ed. Robert Hemenway. Urbana, Ill.: University of Illinois Press.

Hyatt, Marshall. 1990. *Franz Boas: Social activist*. New York: Greenwood Press.

Jacobi, Jolande. 1959. *Complex/archetype/symbol in the psychology of C. G. Jung*, trans. Ralph Manheim. Princeton: Princeton University Press.

Jacobs, Karen. 1997. From "spyglass" to "horizon": Tracking the anthropological gaze in Zora Neale Hurston. *Novel* 30 (3): 329–60.

Jakobson, Roman. 1966. Franz Boas' approach to language. In Thomas A. Sebeok, ed., *Portraits of linguists*, vol. 2: 127–39. Bloomington, Ind.: Indiana University Press.

Johnson, Barbara. 1985. Thresholds of difference: Structures of address in Zora Neale Hurston. In Henry Louis Gates, ed., *"Race," writing and difference*, 317–28. Chicago: University of Chicago Press.

Johnston, Sir Harry. 1920. Haiti, the home of the twin republics. *National Geographic* 38 (6): 483–96.

Jung, Carl G. 1916. *Psychology of the unconscious*, trans. Beatrice M. Hinkle. New York: Moffat, Yard.

———. 1953. *Two essays on analytical psychology*, trans. R.F.C. Hull. *The collected works of Carl G. Jung*. Bollingen Series XX, vol. 7. New York: Pantheon.

———. 1961. *The structure and dynamics of the psyche*, trans. R.F.C. Hull. *The collected works of Carl G. Jung*. Bollingen Series XX, vol. 8. New York: Pantheon.

———. 1964. *Civilization in transition*, trans. R.F.C. Hull. *The collected works of Carl G. Jung*. Bollingen Series XX, vol. 10. New York: Pantheon.

———. 1971a. *The portable Jung*, ed. and intro. Joseph Campbell. New York: Viking.

———. 1971b. *Psychological types*, trans. H. G. Baynes. Princeton: Princeton Univ. Press. [Orig. pub. 1923].

Kaledin, Eugenia. 1993. Henry Adams's anthropological vision as American identity. In David R. Contosta and Robert Muccigrasso, eds., *Henry Adams and his world*. *Transactions of the APS*, new series, 83 (4): 57–75. Philadelphia: American Philosophical Society.

Kinney, Arthur F. 1978. *Faulkner's narrative poetics*. Amherst, Mass.: University of Massachusetts Press.

Krafchick, Marcelline. 1992. All God's chillun play games. In Haiping Lui and Lowell Swortzwell, eds. *Eugene O'Neill in China,* 231–38. New York: Greenwood Press.

Kreiswirth, Martin. 1987. Plots and counterplots: The structure of *Light in August.* In Michael Millgate, *New essays on "Light in August,"* 55–79. New York: Cambridge University Press.

Kuklick, Henrika. 1991. *The savage within: The social history of British anthropology 1885–1945.* Cambridge: Cambridge University Press.

Kuper, Adam. 1988. *The invention of primitive society.* London: Routledge.

Lang, Andrew. 1968. *Myth, ritual and religion,* vols. 1 & 2. New York: AMS [reprint of 1906 ed.].

Levy, Robert I. 1984. Mead, Freeman, and Samoa: The problem of seeing things as they are. *Ethos* 12: 85–92.

Lowie, Robert H. 1937. *The history of ethnological theory.* New York: Farrar and Rinehart.

Lubbock, Sir John. 1895. *The origin of civilization and the primitive condition of man.* New York: D. Appleton. [Orig. pub. 1870].

Ludmerer, Kenneth. 1972. *Genetics and American society.* Baltimore, Md.: Johns Hopkins University Press.

Macgowan, Kenneth. 1923. *The theater of tomorrow.* London: T. Fisher Unwin.

Manganaro, Marc. 1990. *Modernist anthropology.* Princeton: Princeton University Press.

Marcus, George, and Michael Fischer. 1986. *Anthropology as cultural critique.* Chicago: University of Chicago Press.

Mead, Margaret. 1928a. *Coming of age in Samoa: A psychological study of primitive youth for Western civilisation.* New York: William Morrow.

———. 1928b. A lapse of animism among a primitive people. *Psyche* 9: 72–77.

———. 1928c. The role of the individual in Samoan culture. *Journal of the Royal Anthropological Institute* 58: 481–96.

———. 1929. Americanization in Samoa. *American Mercury* 16: 264–70.

———. 1932. An investigation of the thought of primitive children, with special reference to animism. *Journal of the Royal Anthropological Institute* 42: 173–90.

———. 1959a. *An anthropologist at work: Writings of Ruth Benedict.* Boston: Houghton Mifflin.

———. 1959b. Apprenticeship under Boas. In Walter Goldschmidt, ed. The anthropology of Franz Boas. *The American Anthropologist* 61 (5), pt. 2, memoir 89: 29–45.

———. 1965. *Anthropologists and what they do.* New York: Franklin Watts.

———. 1969. *Social organization of Manu'a.* Honolulu: Berenice P. Bishop Museum Bulletin 76. [Orig. pub. 1930].

———. 1972. *Blackberry winter: My earlier years.* New York: Morrow Quill.

———. 1973. Preface to 1973 edition. *Coming of age in Samoa.* New York: Morrow Quill.

———. 1977. *Letters from the field, 1925–1975.* New York: HarperRow.

Melville, Herman. 1968. *Typee: A peep at Polynesian life.* Evanston and Chicago: Northwestern University Press and Newberry Library. [Orig. pub. 1846].

Millgate, Michael. 1987. "A novel: Not an anecdote": Faulkner's *Light in August.* *New Essays on "Light in August,"* 31–53. New York: Cambridge University Press.

Moody-Adams, Michele M. 1997. *Fieldwork in familiar places: Morality, culture, and philosophy.* Cambridge, Mass.: Harvard University Press.

Morgan, Lewis Henry. 1878. *Ancient society: Or, researches in the lines of human progress from savagery through barbarism to civilization.* New York: Henry Holt.

Mullett, Mary B. 1990. The extraordinary story of Eugene O'Neill. In Mark Estrin, ed., *Conversations with Eugene O'Neill,* 26–37. Jackson Miss.: University Press of Mississippi. [Orig. pub.1922].

Nardi, Bonnie A. 1984. The height of her powers: Margaret Mead's Samoa. *Feminist Studies* 10 (2): 323–37.

National Geographic. 1920. Haiti and its regeneration by the United States. Vol. 38 (6): 497–511.

Newman, Louise M. 1996. Coming of age, but not in Samoa: Reflections on Margaret Mead's legacy for Western liberal feminism. *American Quarterly* 48 (2): 233–40.

North, Michael. 1994. *The dialect of modernism: Race, language and twentieth century literature.* New York: Oxford University Press.

Nye, David. 1990. *Electrifying America.* Cambridge, Mass.: Massachusetts Institute of Technology Press.

O'Connor, Mary. 1992. Zora Neale Hurston and talking between cultures. *Canadian Review of American Studies* (special issue): 141–61.

O'Neill, Eugene. 1934. *All God's chillun got wings.* In *The plays of Eugene O'Neill,* vol.4. New York, Scribner's. [Orig. pub. 1924].

———. 1955. *The fountain.* In *The plays of Eugene O'Neill,* vol. 1. New York: Random House. [Orig. pub. 1925].

———. 1965. *Collected poems.* In Ralph Sanborn and Barrett H. Clark, eds., *A bibliography of the works of Eugene O'Neill together with the collected poems of Eugene O'Neill.* New York: Benjamin Blom. [Orig. pub. 1931].

———. 1982. *The theater we worked for: The letters of Eugene O'Neill to Kenneth Macgowan,* ed. Jackson R. Bryer and Ruth M. Alvarez. New Haven, Conn.: Yale University Press.

———. 1988a. *The Emperor Jones.* In *The complete plays,* 1913–1920. New York: Library of America. [Orig. pub. 1921].

———. 1988b. *Selected letters of Eugene O'Neill,* ed. Travis Bogard and Jackson Breyer. New Haven, Conn.: Yale University Press.

Orans, Martin. 1996. *Not even wrong: Margaret Mead, Derek Freeman, and the Samoans.* Novato, Calif.: Chandler and Sharp.

Osterhout, Major G.H. 1920. A little-known marvel of the western hemisphere. *National Geographic* 38 (6): 469–82.

Perloff, Marjorie. 1995. Tolerance and taboo: Modernist primitivisms and postmodernist pieties. In Elzar Barkan and Ronald Bush, eds. *Prehistories of the future,* 339–54. Stanford, Calif.: Stanford University Press.

Pitavy, François L. 1982. *William Faulkner's "Light in August": A critical casebook.* New York: Garland.

Powell, John Wesley. 1970. From barbarism to civilization. In George Crossette, ed. *Selected prose of John Wesley Powell,* 73–75. Boston: David R. Godine. [Orig. 1888].

Pratt, Mary Louise. 1986. Scratches on the face of the country; or, what Mr. Barrow saw in the land of the Bushmen. In Henry Louis Gates, Jr., *"Race," writing and difference,* 138–62. Chicago: University of Chicago Press.

Raleigh, John Henry. 1965. *The plays of Eugene O'Neill.* Carbondale, Ill.: Southern Illinois University Press.

Resek, Carl. 1960. *Lewis Henry Morgan, American scholar.* Chicago: University of Chicago Press.

Richardson, H. Edward. 1969. *William Faulkner: The journey to self-discovery.* Columbia, Mo.: University of Missouri Press.

Ricoeur, Paul. 1970. *Freud and philosophy.* New Haven, Conn.: Yale University Press.

Rieff, Philip. 1979. *Freud: The mind of the moralist.* Chicago: University of Chicago Press. [Orig. 1959].

Rohner, Ronald. 1966. Franz Boas: Ethnographer on the northwest coast. In June Helm MacNeish, *Pioneers of American anthropology,* 149–222. Seattle, Wash.: University of Washington Press.

Ruppersburg, Hugh M. 1983. *Voice and eye in Faulkner's fiction.* Athens, Ga.: University of Georgia Press.

———. 1994. *Reading Faulkner: "Light in August."* Jackson, Miss.: University Press of Mississippi.

Sahlins, Marshall. 1976. *Culture and practical reason.* Chicago: University of Chicago Press.

Said, Edward. 1978. *Orientalism.* New York: Pantheon.

———. 1993. *Culture and imperialism.* New York: Knopf.

Samuels, Ernest. 1964. *Henry Adams: The major phase.* Cambridge, Mass.: Harvard University Press.

Sapir, Edward. 1956. *Culture, language and personality: Selected essays,* ed. David G. Mandelbaum. Berkeley, Calif.: University of California Press.

Sayler, Oliver M. 1922. The real Eugene O'Neill. *Century Magazine* 103: 351–59.

Scheper-Hughes, Nancy. 1984. The Margaret Mead controversy: Culture, biology and anthropological inquiry. *Human Organization* 43 (1): 85–93.

Schwartz, Theodore. 1983. Anthropology: A quaint science. In Ivan Brady, ed., Special section, *American Anthropologist* 85 (4): 919–29.

Seabrook, W. B. 1929. *The magic island.* New York: Harcourt, Brace.

Sheaffer, Louis. 1973. *O'Neill: Son and artist.* Boston: Little, Brown.

Shore, Bradd. 1983. Paradox regained: Freeman's Margaret Mead and Samoa. In Ivan Brady, ed., Special section, *American Anthropologist* 85 (4): 935–44.

Smedley, Audrey. 1993. *Race in North America.* Boulder, Colo.: Westview Press.

Spencer, Herbert. 1897a. *The principles of psychology.* New York: D. Appleton. [Orig. 1855].

———. 1897b. *First principles.* New York: D. Appleton. [Orig. 1862].

———. 1897c. *The principles of sociology.* New York: D. Appleton. [Orig. 1876].

Stepan, Nancy. 1982. *The idea of race in science: Great Britain, 1800–1960.* Hamden, Conn.: Archon.

Stevenson, Elizabeth. 1961. *Henry Adams: A biography.* New York: Collier.

Stocking, George W., Jr. 1968. *Race, culture and evolution: Essays in the history of anthropology.* New York: Free Press.

———. 1974. *The shaping of American anthropology: A Franz Boas reader.* New York: Basic Books.

———. 1987. *Victorian anthropology*. New York: Free Press.

———. 1992. *The ethnographer's magic and other essays in the history of anthropology*. Madison, Wis.: University of Wisconsin Press.

———. 1995. *After Tylor: British social anthropology 1888–1951*. Madison, Wis.: University of Wisconsin Press.

Stowe, William W. 1991. Henry Adams, traveler. *New England Quarterly* 64 (2): 179–205.

Strathern, Marilyn. 1990. Out of context: The persuasive fictions of anthropology. In Marc Manganaro, ed., *Modernist anthropology*. Princeton: Princeton University Press.

Tambiah, Stanley Jeyaraja. 1990. *Magic, science, religion and the scope of rationality*. Cambridge: Cambridge University Press.

Torgovnick, Marianna. 1990. *Gone primitive: Savage intellects, modern lives*. Chicago: University of Chicago Press.

Trautmann, Thomas R. 1987. *Lewis Henry Morgan and the invention of kinship*. Berkeley, Calif.: University of California Press.

Vickery, John B. 1973. *The literary impact of "The Golden Bough."* Princeton: Princeton University Press.

Vickery, Olga. 1964. *The novels of William Faulkner*. Baton Rouge, La.: Louisiana State University Press.

Voelker, Paul. 1992. Eugene O'Neill, world playwright, the beginnings. In Haiping Lui and Lowell Swortzwell, eds., *Eugene O'Neill in China*, 99–109. New York: Greenwood.

Walker, Alice. 1986. A cautionary tale and a partisan view. In Harold Bloom, ed., *Zora Neale Hurston*, 63–69. New York: Chelsea.

Wallace, Edwin R. IV. 1983. *Freud and anthropology*. New York: International Universities Press.

Index

Boldface indicates major treatment of subject or author